CU00663781

1984:
THE YEAR
POP WENT
QUEER

1984:
THE YEAR
POP WENT
QUEER

IAN WADE

NINE
EIGHT
BOOKS

NEB 027

First published in the UK in 2024 by Nine Eight Books
An imprint of Black & White Publishing Group
A Bonnier Books UK company
4th Floor, Victoria House, Bloomsbury Square, London, WC1B 4DA
Owned by Bonnier Books, Sveavägen 56, Stockholm, Sweden

@nineeightbooks

@nineeightbooks

Hardback ISBN: 978-1-7851-2081-7
eBook ISBN: 978-1-7851-2082-4

A CIP catalogue record for this book is available from the British Library.

Publishing director: Pete Selby
Editor: James Lilford

Cover design by Bonnier Books UK Art Dept
Typeset by IDSUK (Data Connection) Ltd
Printed and bound in Great Britain by Clays Ltd, Elcograf S.p.A

1 3 5 7 9 10 8 6 4 2

Nine Eight Books is an imprint of Bonnier Books UK
www.bonnierbooks.co.uk

MIX
Paper | Supporting
responsible forestry
FSC® C018072

For my mum and N with love

CONTENTS

INTRODUCTION

'England's got this incredible craze at the moment for homo-sexuals and lesbians. It's as if they're taking over the world.'
– Malcolm McLaren, September 1984

'Unsuccessful at rugby.' Not my words, but those of my PE teacher in one of my annual school reports. In fact, each year he managed to get around the evidence that I was absolutely useless and uninterested in sport with some ease. The 'appears to enjoy' in the statement 'Ian makes a bold attempt to take part in this activity that he appears to enjoy' is doing some heavy lifting in the sentence about football. Athletics was at least a bit more realistic, with 'unfortunately he lacks strength and technique'. The only thing I appeared to be good at was windsurfing, which I'd 'come on in leaps and bounds in'. That could've possibly been down to the wetsuits. Ahem.

Indeed, looking through the feedback of my academic life is a bit of a minefield of 'lacks concentration', 'tendency to be a bit silly' and outright shade of 'if he would focus more, he's capable of some good work'. Luckily, halfway through secondary school, I'd bucked my ideas up. Music was going well once I binned the violin, and I was showing imagination in English. It wasn't entirely unconnected from hitting puberty and an onslaught of 'new interests' taking position alongside swimming, Lego, *Top of the Pops* and *Smash Hits*.

Saying that I had gaps in my sexual experience at that age would suggest that there'd been at least something, but no. That particular arena was barren and unoccupied. I hadn't been overly intrigued by any subject raised during school sex education lessons. I'd barely taken any notice of any of that caper, as it was still primarily *The Joy of Sex* and some words on an overhead projector. Sex sounded like a right old faff. Having a girlfriend (or even a boyfriend) was barely on my to-do list.

Yet in 1984, all that time spent staring at the swimwear section of Freemans catalogues and looking at pics of Harrison Ford in *Blade Runner* started to make sense. I soon realised that looking at hot dudes having 'a bit of a day' – or, in the case of *Mad Max 2*, realising that the best way to get through a post-apocalyptic oil drought was to raid a sex shop – was telling me something.

Many people of my age will have experience and memories of the handful of homosexuals in culture. John Inman in *Are You Being Served?* Larry Grayson on *The Generation Game.* Danny La Rue dressed up as a lady etc.[1] The late

---

[1] That said, the biggest new comedy series here in the UK was the sitcom *'Allo 'Allo!*, also penned by *Are You Being Served?* writers David Croft and

'70s had thrown Village People into the mix, and what seemed like a blend of choreographed gentleman dressed up in uniforms looked more like a disco employment fair than anything sexual. It's only once you've grown up a little that you spot that the Leather Man was wearing a red hanky in his back pocket (clue: 'into fisting'). Indeed, when you've found yourself in a club witnessing someone ejaculating over a man in army fatigues you get a broader idea of the whole Village People 'concept'.

Sure, I knew that I may not be fully heterosexual. But then I had no concept of homosexuality either. I'd had 'poof' and 'hairy fairy' jibes growing up, and it was seen as the ultimate weakness. I had a decidedly non-macho outlook and that was bully catnip. I was baffled as to why I could be *anything* when I had no idea what it actually was. It wasn't something that you could just drop into

---

Jeremy Lloyd. It began in September 1984 and ran for nine series until 1992. A broad farce that would probably struggle to get commissioned now, it tapped into the 'crazy foreigners' trope and vaguely spoofed the BBC French Resistance drama *Secret Army*. The lead character René Artois (played by Gorden Kaye) was a French café owner and reluctant member of the Resistance during the Second World War. It was Lieutenant Gruber (Guy Siner), a German officer, who appeared to have a crush on René and was implied to be homosexual. Due to the popularity of the show, Kaye was one of the era's biggest stars. He came out as gay in 1989 following a tabloid exposé. And his life was never his own again. Even while he was recovering from brain surgery after suffering near-fatal head injuries in a car accident in January 1990, two journalists from the *Sunday Sport* posed as doctors and took photographs of him in his room at the hospital. He died in 2017.

conversation at the dinner table either. My parents were a lot older than most of my friends' mums and dads, having both lived through an actual war and being a little too old to get involved with rock 'n' roll. They were two generations away from what I was going through, so any questions as regards whatever my sexuality may or may not have been were best avoided.

So, what exactly happened to me upon seeing Frankie Goes to Hollywood's 'Relax' video for the first time? Well ... Was this what a gay bar looked like? Lots of slightly odd-looking gents dressed in school uniforms and fishnets? What was that shiny vest that chap was wearing? Is that what happens when you're gay? Is that part of the recruitment process? And will I, once in an actual gay club, have to deal with the prospect of a tiger launching at me? This wasn't what I was expecting to find at London's homo hotspot Heaven. I'd seen Frankie's adverts in the mags, too – 'making Duran Duran lick the shit off their shoes'. I didn't like the sound of that. At all.

It's not so much that it was a full-on gay invasion; it was more of a 'hovering' over pop culture. Where *Top of the Pops* had been, a year or so before, basically a bunch of amazing crackpots and freaks and nutters, mostly heralding from the era of the Blitz (the club in London, not the wartime German airborne attacks), 1984 saw the arrival of a different kind of expression. New identities and subject matter. An increase in men in dresses and an electronic music that had become slightly harder and more frantic.

The most significant event in pop during the *real* 1984, however, was the emergence of gay culture going over-ground and into the wider consciousness – often by stealth. It was an important twelve months when pop came out of the closet – even if not all of the artists felt that they could at that time – and, in the process, charted the course of the rest of the decade.

1984 is an interesting point of the '80s as it was when the New Pop Dream had started to curdle, and the last of the pop miscreants brought up by Bowie, T. Rex, Roxy Music and punk were starting to show signs of wear or bloating through addictions while wearing overtly ridicu-lous designer garments. That 'bigness' was the goal now, rather than settling for being known for having amazing hair. 1984 also ends with Band Aid and 'Do They Know it's Christmas?' It was sort of the last party of a whole era where the future for some of the acts was wearing large coats at Wembley Stadium and being IMPORTANT and socially aware, with grand albums where guitars sadly came back to the fore and it was now all about issues rather than tunes. It was a key moment in time where Status Quo – positively veterans with not even twenty years in the game at that point – found themselves rubbing up against Marilyn. And yet very few of the acts on that Band Aid single carried on the same level of success afterwards.

The second half of the '80s brought white-boy ersatz coffee-advert soul, charity fundraisers and 'authenticity', along with creepsome gloopy ballads and fucking Bros.

Thankfully, it also had acid house, hip hop, the sample-based doofery of S'Express and the loud, spotty and weird Jesus & Mary Chain. The word 'campaign' was now more commonly being used with artists, rather than some sort of haphazard hoping for the best. The launch of a fully formed Go West seemed joyless compared to the mad evolution of Julian Cope. And having gracefully accepted our finest acts (plus A Flock of Seagulls) as part of the early '80s British Invasion, the US was now giving us bloody Foreigner and Tiffany in return.

The people in this book have been selected due to the impact they had, or were about to have, not just on music, but on a broader cultural context, using their positions to educate, inform or just titillate. It cheers on the allies and the enablers. They were either starting out or dumper-bound or could have already been mainstays of the fabric of pop itself, but they may have made a bigger impact than they realised. To be included, they had to have had a chart entry in 1984 before their impact on people's lives via their success and platforms could be examined. The majority of these findings are based around artists who are/were – openly or not – gay, and/or had an impact on the year, as well as those who allied themselves with gay audiences and spoke to a sector of the pop-buying market that had been perhaps ignored for a few years. As the ideas of the differing realms of homosexuality found a footing in the teen mags, it was increasingly being discussed in a pop context. Even Paul Weller, after fondling his bandmate Mick

Talbot's ear in the video for the Style Council's 'Long Hot Summer', was seen to be questioning his sexuality when he spoke to *Smash Hits*: 'I don't know about actually having gay sex but sometimes I think . . . Well, I wonder what it's like. I'm actually open-minded on the subject.'

1984 saw the chart arrival of a whole host of acts that would all play their part in illuminating gay life. Frankie Goes to Hollywood would shock and appal and titillate in equal measure, laying waste to the year as its biggest stars with a combination of controversy, marketing, sex and horror. The fiercely political Bronski Beat would prove that you didn't need to dress up to show your sexuality and that looking just like you did was a political statement in itself. Madonna turned up in the charts, straight from New York clubland. Within the year, she'd become a massive star and, by the end of the decade, she'd be more than an ally to the LGBTQ+ community. After some gentle momentum, Prince would explode with *Purple Rain*, offering an extremely sexual and liberated take on boring old rock tropes by being a confirmed heterosexual who wasn't afraid to play with feminine imagery, clothing and being a bit camp while fronting a band featuring two lesbians.

The other big pop sensation of the year were Wham!, who seemed to jostle with Frankie for the top spot (between them and Frankie, they spent almost six months at number one) with 'Freedom' and 'Wake Me Up Before You Go-Go', as well as effectively launching George Michael's solo career with 'Careless Whisper' that summer. Having gone from shoving shuttlecocks down their shorts to choreographed dance routines in fluorescent hues with a campness that attracted scores of teenage fans, Wham! would have had a third chart-topper that year with 'Last Christmas', but were denied by the charity juggernaut of 'Do They Know it's Christmas?' (which George appears on anyway, so it wasn't all bad news).

After a few false starts, Pete Burns and Dead or Alive would end 1984 about to become enormous and give Stock Aitken Waterman their first chart-topper with the bombast of 'You Spin Me Round (Like a Record)'. Speaking of which, Stock Aitken Waterman formed when they got together to make a novelty rip-off of 'Relax' called 'The Upstroke' under the name Agents Aren't Aeroplanes, which wasn't a hit but set into motion a production team that would taste future success by producing Divine and Hazell Dean. This would lead to thirteen number-one hits and sales of more than 60 million singles over the next five years, fusing Motown songcraft with a debt to high energy. A London-based duo called Pet Shop Boys, who were keen to work with American producer and high energy innovator Bobby Orlando, would release their debut single 'West End Girls' to mass indifference. And, having charged into the nation's living rooms at the end of 1983, Morrissey and the Smiths would prove be more than a match for their pop contemporaries and would accrue a legion of disaffected youth as fans, combining explicitly gay lyrics ('a boy in the bush is worth two in the hand' etc.) with the insistence that Morrissey himself was celibate.

It was also the year when a host of artists who'd helped open the door for gay visibility, and had previously hinted at a life outside of heteronormative society, were roaming the charts: David Bowie, the architect of the 'Starman moment', when he draped his arm around Mick Ronson on *Top of the Pops*, and who had spent the previous decade offering mainstream pop fans glimpses of an alternative world, was back among his 'children' with a disappointingly straight album; Elton John, who'd battled with his sexuality, drugs and booze before stunning everyone when he decided to marry a woman; Queen, whose flamboyant singer Freddie Mercury had spent the previous decade mincing around in leather, were on the comeback trail after their *Hot Space* album 'flopped' and was slagged off by certain other band members.

Even the new don't-say-gay superstars, who 'still hadn't found the right girl yet', found themselves on the backfoot up against the influx of the out-and-prouders. Soft Cell had split up and Marc Almond had embarked on a solo career, while the comforting provocation of Culture Club, who'd been the biggest act in the world just months before, were gently unravelling as Boy George became the planet's cuddly drag queen, preferring a cup of tea to sex.

So, essentially, it seemed out of all the arts in 1984 – literature, cinema, television – pop music was ahead of them all, burrowing into the collective consciousness with gay themes, issues, ideas and protagonists. It was a not-so quiet revolution that would, in some cases, show a greater degree of tolerance from the public, at least. We were still a little way off from gay kisses in soap operas, and Oscar-winning films and stories where gay characters weren't just the baddies and/or tragic and doomed.

This is all a flipside to what was actually happening in gay people's lives. AIDS was taking its toll on the community, with the initial cases being reported in the UK adding to an ongoing climate of fear and homophobia growing into a hysteria of misinformation. AIDS had become front-page news in 1983, and there would be no let-up, with a general unpleasantness as early cases of the disease in Britain reached three figures, the death toll reached forty-six, and gay men were banned from becoming blood donors. The London Bisexual Group was formed and, in December, ran a conference called 'The Politics of Bisexuality'. The formation of Lesbians and Gays Support the Miners by activist Mark Ashton supported striking miners, starting with collecting donations at the Lesbian and Gay Pride march in London. Bronski Beat headlined the fundraising concert, entitled 'Pits and Perverts', and this alliance would lead to miners' groups becoming the most outspoken allies of the then-LGBT community in the 1988 campaign against Section 28. Small shoots of equality also began with Labour MP Chris Smith becoming the first openly gay MP.

INTRODUCTION

So here I am. Thinking about the fourteen-year-old me again. Thinking about how much I've changed. Thinking about how much the *world* has changed. It turns out that I needn't have worried about tigers being let loose in gay clubs – although, on some occasions, it might have jived proceedings up a bit. I may not still have *Top of the Pops*, *Smash Hits* or even half the Lego that I had back then but, on the plus side, I don't have to tolerate playing rugby. However, I – and all of us – will always have pop music. Because if I've learned anything during my life, *that* is what has helped me navigate my way through it. Pop music is important.

'AIDS is like everything else. When you mess up with nature,
you have it coming to you mate. Homosexuality isn't natural.
And if it isn't natural, it goes against the laws of nature.
It's just another plague. A homo plague'
– Reader's letter, the *Sun*, December 1983

FRANKIE GOES TO HOLLYWOOD

'Make making it your intention.'

It's January 1984, and *Top of the Pops* is celebrating its twentieth anniversary. John Peel and David 'Kid' Jensen are the guides through a selection of the week's hits, while also nodding to the show's past. The line-up isn't, perhaps, the greatest. In fact, you could argue that, despite being four years into the decade, it's like the '80s never happened.

Among the turns that evening are some legends who have been knocking around since the show began. There's Rod Stewart, leering with his top-thirty-two smash 'Sweet Surrender' – which, one would wager, even the man himself can't recall. Be-denimed dinosaurs and *Top of the Pops* regulars Status Quo are on hand with their not-vintage

13

'Marguerita Time' at number five. And, a decade on from their Super-Yob and gurning, mirror-hatted pomp, Slade are enjoying a brief return to fortunes in the top three with the scarf-waver 'My Oh My'.

This being the first show after Christmas 1983 unfortunately means that unappealing a cappella act Flying Pickets are still at number one, ba-ba-ba-ba-ing through their version of Yazoo's 'Only You'. There's also the rum inclusion of Frank Kelly – who, a decade later, would become better known as Father Jack in the sitcom *Father Ted* – performing 'Christmas Countdown', which feels as welcome as a stray sprout found behind a radiator. Grim all round. *Top of the Pops* traditionally showcases numbers that are climbing the chart, and to be honest, it's thrill-free slim pickings looking at the other opportunities on offer in the Top 40 that week. There's Macca's 'Pipes of Peace', en route to the top for one week, only really leaving unappealing festive novelties such as Roland Rat, George Cole & Dennis Waterman, and Black Lace.

But among all this light entertainment fare, one genuinely new band appears and opens the show with their debut single – a rambunctious romper entitled 'Relax'. It had finally staggered into the Top 40 at number thirty-six, having knocked around the lower reaches since its release the previous October. Unsurprisingly, given the post-festive gruel on offer, Frankie Goes to Hollywood's debut appearance feels genuinely revolutionary.

But let's start at the very beginning. Frankie Goes to Hollywood were just another Liverpudlian group when they formed in 1982. Their lead singer Holly Johnson had some form as a face on the city's post-punk scene, having released a pair of non-selling solo singles. He'd also played bass in the group Big in Japan alongside future Lightning Seed Ian Broudie, KLF-er and impresario Bill Drummond, and yet-to-be-a-Banshee drummer Budgie. Frankie's back-up singer and dancer Paul Rutherford did time in Hambi and the Dance, a troupe that barely got anywhere, despite signing with Virgin in 1981. In fact, the only other Hambi alumnus of note was producer Steve Power, who'd go on to twiddle knobs for the likes of James, Blur and, most notably, Robbie Williams. Then there were the other three, or The Lads as they became known: drummer Peter 'Ped' Gill, bassist Mark O'Toole and guitarist Brian 'Nasher' Nash, who had been associated with Johnson's earlier musical endeavours, and joined up to, well, be the musicians.

From the start, Frankie was all about SHOCK. Paul and Holly were very comfortable fruiting about in sex gear. More often than not, they were accompanied by the Leatherpettes, a pair of clothing-optional ladies brandishing whips and sexy paraphernalia. Frankie soon set about supporting the likes of punk remnants the Ruts DC, while trying to make impressions with record labels such as Phonogram and Arista, albeit unsuccessfully.

The first of two John Peel sessions were recorded in November 1982 and featured an infant version of 'Two

Tribes', as well as 'Krisco Kisses', 'Disneyland' and 'The World is My Oyster'. Yet, still, no labels were scrambling to secure their signatures, despite Peel taking the band on his roadshow at Warrington. After Channel 4 music show *The Tube* offered the band a slot, they filmed a performance of 'Relax (In Heaven Everything is Fine)' at Liverpool's State Ballroom. This also included being interviewed by a slightly perplexed Jools Holland. Their film was broadcast in February 1983, offering the nation a first proper glimpse of their *Mad Max*-meets-Tom of Finland image.[1] Of that moment, Holly reflected: 'The time we played *The Tube*, Jools Holland was sitting around moping all day. I think he's sort of bitter because he's a real muso and he's on the other side of the camera. Very sad. He needed cheering up, so we bound the Leatherpettes in pink ribbon and

---

[1] A key figure in the development of the leather lifestyle was Finnish artist Tom of Finland (real name Touko Valio Laaksonen), whose early drawings for men's physique magazines saw him gravitate from manly images of lumberjacks to athletic beefcakes whose clothes kept falling off. It was a fine line between offering images of the healthy ideal man and soft porn. However, as the pornography laws were relaxed towards the end of the '60s, Laaksonen's work became more explicit with the invention of *Kake* comic books. These ran from 1968 until 1986 and featured 'the hypermasculine leatherman' who would 'meet' various well-endowed muscly types (usually archetypes of police officers, cowboys, builders, sailors and such) and end up bumming them. While Laaksonen wanted to portray Kake and his conquests as 'proud men who were happy having sex', he also wanted to show elements of affection between his characters, rather than pages of just non-stop cock.

gave them to him. He brought them back to his hotel and showered them with champagne.'

Fortunately, watching *The Tube* that evening was producer Trevor Horn, who was looking for turns to sign to his new label, *Zang Tumb Tuum* (ZTT). He tracked the group down and snapped them up in May 1983, after convincing his business partner, the former journalist Paul Morley, that they were the future. At this point, Trevor Horn was having, what could be termed, a *very* successful '80s. Not only had he had enjoyed having, as one half of the Buggles, the first song played on MTV with 'Video Killed the Radio Star', he'd also dragged proggers Yes into the twentieth century and rescued hapless end-of-pier turn Dollar from the dumper by turning them into a futurist pop force. And, as if that wasn't enough, he'd co-curated Malcolm McLaren's visionary *Duck Rock* album, and was fresh from hitting the jackpot with his production on ABC's globally huge debut album, *The Lexicon of Love*.

Of Frankie, Paul Morley was less than convinced. He was a bit sniffy about the whole enterprise, later telling *Record Collector* that 'my kind of '80s English funk-punk at the time, being an *NME* snob of some standing, was more Clock DVA, 23 Skidoo, A Certain Ratio and the Pop Group.

'But this lot – as well as being very Liverpool-dandy – seemed very corny and ramshackle and also draped inelegantly with semi-naked go-go ladies, which offended me. Or at least it was a bit boring and obvious and Mayfair, not very transgressive at all . . . But I could see them through Trevor's eyes as a riotous piece of showbusiness and something that got him very excited.' After weighing up his pros and snooty cons, Morley eventually ditched his preconceptions and was soon onboard with turning the Frankies into A Thing.

'We used to know Paul Morley when he was in Manchester and he was working for the *NME*,' said Holly in 1983. 'We used to hate him, to be quite honest. He was like this div from Manchester. He made people like Howard Devoto, created their whole standing as far as the press were concerned. Made them out to be much bigger than their capabilities, which was a shame because Howard Devoto was quite talented. Maybe now he's doing the same thing with us in a way. I guess we fitted into his little fantasy, and he fitted into ours.'

When the band signed to ZTT, Horn reckoned he could probably reswizzle 'Relax' into *something*. He and Morley persuaded the band not to perform live while he was tinkering with their new, upgraded sound. Morley got out his thesaurus and set about applying his theories and ideas on the launch of the band, talking of how pop music could in fact be a lofty affair with references to more elaborate concepts than usual. Speaking in 2010, Morley reflected on ZTT, explaining that he 'loved the thought of inventing a label, and this was a time when pop labels were being invented that had artistic sensibility, philosophical personality, and very individual looks – they were all a combination of sound and design, and the music on these labels was completed by how the records looked as objects, and you could tell from a design what the label stood for, and each label was separate from the other.

'I loved the idea of a record label being itself a kind of work of art, with a very definite set of ideals, based around a manifesto or two, and having written about music for a few years but always being interested in action and ideas and provocation, the invitation seemed perfect.

'I really did fancy and then fantasise the idea that I, as an *NME* journalist interested in experimental pop music and the post-surreal history of twentieth century art from Duchamp to Beuys, would start up a very distinctive and somehow articulate and even argumentative record label inspired as much by Warhol's Factory as Manchester's Factory, which had Trevor Horn as its house producer.'

Holly had a specific vision of how he wanted the band to look and sound. 'David Bowie, or the fictional Spiders From Mars, was the inspiration for forming a band,' he surmised in his autobiography, *A Bone in My Flute.* 'After the music and songs were written, it came to me in a kind of LSD vision while watching Bow Wow Wow play in [Liverpool's] Sefton Park. We decided to incorporate the *Mad Max* warrior look with Tom of Finland, and create a kind of post-apocalypse, S&M punk look. We were bound to get attention and have lots of fun that way.'

Holly would reminisce to *Q* magazine that the band was 'totally blown away, because [Trevor] was the most technologically advanced producer in the UK at that time. By then, we'd been together for ages, and all my mates in Liverpool seemed to be getting famous, and we were going nowhere.

'We were on a downward trail. If Frankie hadn't taken off, I and the other members of the band could easily have been dragged into the sewer or I was going to go to art school ... The only other interested label was Beggars Banquet. They offered us £40 a week each for the next year, but *they* didn't have Trevor Horn. So, we signed to ZTT with a very unfair £250 recording advance between the five of us, and then we had to wait four months in the summer of 1983 for Trevor to become available.'

Naturally, the first thing that Trevor thought he'd lay down on tape, after he decided that 'Relax' should have a very classic 'shagging' 4/4 beat with elements of Donna Summer to it, was a recording of the band jumping into a swimming pool. 'It was the first thing we did at Virgin Manor Studios. I just thought it might be useful, and we did eventually use it in the Sex Mix.' For the uninitiated, the Sex Mix was a sixteen-minute doof odyssey of splashes, zips and Holly listing the names of various Amsterdam fetish clubs. This was definitely not the sort of thing you got with other chart staples of the day.

Despite having been a great live affair, Horn wasn't going to let the small detail of Frankie not being terribly good in the studio spoil the launch of his label. 'I brought in Ian Dury's backing band, the Blockheads, to give the

Frankies an example of another way to approach the song. That was when the Blockheads' bass player, Norman Watt-Roy, came up with a descending three-note bass part that I decided to include.'

An exasperated Holly was understandably losing patience. 'We'd already spent three months in SARM West, recording and scrapping two complete versions. It cost £30,000 while I was travelling back to Liverpool every week to sign on.' However, in the end, after the backing track had been completed, Horn remembered that 'Holly ran down to Studio One. When they heard it, him and Paul immediately started to dance, and so did the rest of us, just dancing around the control room. When it stopped, Holly said, "That's fantastic." I felt we'd snatched it from the jaws of disaster . . . I put a huge orgasm in the middle, the biggest orgasm that had ever been had by anybody, which we achieved with a sound Andy Richards had worked up on the keyboards some while before.'

At the time, Holly correctly described the results as being 'like these untamed creatures meet Trevor Horn and his stamp is all over it. Because it was our first single, and there's no ready-made market, we just had to have as much fun as we could when we were making it.'

There was then the small matter of conjuring up a video that would showcase 'Relax' and the full Frankie Goes to Hollywood experience. Ahead of making it, Holly told *NME* that 'the basic idea is that there's this virginal character, Frankie, and his girlfriend's just left him . . . He's never had sex and he's walking down the street, and gets lured into an orgy scene by this character in black . . . It's going to be a club scene, the sort of clubs we like to go to.'

'It was really great,' said Paul Rutherford. 'We had to go out and give out twenty invitations to act as extras in our video. So it was like going out and being told to pick up twenty men.'

'For us, it's just like getting someone else to pay for our fantasies,' suggested Holly. 'That's the whole idea. We're just having a party. It's such wonderful imagery to use, though if you haven't been in an Amsterdam leather bar you won't quite understand.'

'It's interesting drawing a comparison with the Soft Cell thing.' Holly said to the *NME*, 'Where they pantomimed it, we're going to do it for real.' Paul stressed that it was *art*, actually (darling), by offering that the video was full of 'really strong images, like a Fellini film'.

'Our main purpose is pleasure, to communicate a good feeling,' Holly reckoned. To the *NME* he said, 'Sex is part of it, sex is enjoyable, isn't it? It's about not being hung up or feeling guilty about any particular so-called deviation you'd like to get into. It's quite normal. The gay/S&M angle is regarded as taboo, but it's just people getting down, getting into enjoyment because it's not long that we are here . . . I met this Irish guy in a pub once and he asked me was I into M&S, it was really lovely. So sweet.'

Completed in considerably less time than it had taken to make the actual single, the promo for 'Relax' reflected the giddiness and perving phwoar-ness of the song itself. Filmed by Bernard Rose in a disused warehouse, the 'Relax' promo opens with a rubber-vested Paul Rutherford as a doorman having a snout at the door of an anonymous bar, as a suited Holly (as the 'Frankie' character) is wheeled up on a cart. Instead of Holly paying admission, an unhygienic Paul cheerily spits in the face of the attendant and leaves Holly to his devices as he ventures into a bar populated by drag queens, various types whose clothes have fallen off and several gentlemen at the bar 'keeping themselves entertained' with bananas. There are men waving torches about, harking back to a time in the '60s when same-sex dancing was illegal and when police would carry torches when undercover (or otherwise) in nightclubs, to shine in the dark to see if two men were dancing together.

A Nero-type character is then brought in. Holly would excitedly explain that 'it's Emperor Nero in this club, a huge man who gets his whole body shaved for sexual kicks and feeds people to tigers and lions. We're using the actual Esso tiger . . .' Indeed, the biggest star in the video at that time was actually the tiger. As for the Nero figure, he was someone they'd hired from a then-popular modelling service called the Ugly Agency, who specialised in representing 'differently attractive' and unconventional models.

While various poor patrons find themselves caged or locked up in medieval iron maiden torture devices, most of the bar are more into throwing drinks over each other than actual drinking. Nero soon summons the punters to bring Holly over to the stage to be fed to the tiger – not ideal as a night out by any means. However, despite the various clones and queens egging the tiger on, Holly manages to befriend it and doesn't end up as a snack.

The next thing you know, Holly and Paul are tied to a wheel and Nero appears to start pissing on them. This sends the club barmy, with everyone going wild and joining in with the pissing and throwing straw about. As the bacchanal reaches its zenith, Holly is next seen astride Paul with his tie around his neck, while Paul manhandles one of the Leatherpettes whose fright-wig is coming apart.

The video managed to tap into an entire subculture, driven by a world that Holly and Paul knew. They would have been very much pushing the ideas; Paul Morley was unlikely to have known what the inside of Amsterdam's Argos bar, or even the Coleherne in Earl's Court, looked like.

The gay scene in London, or at least that part of it which tried to imitate the hardcore backrooms of New York, centred around the Coleherne. It was originally split into two bars, one for straights and one for the gays, creating a 'man only' space when homosexuality was still illegal. But, by 1965, it was known more as a leather bar with blacked-out windows; the likes of Freddie Mercury, Kenny Everett and Rudolf Nureyev were among the celebrity revellers. It had its fair share of controversy, with local residents trying to close it down, as well as becoming known as the place where gay serial killer Dennis Nilsen picked up men.

It would later be where another mass murderer, Colin Ireland, befriended his victims. There was also Subway near Leicester Square, which attempted to recreate the vibe of New York's Mineshaft. According to Guy Burch, an artist who was wooed to London by both art school and the gay scene, 'you went down steps and an army jeep was parked on the landing where you paid. In the basement were two backrooms, one large right by the bar and another that was like the Black Hole of Calcutta, so cramped and packed and smelling of poppers you thought you wouldn't get out alive!'

Down in south London, there was the Market Tavern that had a late licence and became known as a gay bar in 1983, offering a selection of specialist nights. Guy recalls it as 'a scuzzy pub used by market traders, so had one of those exceptional late licences. It catered to the harder end of the market of leather, rubber and skinheads. After we left there, we'd go to the derelict Meat Stores. Very creepy and dangerous: hardly a weekend passed without some queen falling from one of the levels and breaking a leg.'

London's longest-running men-only fetish club, the Backstreet, would arrive in Mile End in 1985 and remain there for thirty-seven years until 2022, when the twin evils of Covid and a demand to redevelop the area in order for yet another bloody Tesco put paid to it.

The iconography of the Leatherman, a symbol of strength and idealised manliness – the clone – played a significant part in the 'Relax' video, emphasising a shorthand of fetish, as well as giving the promo, and Frankie, a certain toughness. The leather subculture was a way of signifying that the participants distinguish themselves away from traditional notions of homosexuality. While it has long been associated with BDSM, for many it was a way of expressing a heightened masculinity and an added power. The fetish grew from the motorcycle clubs of the late '40s/ early '50s, with gay men aping the look of Marlon Brando's 1953 film *The Wild One*, and was adopted by gay men as a way of moving away from 'camp'. While the first gay leather bar opened in Chicago in 1958, it found its true home in San Francisco in 1961 in the South of Market district when the club Tool Box opened, primarily frequented by gay bikers. The club would go on to be featured in a *Life* magazine article called 'Homosexuality in America' – the first time a national publication had ever reported on the gay experience. While the club was keen to dispel the myths of all gay men being effeminate, the article helped to turn San Francisco into both a destination for leather men and the gay capital of the country. This subculture had already gained broader acceptance in *Drummer* magazine which, when first published in 1975, proffered an entry into the gay leather lifestyle.

It didn't take long for Berlin to catch up with what was happening in San Francisco. A range of clubs opened around Nollendorfplatz in the early '70s and the area continues to host fetish-themed weekends. The sexual fetish of uniforms, leather and rubber allows gay men to attain an agency of masculinity otherwise absent and, in some way, can be seen as 'dressing up like your oppressor'. Meanwhile, the skinhead scene evolved from the original mod scene in the '60s, championing a working-class 'bit of rough' culture. The skinheads were also prominent in the popularity of ska music, with Symarip's 'Skinhead Moonstomp' being adopted as something of an anthem. By the end of the '70s, however, skinheads were more associated with right-wing and fascist movements, becoming increasingly racist and homophobic. The gay fetish appropriation of skinheads can be seen as an adoption of a more extreme masculinity as skins were tough and violent. In other words, a massive turn-on.

While leather found its place in gay culture, it was subsequently also near-parodied in the mainstream; witness the Village People leather clone Glenn Hughes, or Freddie Mercury mincing about in leathers for 'Crazy Little Thing Called Love'. Even in William Friedkin's wonky 1980 movie *Cruising* where Al Pacino plays a detective who goes undercover into a world of gay sex clubs to track down a be-leathered killer.

The 'Relax' video stands the test of time and now, some forty years on, there is almost nothing that dates it. No big hair or fashions of the day. You could walk into any gay club from Paris to Berlin, New York to London, and find the exaggerated masculinity of the Muir cap and leather uniform. It was the video's thrusting of an entire netherworld into the open that helped secured its iconic status.

Director Bernard Rose's only other video had been for UB40's 'Red Red Wine' – one not knowingly laced with such totems of homosexuality. He would also go on to direct the promo for Bronski Beat's 'Smalltown Boy'. As he revealed to *DMovies*, 'what was wonderful about them, especially in the early 1980s, was the record companies pretty much let you do what you wanted to do, because it was so new to them'.

As might be expected, 'Relax' didn't get much traction on MTV, and no one from regional television was hounding Frankie down to appear on Saturday-morning telly. Not that the record-buying public were necessarily pounding the doors of the nation's record shops in order to get a copy, either. 'Relax' was seemingly stapled to the shelves. After it was released in October 1983, it took an almost comically long time to crawl up the Top 75, even dropping on some weeks. It is likely that potential buyers were put off by the array of adverts in the press trumpeting messages of suggestive filth. With headlines such as 'All The Nice Boys Love Seamen' and copy suggesting 'Relax' 'makes Style Council seem like the last line in a Barbara Cartland novel' could be considered transgressive for a teenage music mag in the '80s. While it echoed the shock of punk, there is no way advertisers would get away with it today. In addition, the cartoon semen, and Paul and Holly leering out with their rubber and sheer abandon, was definitely not something the pop kids had previously experienced with the flimsy old comically haired likes of Kajagoogoo. This hadn't gone down well with the rest of the band, either. No one was keen with the emphasis on making Paul and Holly look like a pervert Wham! and denying the existence of the lad faction.

The entire launch of Frankie appeared to be hitting the buffers somewhat. After entering at number seventy-seven in November 1983, 'Relax' spent the next couple of months fart-arsing about before crawling into the Top 40 at the very start of the new year – something of a result for a record mostly unplayed by daytime radio and only picked up by early adopters. It was that fortuitous decision of *Top of the Pops* to ask the band to perform on that 20th-anniversary show that really gave the single its wings and the momentum it needed. That appearance had propelled it from number thirty-five to number six in a single week. You'd have thought it was inescapable on the airwaves. However – uh-oh – trouble loomed. And not just from any potential grief from the dole office seeing Holly and chums fruiting it up on national television, but from the BBC themselves.

The *BBC* 'ban'[2] was brought about by Radio 1 breakfast DJ Mike Read, whose show had the ears of millions of

---

[2] There was also John Peel's alleged 'ban' of 'I, Bloodbrother Be' by Shock Headed Peters, due to its homosexual lyrics ('I wanna walk through Sodom with a boy on my arm / Who's so damn pretty I don't know where I am'). Peel disputed this as something their record company had dreamt up, saying at the time that 'it's one of these things where I suppose, it's good publicity to do this but it's certainly not the case at all. I just didn't think it was a good enough record to play. I don't play Des O'Connor records, but you don't see Des O'Connor being interviewed in the papers and saying 'John Peel's a bastard and he's banned my records'.

listeners tuning in. While playing that week's chart run-down, he spotted the sleeve, looked at some of the lyrics and rather sniffily said that he wasn't going to play it. He has since gone on to claim – with all the air of some self-righteous politician – that 'many people came up to me and said they were really pleased I had done so'. With hindsight, it all feels a little prudish, if not ridiculous.

Radio 1's then-controller Derek Chinnery backed up Read, claiming that 'we could have said there was a dual meaning to the song, that it's a nonsense song about relaxing. But when the band confirmed that it referred to fellatio and ejaculation, then it didn't seem to me appropriate that we should play it at all'. It's a good thing that Mike Read had only discovered it at that point, because the self-appointed moral majority would have had an absolute nervo after seeing the initial adverts for the song. Fortunately, it backfired on him, making him seem even more of a square.

It was a drag for the band to be at number one and not actually be able to perform it on TV – and no doubt was as annoying for the thousands of punters buying it, especially when it spent five weeks at the top of the chart. Paul Morley claimed that 'when it was banned, we were shocked, from the point of view that we'd got away with it for so long. It didn't upset me, 'cos my taste lies in line with things like that.'

While it shot up the chart, Frankie made another video for 'Relax', a straightforward performance affair that lacked any semi-naked emperors, torture or people pissing. Talking to Radio 1 presenter and self-styled hip uncle Peter Powell on the *Oxford Roadshow* about it, Holly claimed that 'the ban is not a good thing. For our first single, it's like a little black mark against us. That's what it feels like.' Powell also showed himself up terribly when he suggested the band's music is 'camp or glam rock', to which a chortling Holly corrected him. 'I think it's more closely related to New York disco or funk, but it is something that is kinda English to show we can do it as good as those boys.'

Holly was also on good form when Dave Atkey, Peter Powell's producer, was asked about the ban. 'Normally Radio 1 never bans anything,' said Atkey. 'It's usually down to the individual producers who have a responsibility to their audience to make the decision whether they play a record or not. The record came in to me, and I found the lyrics objectionable and I felt that the record could offend the majority of our listening audience, so I made the decision not to play it. When the record originally came into the office, it was a promotional copy in a white cover. The actual copy that went to the shops had the lyrics on the picture bag [and] confirmed my original opinion about the record. And when I saw the video, I thought that it was tasteless and nasty.'

Holly was right to ask the question, 'why did we get on *Top of the Pops* and have ninety-two airplays on Radio 1?

And then, all of a sudden, it's banned? I'm quite outraged by the way I've been slandered as someone with disgusting lyrics, and that only someone with the mind of a sewer could see those as obscene.' Atkey, doing his best not to morph into Mary Whitehouse, fumed that there was 'no other interpretation you could take of those lyrics. It is the description of a sexual act.' 'It's "Relax", DON'T do it,' appealed Holly.

Fortunately, the ban was only a BBC ruling; commercial stations were still playing the song. It was a significant moment in the 'groovy, youth-led' station's history. Radio 1 was now seen as this stuffy moral arbiter, and 'Relax' was now in the lineage of banned songs that had previously included Tom Robinson's 'Glad To Be Gay' and the Kinks' 'Lola' (although that was actually about the product placement of Coca-Cola), and which would later be joined by George Michael's rumpo-loving 'I Want Your Sex' in 1987 and Lil' Louis's heavy-breathin', asthma-houser 'French Kiss' in 1989.

The nation's supposed favourite clearly didn't want songs that were about sex on their station – which, if we're going to get arsey about it, would preclude much of music itself. This is the station that would, on 21 January 1991, issue a blacklist of inappropriate songs to play during the Gulf War. The list scuppered Massive Attack's chart climb with 'Unfinished Sympathy' (they ended up being called Massive for a bit), edited out the gunfire at the beginning of the KLF's '3AM Eternal', royally buggered up Bomb

The Bass's career and denied the listeners the chance of hearing Jona Lewie's festive treat 'Stop The Cavalry' in February.

Taken in context with the advertising AND the video, Radio 1 may have had a point, but ultimately their job was to just play the record, not critique the marketing of it. Mike Read's disgust was based on the illustration of a man and a woman drawn by Yvonne Gilbert that originally appeared in the June 1983 edition of perv-rag *Men Only* magazine, accompanying an article called 'Breastfest'. 'I would have drawn Paul and Holly in their fetish gear if I'd had the time,' recalled Yvonne to *Q* in 2001. 'We were big fans of Tom of Finland,' said Holly, 'as she was, and we thought it would be perfect. So, we put it under the record company's nose. It wasn't very fashionable in 1983. I don't know of any other pop groups until then who'd discussed sado-masochism or gay sexuality with the music weeklies before in such an in-your-face way.'

Once 'Relax' had seen off Paul McCartney's 'Pipes of Peace' from the top spot, Frankie Goes to Hollywood were now officially pop stars – albeit, admittedly, pop stars who had the same appeal of sick filth and outrage that had briefly sustained the Sex Pistols a few years earlier (although in the case of Frankie they managed to sell far more in the process).

Holly also proved to be a refreshing change from the usual pop interviewee. He answered queries in a 'Personal

File' feature in *Smash Hits* with the sort of frankness that you didn't get from the Thompson Twins.

FAVOURITE ITEM OF CLOTHING: 'Brogue shoes. And I love a leather jockstrap.'
  WHAT HAVE YOU GOT IN YOUR POCKETS: 'Receipts from Expectations, a rubber shop in the East End. And a packet of Extra Strong Mints and my favourites, Lemon Fruitellas.'
  FAVOURITE CLOTHES: 'Denim and black things. I like wearing suits as well – I had this gorgeous one that got wrecked in the vid. And rubber, of course.'

From their convoluted beginnings, and their crowning as the harbingers of BumPop, Frankie Goes to Hollywood would spend the rest of 1984 ruling the charts. They took up a quarter of the year at the number-one spot with nine weeks for 'Two Tribes' across the summer, and another week in December for their third single, 'The Power of Love', which had its Christmas number-one ambitions scuppered by 'Do They Know it's Christmas?' (which also had a contribution from Holly on the B-side). The majesty of 'The Power of Love' has grown ever since; it was seen as being festive-adjacent, due to the nativity story theme of the accompanying music video. Their debut album – a double, no less – *Welcome to the Pleasuredome* was also a number one on its release, with reported advance orders of more than a million copies. It contained the song 'The World is My Oyster'. For Frankie, it most certainly was.

Frankie did actually go to Hollywood. The group appeared in Brian De Palma's erotic thriller *Body Double* in 1984, in a 'film within a film' scene where main character Jake (Craig Wasson) goes undercover to find Holly Body (Melanie Griffith) on the set of a porn flick in a nightclub. Jake is welcomed into the club by Holly Johnson, who is then picked up by some gents and placed on top of the bar where a dominatrix walks over him. The patrons of the venue seem to be making a very American fist of a sex club. It's as though somebody described the 'Relax' video to the ensemble, but they didn't quite get it. There are a few punky types, a random woman pouring water over herself (presumably a *Flashdance*-esque moment) and, in a nod to the *Rear Window* voyeurism of the film, Holly and Paul peer into a telescope to watch the shenanigans. Although Melanie Griffith was nominated for a Golden Globe, the $10 million-budget film didn't particularly set the box office alight, scraping 'only' $8 million in total.[3]

---

[3] One of the biggest films of 1984 was *Police Academy*, a bawdy tale of misfits signing up to join the police force. One of the recurring themes of the franchise, that would eventually run for another six sequels, was the Blue Oyster 'salad bar' ('salad bar' presumably to indicate the perceived effeminacy of lettuce). This would cause a level of panic in the main characters whenever they had to attend the place because it was home to an army of leathermen who seemed only to want to waltz and tango. It was very odd, a bit shitty and obviously hilarious for any homophobe whose worst fear was the gays.

By December, Frankie found themselves among the big-league poll winners Duran Duran, Wham!, Culture Club and Spandau Ballet in *Smash Hits*' annual awards. They also found themselves at the receiving end of sniffy remarks from some of pop's leading lights. 'Who knows where Frankie will be next year?' asked Boy George. 'Frankie's a weird one,' said Spandau's Gary Kemp. 'I find it hard to think of them as a group, although they make great records.'

The wheels of the Frankie operation began to wobble by the time of their fourth single. The title track of *Welcome to the Pleasuredome* was billed as 'Frankie's fourth number one' in early 1985, but 'only' reached the lowly number two spot. Keen to step out of Trevor Horn and Paul Morley's shadow, they set about recording their second album, but cracks were beginning to appear. The two factions of the band – Paul and Holly, and the three lads – were increasingly on different planets. When they returned in August 1986 with the single 'Rage Hard', public interest was muted. Things didn't improve with the release of the album *Liverpool* that October. The band imploded and, by March 1987, it was confirmed they'd split.

Despite all this, according to Official Charts Company data, 'Relax' has now sold more than 2.08 million copies. It's one of the biggest-selling singles of all time and one of the biggest-selling debut singles ever. Add the 1.8 million sales of 'Two Tribes' and it was clear that no other band would have quite such the chart impact that Frankie had in 1984.

Did Frankie set out to be controversial? Or was it handily adjacent to an already amazing piece of pop? Was the 'ban' the icing on the cake, adding a frisson of controversy? Well, yes and no. There's no doubt that ZTT were focused on ensuring the band made as much of an impact as possible. And there's no question that, when taken as a whole, 'Relax' certainly did that. The second, less controversial video, made as the single shot up the charts, was obviously an attempt to give the whole thing legs and to avoid further prohibition. But it was Mike Read's decision to ban the record – doing what he did when he did – that turned the record into much more of an event.

It also led to pressure for the band to 'follow that'. Like it or not, the expectation of shock was presumed when 'Two Tribes' arrived. It was a colossal banger already, aided by umpteen remixes, T-shirts and some terrifying advertising that explained how many people would die when a nuclear warhead came to their town. And, of course, another banned video. It all tapped into a wave of paranoia that swept through culture. Some law was clearly passed where everyone in pop, from Kim Wilde to Ultravox and the Human League, had to have some sort of nuclear panic-themed promo. That's not forgetting the gruesome TV drama *Threads* as well, which scarred and scared a whole generation for life. You can almost begin to understand why Black Lace's 'Agadoo' was so popular, feeling like welcome relief from all this *Protect and Survive*-chic.

As Holly pointed out to *Record Collector*, 'the whole multiple remixes of the 12-inch single was something that hadn't really been done before and became standard practice in the music industry. It wasn't just the first album either – it was the presentation, the appearances on *Top of the Pops* and *The Tube*, the midnight showings of the video of 'Two Tribes' because of its controversial content. These things all seem standard now, but with Frankie Goes to Hollywood, it was the first time that had happened. You had to be fourteen in 1984 to truly appreciate the excitement it generated. They just don't make them like that anymore.'

And Holly is right. Frankie Goes to Hollywood was a perfect amalgamation of shock and mass marketing, which far eclipsed anything that had gone before, and a media manipulation where the stars aligned way beyond Frankie and ZTT's wildest dreams. What looked like a blitz of hype and T-shirts was backed up by the music, by three iconic chart-toppers that sound dateless four decades on.

Now, when 'Relax' pops up on the radio, no one is running to complain. Instead, it just stands as a sizzling, thrusting, utterly brilliant piece of music and revolution that elicits fond memories from anyone who lived through the era. The Mike Read hubbub, even in an environment where sexuality has become a culture war go-to, feels like a moment of pearl-clutching ridiculousness. When a DJ pops the Annihilation mix of 'Two Tribes' on in a nightclub, it packs the apocalyptic oomph it always had and the opening HRRNK of the air-raid siren alone will ram the dancefloor. Hearing 'The Power of Love' piped through a shop in December, or indeed any other time of the year, it still gloriously swoons as the perfect love song. Its, um, power was also used magnificently in the 2023 film *All of Us Strangers*, provoking outbreaks of blubbing in cinemas.

As a cheery update to this tale, Frankie Goes to Hollywood reformed for a one-off performance as part of the Eurovision Song Contest celebrations in Liverpool in 2023. During a concert outside St Georges Hall, featuring the likes of other local turns such as The Lightning Seeds, the original fivesome performed 'Welcome to the Pleasuredome' and . . . er, that's it. The all-too-brief reunion might have seemed a little bit of a cop-out to some. To be honest, what else could they have played? Eurovision was being held in Liverpool after the UK had stepped in to host the event following Ukraine's inability to because of the Russian invasion, and so 'Two Tribes' would have been a little on the nose. However, the sheer joy and outpouring of love after their performance was broadcast was palpable. Many people remembered why they were so magnificent, and the warm reception allowed them to leave on a high. The buzz of love for Frankie and their catalogue was evident.

But the whole adventure all kicked off with 'Relax'. It not only sounded like the most exciting thing on Earth, but it also caused ripples in general during their five-week internment at number one when it made a returning rock band – also featuring a gay lead singer not averse to dressing up – absolutely *furious* when their comeback was reduced to making do with the runners-up spot.

In January 1984, The Terrence Higgins Trust, named after
Terry Higgins who was one of the first people in the UK to die
of an AIDS-related illness in 1982, gains charitable status.
It becomes the first charity in the country to be set up in
response to the HIV epidemic and has been at the forefront
of the fight against HIV and AIDS ever since.

QUEEN

'But life still goes on . . .'

It's January 1984, and Queen are back. Back. BACK! They'd not actually been away that long in all honesty, but required a reset after the relative failure of their previous album. They returned in a spectacular fashion, a step-up into enforcing their legend as one of the world's greatest rock bands.

Formed in London in 1970, the original quartet of Queen – aka Freddie Mercury, Brian May, Roger Taylor and John Deacon – spent the next decade becoming one of the world's biggest bands. There were significant highs; the original single release of 'Bohemian Rhapsody' in 1975 for one, spending nine weeks on top of the charts, ushering in the age of video, and generally becoming one of the most-played songs of all time would be enough for one turn as it is. There was also the parade of huge, huge albums, the invention of the stadium act, and the studious application of creating anthems. 'We Will Rock You' and 'We are the Champions' are prime examples of that stompsome, arms-aloft format. Then there's the cavorting about on the shoulders of someone dressed as Darth Vader, Brian May's homemade guitar, his fondness for clogs . . . Queen were pioneers on many levels. They were in the right place at the right time on so many occasions: supporting Mott the Hoople; the glam adjacent stylings of 'Seven Seas of Rhye', which gave them their big break on TV on *Top of the Pops* when they stepped in last minute as a replacement for an otherwise unavailable David Bowie; the 'disco rock' moment that was 'Another One Bites the Dust', which became the bedrock of several early hip hop tracks. It's not for nothing that their first *Greatest Hits* is, at time of writing, the biggest-selling album of all time in the UK with more than 7 million sales. It's a title they are likely to keep into the foreseeable future, unless the next-closest LP, *ABBA Gold,* lays siege upon it.

Back in the '80s, though, Queen were in a rum spot. They'd entered the decade cheerily with *The Game,* a 4-million seller that finally saw them dismiss their snooty 'no synthesisers are on this record' gambit. They looked to embrace the next ten years with a host of singles such as 'Play the Game' and 'Save Me', together with the marginally more successful 'Crazy Little Thing Called Love' and 'Another One Bites The Dust', which were their only two number-one singles in the US. These were hastily followed up with their soundtrack to the camp-as-tits remake of *Flash Gordon*.

By 1981, buoyed by 'Under Pressure', a UK number-one duet with David Bowie, they released their first *Greatest Hits* album the same week. They neglected to actually include the track on the UK version, which seemed a bit barmy, but everything was fairly rosy in the garden of Queen career-wise. While the *Greatest Hits* was doing the business, the band were in the process of working on what would become *Hot Space*, ahead of its release in May 1982.

Now, *Hot Space* has its knockers. Although maybe not quite as many knockers as Roger Taylor would've liked. It was the first sign of an – until then – otherwise sturdy outfit having their 'we hope you like our new direction!' moment. It saw the band embarking on more 'disco' – or as Freddie, um, *gallantly* called it onstage, a more 'black'-sounding record. However, *Hot Space* was, and still is to an extent, viewed by both its makers and fans as something of a hot mess. It was even listed on a *Q* magazine chart as an example of where great bands lost the plot. Made in Munich and Montreux, and embracing – well, 'embracing' may not be so much the word as far as some members were concerned – more electronics and synths, it was also the first occasion where the quartet were recording separately rather than all together.

It didn't help that the members were indulging in various excesses, be it drugs, drink or women. Since reflecting on the album, Roger Taylor has been openly critical that Freddie's personal manager, Paul Prenter, had considerable influence over the singer, and was denying the rest of the band access to him. '[Prenter] wanted our music to sound like you'd just walked in a gay bar . . . and I didn't.' At the time, though, he more professionally offered that 'we never tried to pander to what we feel people want. A lot of people want to hear rehashes of what they liked in the past, but that would be death for us. That's really unfair, because we have changed a lot.'

Brian May retrospectively suggested to *Uncut* that the band 'moved out to Munich to isolate ourselves from normal life so we could focus on the music. We all ended up in a place that was rather unhealthy. A difficult period. We weren't getting along together. We all had different agendas. It was a difficult time for me, personally – some dark moments.' Even Freddie was initially on the offensive. 'We weren't extremely disappointed. But we're conceited enough to believe that the music isn't less popular, and we are prepared to fight to show that it isn't.'

Putting it mildly, *Hot Space* was Queen at their gayest yet. Yes, even after a decade of songs about fairy kings and old-fashioned lover boys, this departure into a groovier direction had Freddie's hands all over it. It wasn't all doom and gloom – the biggest hit from the album (if you discount the inclusion of 'Under Pressure') was 'Body Language', which reached number eleven in the US. In the UK, though, the three singles – 'Body Language', 'Las Palabras De Amor' and 'Backchat' – fared quite badly in comparison, reaching twenty-five, seventeen and forty respectively. 'Under Pressure' had actually been tacked on at the end as a last-minute addition to the album.

Queen's attempt to 'get with it' and get funky was woefully misjudged by at least two years. '*Hot Space* was a mistake, if only timing wise,' May reflected to *Sounds* in 1989. 'We got heavily into funk and it was quite similar to what Michael Jackson did on *Thriller*. But the timing was wrong. Disco was a dirty word.' Michael Jackson himself claimed that *Hot Space* had been an influence on *Thriller*, which went on to sell considerably more copies. Sixty-six million more.

Burned by the album's reaction, and in an attempt to regain their position, 1984's follow-up *The Works* – said to be a quote from Roger Taylor saying, 'Let's give them the works' – was a serious concerted effort to recapture the public. It was Queen back to being the band that the public had spent the previous decade buying squillions of. It's almost hilariously precision-made to the nth degree to re-establish the brand.

Heralded by the first single off the album, 'Radio Ga Ga', which was aided with a video specifically designed to get screened on the increasingly important MTV, it was as if the band had never been away. 'Radio Ga Ga' was a straight-in-the-top-five return, although it was denied the top spot by Frankie Goes to Hollywood's 'Relax'. It was as if the band who'd fought so hard against the 'faggy' previous album were ironically held off the top spot by possibly the most homosexual record ever made. Still, it's responsible for influencing a certain Stefani Joanne Angelina Germanotta who took part of the song's title for her stage name some years later.

It was the follow-up that would cause the band a new headache, however. Released in April 1984, the John Deacon-written 'I Want to Break Free' came with a video that was destined to be all over MTV. Only trouble was that the video – a representation of the band dragged up as nods to various *Coronation Street* characters, with Freddie as an exaggerated Bet Lynch pushing a hoover around the other members, Roger Taylor (as Suzie Birchall), John Deacon (as Ena Sharples) and Brian May (as Hilda Ogden) – didn't go down terribly well outside the UK. While it may not have been entirely faithful as regards looking exactly like the cast, the video's setting suggested as much, and as far as British viewers were concerned, it was an affectionate piss-take of one of television's longest-running soap operas. It was Roger Taylor's idea, despite not being a big fan of making videos. 'We had done some really serious, epic videos in the past, and we just thought we'd have some fun,' he said. 'We wanted people to know that we didn't take ourselves too seriously, that we could still laugh at ourselves. I think we proved that.' Even May recalled that 'it was hilarious to do it. And all around the world, people laughed. And they got the joke, and they sort of understood it.'

All around the world except North America, that is. MTV banned it. 'I remember being on the promo tour in the Midwest of America and people's faces turning ashen and they would say, "No, we can't play this. We can't possibly play this. You know, it looks homosexual." And I went, so? But it was a huge deal. And I know that it really damaged our sort of whole relationship with certainly radio in this country and probably the public as well . . .' said May.

Claiming that a video is promoting cross-dressing seems almost archaic now, and there's no mention of the middle section, featuring members of the Royal Ballet and a parody of Nijinsky's *Afternoon of a Faun*. In one strike, the video derailed Queen as chart-goers in the US. 'Fans' even lobbed missiles (well, bottles and coins) at the band when they played it in Brazil. Frankly, it all seems a bit daft.

The song managed to crawl to number forty-five in the US, which in view of how well they'd been doing, was something of a disaster. Things were never really the same again as regards their US profile, at least not until a post-Freddie-death/*Wayne's World*-related re-release of 'Bohemian Rhapsody' returned them to number two in 1992.

Also in 1984, Freddie set about launching his own solo career with the song 'Love Kills', recorded for Giorgio Moroder's new soundtrack for the restoration of Fritz Lang's 1927 film *Metropolis*. Queen were allowed to feature scenes from the original film in the video of 'Radio Ga Ga', permission they received in exchange for Freddie's contribution to the Moroder soundtrack. Reaching number ten in the UK that September, 'Love Kills' fared somewhat better than the film did. Unsurprisingly, it was a hit in gay nightclubs and prophetically a song that would be very of its time due to the encroaching grip of AIDS. Although it had been originally considered for inclusion on *The Works*, it must have seemed a bit too *un*-Queen at the time. However, twenty years later and short of anything new to flog, it was reworked by Queen themselves, who recorded a new musical backing for it for their 2014 compilation *Queen Forever*.

The Works did its thing, spending an initial fifty-seven consecutive weeks in the chart, in the process becoming one of Queen's biggest studio albums. It was invariably helped by their military-precision appearance the following year at Live Aid. Queen had pretty much rescued their career from the *Hot Space* blip. Live Aid itself renewed interest in the band's catalogue, catapulting the *Greatest Hits*, *The Works* and even – tenuously – Freddie's solo debut album *Mr Bad Guy* back into the charts. From that point on, if anything, Queen were possibly bigger than they'd even been – a global audience of a billion or so kind of helps like that – and their performance on that July day in 1985 was widely considered to be the highlight. That was all fabulous. Well done, Queen.

However, it's the light airbrushing of Queen's gay legacy that seems to have been glossed over. One could say that the movie of *Bohemian Rhapsody* needed to be as big as possible. Reenactments of Freddie leathered up and taking Kenny Everett to leather bars in London, being a regular at Heaven, and basically moving into fisting-friendly venue The Anvil in New York were never going to be suitable for an Academy Award-winning multiplex-filler. It's not like Freddie wasn't backward in coming forwards about his sexuality; he claimed he 'did everything with everybody'. Even in the early days of Queen, he was open about being bisexual while living with his girlfriend Mary Austin. The rest of the band claimed that Freddie was extremely private about what he got up to, and they never really pushed him about it. Yet by wearing T-shirts from gay bars, mincing about in leotards or Muir caps, and wearing that handlebar cockduster moustache, he'd made it almost *too* obvious.

But it mattered not a jot as regards their popularity. Even when tabloid newspapers, at their most vicious and invasive and really fucking unpleasant, were circling Freddie's house during his last days for papped images of him looking ill, or printing 'exposés' about the bars that he frequented during the early years of the AIDS pandemic, Queen were still untouchable in their fans' eyes. Freddie's non-adherence to being neither one thing or another added to the appeal of the band. The Queen 'brand', as it was, did not appear to suffer any major denting, even after Freddie admitted to German magazine *Popcorn* in 1984, 'I'm gay, so what? I admit that, just as I also admit the fact that I'm not a particularly happy person. I'm actually a very sensitive, romantic guy, but I was often disappointed.

My heart has many scars. Nowadays I only have casual sex without emotions.'

The ultimate betrayal came when Paul Prenter, in what seemed like an act of retaliation after being sacked by Freddie, sold his story to the *Sun* in 1987. With such tabloid-fodder as 'Freddie was so scared he would catch it', Prenter went full shade with bitchy insights such as 'It was more likely that I would see him walk on water than go with a woman', and 'While we were touring, there would be a different man every night. He would probably go to bed by 6am or 7am – but rarely alone.' Miaow.

While Prenter was no doubt paid handsomely for his betrayal, Freddie understandably cut him off completely. As Freddie's then-lover Jim Hutton said in his own autobiography, 'we later learned that Prenter had been paid about £32,000 by the paper for his story. Freddie never spoke to him again. For the next few days, there was more in the *Sun*, and at each episode of Prenter's story, Freddie became angrier. Prenter sold the paper several photographs of Freddie with various lovers and these were thrown over two pages under the heading "All The Queen's Men".'

Prenter himself would die of AIDS a few months before Freddie did. You can kind of understand why he was presented as the villain in the film, and no doubt the remaining members of Queen felt the story needed to anchor around a bad guy. Certainly, by any metric of privacy and disclosure, it was a shitty thing for Prenter to have done.

You have to remember that these were very different times. The demonisation of AIDS, and misunderstanding of the disease, was rife throughout the decade. Having gone from just a handful of deaths at the start of the '80s, it had grown into a terrifying and harrowing epidemic – and was something that was shorthand for 'unclean' and 'depraved'. Any great leaps made by the gay movement were pushed back into the closet with the door firmly held closed. The mood was fed by an unpleasant, homophobic government and a sensationalist press, which was happy to perpetuate a culture of fear, one where misinformation was the order of the day.

Freddie himself was a mass of contradictions. Despite his very public flamboyant persona, he was a very private man. His matter-of-fact approach in later life, and his focus on getting as much work done 'until he dropped', offers up the view that he himself didn't want to be defined by his sexual preferences. He had a platform, and some have suggested that Freddie could have helped shape a whole generation of attitudes to homosexuality and AIDS had he discussed it openly, rather than announcing his illness the day before he died. He chose not to for the band's sake, issuing the following statement: 'Following the enormous conjecture in the press over the last two weeks, I wish to confirm that I have been tested HIV-positive and have AIDS. I felt it correct to keep this information private to date in order to protect the privacy of those around me. However, the time has now come for my friends and fans around the world to know the truth and I hope that everyone will join with me, my doctors and all those worldwide in the fight against this terrible disease.'

As Elton John said in his book, *Love is the Cure: On Life, Loss and the End of AIDS*, 'Freddie didn't announce publicly that he had AIDS until the day before he died in 1991. Although he was flamboyant on stage – an electric frontman on a par with Bowie and Jagger – he was an intensely private man offstage. But Freddie told me he had AIDS soon after he was diagnosed in 1987. I was devastated. I had seen what the disease had done to so many of my other friends. I knew exactly what it was going to do to Freddie. As did he. He knew death, agonising death, was coming. But Freddie was incredibly courageous.' May recalled to *The Times* that 'He said, "I suppose you realise that I'm dealing with this illness." Of course, we all knew, but we didn't want to. He said, "You probably gather that I'm dealing with this thing and I don't want to talk about it, and I don't want our lives to change, but that's the situation." And then he would move on.' Only a handful of people knew just how ill Freddie had become, but that's how he wanted it to be. 'He was a very private person. People should remember him for his music and the happiness he brought to the world.'

That's undisputed. Freddie was indeed the ultimate performer and, since his death, has become shorthand for an iconic totem of rock showmanship, referenced in advertising, songs and films. As stories and first-hand accounts began to correct any myths, he was truly one of a kind and an inspiring individual.

Much has been said about Queen's gay-washing and how Freddie's excesses have been carefully curated so as not to upset their place in music history. The biopic *Bohemian Rhapsody* may be a case in point. It's alarming how commercial interests can reshape timelines and the narrative of people lives. As Alexis Petridis said in the *Guardian* about the film: 'For one thing, few artists have been so hawkish in posthumously extending their brand as Queen: since Freddie's death in 1991, there have been jukebox musicals, umpteen archive releases and documentaries, as well as attempts to reboot the band without him. For another, Mercury's story is clearly one worth telling. If anything, he seems a more remarkable figure in hindsight than at the height of his career.'

Freddie Mercury was indeed a remarkable figure. And while nothing is ever likely to damage the reputation and legacy of Queen, you rather hope that some addressing of who the man himself actually *was* could only enhance it in the long run.

If Freddie were still around now, he'd no doubt have been able to fully embrace being his authentic self – probably romping around Instagram, posting photos of him and his cats, and digging out occasional snaps of when he was at his fruitiest. But he wouldn't be the only gay, leather-friendly rocker. Over on the heavier side of the rock spectrum in 1984, a Metal God's 'real' self was also hiding in plain sight.

In February 1984, the album of Eddie Murphy's comedy special Delirious *wins Best Comedy Album at the Grammy Awards. It features routines about homosexuals and AIDS, and takes a carefree approach to the use of the word 'faggot'. For example: 'It petrifies me because girls be hangin' out with them. And one night they could be in the club havin' fun with their gay friend and give them a little kiss and go home with their AIDS on their lips.' Murphy later apologised in 1996 for causing offence.*

JUDAS PRIEST

'Squealing in passion as the rod of steel injects.'

For many years, in the world of heavy metal, much like professional football,[1] there were pitfalls in expressing your sexual preference for fear of abuse and being outcast.

You'd have thought that a musical form such as metal — populated by men whose hair knew the benefits of a good conditioner, and who were dressed in leather and

---

[1] Britain's first — and seemingly only (at that time) — gay footballer Justin Fashanu had risen spectacularly through his humble beginnings as an apprentice at Norwich City, turning professional in 1978. Despite his scoring abilities,

spandex — that there'd have been no end of queens, but no. Heavy metal fans weren't considered to be accepting of such matters, and the closet ended up as the place to be for most of the music's gay practitioners. The thing was, however, that not many, if any, of those fans out the front at Judas Priest concerts, or purchasing the band's albums, had an inkling that lead singer Rob Halford was gay.

That was the thing with metal. Many acts played around with make-up and long hair and tight garments, but it was the de facto look. This is why the US never really adopted the otherness of Bowie or T. Rex in all their pomp, yet were fine with the theatrics of the likes of Alice Cooper, who was more about shock and outrage. While these acts would liberally borrow from their girlfriends' and wives' wardrobes, and took tips on what eye shadow suited them

---

he couldn't stop Norwich being relegated and so, in 1981, he transferred to Nottingham Forest, becoming Britain's first million-pound black footballer. However, his tenure at Forest wasn't all rosy, as his relationship with manager Brian Clough deteriorated when his previous form deserted him. Rumours of Fashanu attending gay nightclubs became part of Clough's ire towards the player and, when confirmed, Clough barred Fashanu from training with the side. Fashanu's career went through various dramas — it wasn't helped by the crowd's ugly homophobia, and despite his teammates being fairly accepting of his sexuality, there'd always be the occasional barb in the changing room. Fashnau publicly came out in 1990, or at least in an interview with the *Sun*, after which no club would touch him. He committed suicide in 1998 following allegations about underage sexual assault during his time in Maryland, which he denied and which he claimed were entirely consensual.

best, there was no androgyny or perceived effeminacy. The lack of femininity was the point. Examine how Queen were perceived when Freddie was dressed in full leathers looking like he was off out for an enjoyable night of man-fun. That was fine. But the minute they dragged up, as in the video to 'I Want to Break Free', that was a step too far and the audience were OFF. The leathers were, for Priest, a uniform, a way of making them look tough, hard and not to be fucked with. It's what men who engage in fet-ish would consider their 'superhero' look, that you could transform your normality into something untouchable, yet still wanted to be touched, to become something other.

Judas Priest's singer Rob Halford was born on 25 August 1951 in Sutton Coldfield, and grew up in nearby Walsall, where he was raised on the Beechdale housing estate, which was also home to Slade's lungsmith Noddy Holder. Before Priest, Halford had been the manager of a men's clothing shop, but binned that once he made his live debut with the band in May 1973.

After forming in Birmingham in 1969, the tumultuous nature of Judas Priest's early years had seen numerous line-up changes, but when the remnants of the band discovered Rob Halford and drummer John Hinch rocking out in some outfit called Hiroshima, they persuaded the pair to join them instead. After a few more years of grafting at the metal coalface, things looked up for the band when they signed to CBS in 1977 and broke into the album chart with third album *Sin After Sin*. They also started making inroads in the US with the follow-up, *Stained Class,* but it wasn't until 1980's *British Steel* that they gained a wider fan-base, with tracks such as 'Breaking the Law' and 'Living After Midnight' becoming hit singles.

After a long-winded, decade-long, dues-paying ascendancy, by the time the band released their ninth album *Defenders of the Faith* in 1984, they could rely on a world-wide welcome reception. But by now their new fame had firmly put them in the firing line, in more ways than one. Most Priest afficionados would cite *Defenders of the Faith* as a copy of their 1982 international breakthrough album *Screaming for Vengeance* and, to be honest, they'd be sort of right. The band had found a formula, become extremely successful with it and carried on with aplomb. A Top 20 album in both the UK and US, Sweden fucking *loved* it and it reached number two. But *Defenders . . .* contained a particular track that would gain Judas Priest a whole new level of notoriety.

Now, Rob Halford was gay, and his sexuality was known by the band. However, heavy metal, as we've established, wasn't the arena for such things at the time. Rob would buy his stage gear from sex shops – he even worked in one for a bit – and it was actually guitarist K K Downing who hit upon the idea of the band wearing leather. As Halford explained to *Loudersound*, 'I swear, I never drew a parallel. I was clueless about the filth and the depravity and the debauchery. I'd love to say I was leafing through *Bad Boys In Bondage* and suddenly went, "Oh, I like the way he's looking", but I never did. It was purely this great experimentation, just seeing what worked.

'Something happens when I put my gear on. It's just a wonderful feeling. You change.' The band were absolutely fine that their excesses and proclivities with women were being shared by Rob, except his was with men. They knew about his antics of cruising truck stops on tour in the States, and were accepting of his lifestyle. Rob also knew that to be out publicly would affect his band's success and so kept things on the downlow for their sakes.

Being the singer and key lyricist for Judas Priest, he managed to give out certain signals as to his sexuality in the band's music in songs like 'Living After Midnight' (basically about cruising), 'Hell Bent for Leather' ('Seek him here, seek him on the highway / Never knowing when he'll appear') and 'Jawbreaker' ('And all the pressure has been building up / For all the years it bore its load'). There were also 'love' songs such as 'Turbo Lover' (about going to bathhouses), 'Before the Dawn' (Halford's first serious gay relationship) and 'Out in the Cold' (about Halford's boyfriend Brad who committed suicide in 1986). The lack of any pronouns or attempt to address any particular gender made them all the more ambiguous.

The *Defenders of the Faith* track 'Eat Me Alive' was another. It makes 'Relax" sound like 'The Frog Chorus'. Despite never being released as a single, 'Eat Me Alive' soon found itself in a chart, albeit not one that anyone was aiming to be a part of.

The Parents Music Resource Center (PMRC) was founded in the US by various politicians' wives: Tipper Gore, wife of Senator and later Vice President Al Gore; Susan Baker, wife of Treasury Secretary James Baker; Pam Howar, wife of Washington realtor Raymond Howar; and Sally Nevius, wife of former Washington City Council Chairman John Nevius. The group also received financial backing from Beach Boy Mike Love (just in case you'd run out of reasons to hate him) and created a Filthy Fifteen list of songs that they considered to be lewd or provocative. The song that kicked the PMRC into action was Prince's 'Darling Nikki', which Tipper discovered when her then eleven-year-old daughter brought home a copy of *Purple Rain*. She was so shocked that she felt she needed to inform other parents about this album which had spent pretty much half of 1984 at the top of the Billboard chart. Understandably, any mother of a pre-teen overhearing those lyrics for the first time would be alarmed. The opening couplet of 'Darling Nikki' is quite racy, to put it mildly. So, with this as the touchpaper, Gore formed the group and set about investigating other problematic music.

The rest of the Filthy Fifteen was chosen based on tenuous connections to devil worship, drug taking, sex, and generally the sorts of things a concerned parent would not be keen on. W.A.S.P.'s 'Animal (Fuck Like a Beast)' is fairly self-explanatory for the sex/language/violence category and fulfils that brief, as does AC/DC's 'Let Me Put My Love Into You' as far as sex is concerned. In fact, the Filthy Fifteen didn't appear to know its arse from its elbow if they selected that as the sole AC/DC entry. Others, such as Def Leppard's 'High 'N' Dry (Saturday Night)' and Black Sabbath's 'Trashed', are pretty basic, while the very idea of Madonna's 'Dress You Up' featuring on the list seems quite quaint seeing as what she had in mind with *Erotica* a few years later. As Twisted Sister's Dee Snider argued at the Senate hearing, when defending his own 'We're Not Gonna Take It', which was accused of promoting violence, the PMRC seemed to confuse what a video conveyed rather than the actual lyrical content. In short, it was all a bit pearl-clutchy and reactionary, the sort of thing that has fuelled moral panics since the beginning of time.

Reflecting on the palaver to *Rolling Stone* in 2015, Rob Halford said: 'For me, it was a fun S&M/rock/sex song. But the PMRC twisted it into some kind of snuff song, which is ridiculous. The PMRC's suggestion of giving people some guidance was okay to me. It was just common sense from my perspective for young kids at the time. But the fact that there was this scary political screaming and yelling and shouting at the forefront was smothering the whole message. It was like, "God this is just so stupid." The heart of the message is a valuable idea, but all the other extraneous screaming and yelling – "Bands are out to kill your kids" – and the telethon Christians, adding that extremism in the mix with crazy people. Crazy people diluted the message.

'We wrote "Parental Guidance" and "Private Property" after all of that. Priest has never been that kind of a band, but they kind of forced our hand in that respect, you know? "We don't need no parental guidance." What we were saying was just what the younger fans were saying: "Your mom and your dad don't like your music. They never have and they never will." We're on your side as it was then and I think to some extent how it is now.'

The legacy of the PMRC was that the RIAA (Recording Industry Association of America) agreed to put Parental Advisory stickers, which were introduced in November 1985, on albums to supposedly warn parents that the music their kids liked might not be up their street. The sheer lunacy of all this is that it gave parents the last word, and was the very antithesis of rebellion. In fact, it actually worked as free advertising for the artist, revelling in their forbidden-ness. If anything, a Parental Advisory sticker ended up attracting more purchasers, luring them in with the promise of sex, swearing and/or violence.

Throughout the history of rock 'n' roll, the very tenet of it has been that it was music your parents/older generations didn't like/understand etc. The idea that, having lived through Elvis Presley, Alice Cooper, punk and whatnot, parents were now expected to police their children's lives and cultural intake bordered on the absurd. Rebellion is the very essence of rock music, it's the lifeblood, yet these measures seemed a little over the top, and the start of a very slippery slope. However, the Parental Advisory sticker had a reverse effect on the sales of albums. While many record shops would sell these stickered records by discretion, it actually became a badge of honour for some hip hop and metal acts, and even helped to promote those albums. This included acts such as Ice-T, Metallica and Sonic Youth either referencing PMRC in song or artwork. On the Lollapalooza tour of 1993, Rage Against the Machine protested against the PMRC by standing naked onstage with duct tape covering their mouths and the letters PMRC on their chests. There's a lengthy playlist to be made about PMRC/Tipper Gore mentions in metal and hip hop, but it wouldn't be particularly listenable.

It wouldn't be the last time that Judas Priest would have issues with their lyrics. In 1990, the band were involved in a high-profile subliminal message trial. A civil action[2]

---

[2] The track in question was Judas Priest's cover version of Spooky Tooth's 'Better By You, Better Than Me' on their 1978 album *Stained Class*. The parents believed they could hear 'do it' hidden within the music, and it was a belief in these hidden messages that prompted the parents to sue. Unsurprisingly, there were no such messages and Judge Whitehead dismissed the case against Judas Priest and their record company. While the sheer amount of energy spent on trying to make Judas Priest guilty was questionable, at the end of the day, two young men died very tragically. You can't Brightside that in any shape or form. 'It tore us up emotionally,' said Rob. 'Hearing someone say to the judge and the cameras that this is a band that creates music that kills young people. We accept that some people don't like heavy metal, but we can't let them convince us that it's negative and destructive. Heavy metal is a friend that gives people great pleasure and enjoyment and helps them through hard times.'

against the band was brought by the parents of twenty-year-old James Vance and eighteen-year-old Ray Belknap, who claimed they were responsible for the suicide attempts, and ultimate deaths, of their sons. In December 1985, the two boys were said to have spent the day getting high and drunk while listening to Judas Priest. The pair travelled to a local playground where Belknap put a 12-gauge shotgun under his chin and pulled the trigger, dying instantly. Vance attempted to do likewise, but due to the gun being slippery with blood, he shot away the lower half of his face. He survived, but was severely deformed and lived in constant pain. Three years later, he slipped into a coma and died.

Had the families won the lawsuit, it would have created a whole world of shit for musicians, especially those operating in arenas of metal and hip hop where anybody could come along and cite a lyric that had caused a murder or a rape or any other heinous crime. While such an experience could break lesser bands, Judas Priest had two decades' worth of skin in the game. They survived and continue to make new music – sometimes with Rob Halford, sometimes without. Either way, they remain one of the greatest metal turns of all time.

It was in 1998, during one of Rob's hiatuses from the band, that the truth about his sexuality emerged. While promoting his new act 2wo on MTV, he outed himself. Fielding a question about his sexuality, Rob told the interviewer: 'I think that most people know that I've been a gay man all of my life. It's only been in recent times that it's an issue that I feel comfortable to address, an issue that has been with me ever since recognising my own sexuality. [It's] something that I've been comfortable with forever, something that I feel has a moment. And this is the moment to discuss it.'

Halford took control of the situation, addressing the fact that he kept his sexuality a secret for the band's sake, and acknowledging that metal wasn't the world for gay men, explaining that 'a lot of homophobia still exists in the music world' and 'if we have a problem with it, I think we should seek help and find out why we do have a problem with it. Because if you have a problem with gay and lesbian people, maybe you have a problem on a racist level, maybe you have a problem on a religious level. I think that every individual should seek out their own humanitarian qualities and just be who they want to be and leave it alone.

'If you want to go through your Priest collection, you'll be surprised to see how many innuendos, how many metaphors I used, some obvious and some not so obvious.' The signs were there all along, but it still came as a complete shock to the fanbase. Reassuringly, aside from a handful of morons, they completely accepted him. In fact, the idea that Halford had dabbled with synthesisers divided fans far more than what capers he got up to in his private life. Halford rejoined Judas Priest in 2003, after further solo dalliances, and found the reception to his announcement extremely positive. The Metal God himself saw that fans loved him, possibly even more so, and he was now held in even higher regard.

So, aspiring rockers take note: if Rob Halford isn't on your inspiration moodboard – a leathered-up screamer who arrives onstage on a motorbike, has a fruity Instagram where he occasionally posts pics of him in leather chaps with his bum out (and lots of cats – although not together), someone who even convinced his band to record with Stock Aitken Waterman – then give up right now.

In March 1984, Canadian flight attendant Gaëtan Dugas, who was labelled 'Patient 0' in the US, dies. For decades he was wrongly labelled, and even demonised, as 'Typhoid Mary', for setting in motion a deadly epidemic by spreading the HIV virus to hundreds of other men. Originally named 'Patient O' for 'outside Southern California', a simple typo of '0' rather than 'O' wrongly implied that he had kicked off the AIDS epidemic when he was in fact Patient 57.

CYNDI LAUPER

'If you're lost, you can look and you will find me.'

Following their nascent success in the US throughout 1983, both Cyndi Lauper and Madonna made their first impressions on the UK in early 1984. They even entered the charts the same week: Cyndi's debut 'Girls Just Want to Have Fun' at number fifty and Madonna's 'Holiday' three places below. It was a perfect entry point into a marketplace bored with festive fare and desperate for the New Year New You of freshness.

Cyndi and Madonna were two sides of the same pop coin: Madonna came from disco and Cyndi was new wave-adjacent. They had an eye on pop domination with a very American aesthetic and a take on what they'd witnessed from the British invasion of the US. Both were accessible and relatable, long before relatability became an asset for a pop star. Both dressed cheaply and trashily, although Madonna's Keith Haring skirt set her among the trendier art set, while Cyndi looked as though she'd been given a thirty-second fashion challenge in a charity shop. They were the girls next door who'd you see hanging around the clubs or outside the chip shop, or the five and dime in their case. Young British fans could easily nip to Tammy Girl or C&A for its Clockhouse range to hoover up bangles and trinkets to emulate either.

Obviously, being female, the pair were pitted against each other. They were part of a confected rivalry that emerged from a culture not used to seeing strong independent women. Both would eclipse their beginnings in varying ways, and even by the end of 1984, the chasm between their offerings would deepen.

However, at first Cyndi seemed the racier proposition. Madonna's debut album was a smooth, joyful array of dance sensations and foresaw nothing of the saucing around that she'd become known for in later years. Cyndi, on the other hand, was pushing the pervery and female empowerment from day one.

Cyndi Lauper was an ally from the beginning; she had grown up surrounded by LGBTQ+ lifestyles. 'My sister was gay, my best friends were gay, so I figured I had to be gay,' she explained in 2008. 'So, I did everything they did. I tried kissing girls. But it didn't feel right for me and eventually I was forced to come out as a heterosexual.

'It's ridiculous thinking back on it as an adult, because it's opposite from what happened to all my gay friends.'

Cyndi was born in Brooklyn. She had paid her dues playing in cover bands through the '70s and, in 1978, she met saxophonist John Turi, with whom she formed Blue Angel, a popular turn on the New York new-wave circuit. Despite a slew of offers to go solo, Cyndi held out in order to involve the whole band and they went on to release their debut album in 1980. Not much of a success in their home country, their cover of the Barry Mann and Cynthia Weil-written 'I'm Gonna Be Strong' nonetheless charted in the Netherlands. It is fair to say that it wasn't plain sailing by any means. Despite recording a second album, the band fell out with their manager. They also, unfathomably, turned down an opportunity to work with Giorgio Moroder for 'not being rock and roll enough'.

Blue Angel were dropped by their label after a change in management, which led to bankruptcy. And, to make things worse, Cyndi lost her voice due to an inverted cyst on her vocal cord. Inevitably, the band split in 1982, bidding showbiz adieu with a final show at Studio 54. As a result of the financial insolvency and to pay the bills, Cyndi worked in retail, in kennels, took secretarial and waitressing work, and sang in local bars. It was during this period that her star potential was spotted by David Wolff, who became her manager and secured her a contract with Epic subsidiary Portrait Records.

Cyndi's debut album *She's So Unusual* was released in the US in October 1983, peaking at number four in February 1984. Her first single from the album, 'Girls Just Want to Have Fun', reached number two on both sides of the Atlantic in the same month. The album was a mix of covers and originals, with versions of the Brains' 'Money Changes Everything' and Prince's 'When You Were Mine', which was turned into a *Footloose*-ian synther. *She's So Unusual* is quite possibly the most 1984-sounding album ever.

While 'Girls Just Want to Have Fun' had been written in 1979 by Robert Hazard, Cyndi altered the lyrics as she felt the original was a bit misogynist. 'I changed the words,' Cyndi told *Rolling Stone*. 'It was originally about how fortunate he was 'cos he was a guy around these girls that wanted to have "fun" – with him – down there, of which we do not speak lest we go blind. I tore it apart.' She also informed *Smash Hits* that she was 'super super pleased that it's my record. It's so great because it's done by a woman but written by a man and, when two genders say the same thing, things change.'

Way before the days of media training, Cyndi wasn't afraid to air opinions that today's stars would be advised against, such as telling *Record Mirror*: 'I really admire the

Greenham women[1] for standing up for their principles. Sure, I'd love to do a concert for them if the rest of my band were here.'

Cyndi became the first woman to score four top-five hits on the Billboard Hot 100 chart with tracks from a debut album. She connected with young girls, thanks to her brew of rocky new wave and her impressive four-octave roller-coasting voice that exuded kooky fun and jokey, carefree abandon. She could sound like a yelpsome Betty Boop one minute, as throaty as Pat Benatar the next, and then as smooth as Karen Carpenter. She also came with a tough-ness that was hard won by her first bruisings with fame and of the struggles of 'making it'.

The follow-up, 'Time After Time', became her first chart-topper in the US and is widely considered one of the greatest love songs of the era. Paired with 'Girls . . .', it

---

[1] In 1981, a group of women set up the Greenham Common Women's Peace Camp in response to the decision to store cruise missiles at the site near New-bury in Berkshire. Over the next few years, they tried to stop construction work with a series of sit-ins, blockades and fence removals. By December 1982, 30,000 women joined hands around the site, but the first cruise missiles were already arriving. While the peace camp fended off many attempts to close it down, a small band of hardcore protesters remained throughout the '80s, with the last protest happening in September 2000. As part of the media campaign to discredit the protesters, the women were usually labelled with derogatory remarks in the press and in early 1984, the *Sun* claimed that 'four out of five [protesters] are lesbians'. This is an age-old device of labelling those who disagree with you as gay, suggesting their opinions are less worthy and not to be taken seriously.

presents one of the great one-two openings to a career as far as arrival/confirmation-of-versatility passages go. As if that display of ability wasn't enough, Cyndi's third single, 'She Bop', was about wanking. The ode to female masturbation was inspired by finding a copy of the gay porn magazine *Blueboy* in the studio, which is mentioned in the song's first verse, and came accompanied by a video with numerous images of mayonnaise bottles squirting, a large sign saying 'Self Service' and a blind person winning a game of something called Masterbingo. It will come as no surprise, then, that these antics saw the song added to the PMRC's Filthy Fifteen list of objectionable songs.

Cyndi's 1984 was a bit of a triumph. She scooped the Grammy for Best New Artist at the 1985 Awards, where *She's So Unusual* also received nominations for Album of the Year, Record of the Year, Best Female Pop Vocal Performance (for 'Girls Just Want to Have Fun'), and Song of the Year (for 'Time After Time'). As part of her anointment into pop's higher echelons, she was invited to join the star-studded ranks recording 'We are the World' for USA for Africa.

'People have always said I couldn't sing,' Cyndi told *Rolling Stone*, 'always tried to label me. I ain't worried about them, because the minute I open my mouth and sing, I can blow them right offa their chairs. They can't take your talent away from ya. I am not a Broadway singer, and I am not a movie-TV person. I ain't into that shit. I'm no dummy. I'm not a puppet. And all the people that make fun of me, or call me a cartoon . . . They're talkin' outta their ass.

'You know what I always say? No balls, no glory. I feel it's a great message . . . I want to really communicate with people and touch humanity and complete my creative process and become a complete artist. Project a reality, a sense of art. I think art should reflect life.'

Cyndi's allyship to the LGBTQ+ community would soon make itself more known when she released the follow-up, *True Colors*, in 1986. The title track was written by Billy Steinberg and Tom Kelly and the initial arrangement was said to be not unlike that of 'Bridge Over Troubled Water' until Cyndi rearranged it to make it her own. She had recently lost her friend Gregory Natal to AIDS when she heard the demo. 'He said to me, "Cyn, you gotta write a song like 'That's What Friends Are For'[2] for me." I'm thinking, *Oh, great. Burt Bacharach, one of the greatest American songwriters, wrote that!*'

She was thinking of Bacharach when she came up with her approach to the vocal. 'I realised it had to be a voice that whispers to you,' she told *60 Minutes*, 'a voice that's almost childlike so it will speak to the softest, most gentle

---

[2] Written by Burt Bacharach and Carole Bayer Sager, 'That's What Friends Are For' had originally been recorded by Rod Stewart in 1982, but became better known when covered by Dionne & Friends (Dionne Warwick, Elton John, Gladys Knight and Stevie Wonder). Released at the end of 1985, it became the biggest-selling single of 1986 in the US. The charity single raised more than $3 million for the American Foundation for AIDS Research.

part of a human being. It's a voice whispering to you, telling you it's going to be OK.' 'True Colors' would become her second chart-topper in the US and reach number twelve in the UK.

Cyndi later explained the impact of the song to *Billboard*. 'I was reading a lot of emails in '96 and '97 from people who were disenfranchised from their families and their homes, and their jobs, and their friends when they came out and how they felt suicidal, and then they heard "True Colors" and it kind of saved their lives. I kind of understand what that feels like because there are certain songs that I listened to when I was younger that I always felt like, "Gee, that song saved my life".'

Cyndi went on to tour in 2007 under the banner of 'True Colors', with the hope of supporting gay rights and fighting hate crimes. The line-ups included acts such as Erasure, the Dresden Dolls, Debbie Harry, and Tegan and Sara. The following year, she launched True Colors – with Lisa Barbaris, Jonny Podell and Gregory Lewis – as a non-profit organisation advocating for LGBTQ+ youth, working with communities to make sure their shelters and youth centres are inclusive. They're also involved with lobbying work in Washington, advocating for legislation that supports and protects the LGBTQ+ community. 'I really tried to look conservative and speak clearly, you know, and listen and try and represent the best I could for people without a voice. If you've got a big mouth, you might as well use it for something good, like for people who have no voice.

'With the work that I've been doing with the True Colors Fund, it really started with the "True Colors" tour and the opportunity to create a tour that was totally inclusive and have all different kinds of people on tour with you – not just famous people, but all kinds of people. It was exciting to me. I always thought that multiracial tours were good because even that created a community of inclusivity, but to also include LGBTQ+ people was a big deal.'

So, much like one-time 'rival' Madonna, Cyndi has become something of an ally to the LGBTQ+ community. For someone who was potentially seen as a bit of a joke, she has managed her career magnificently and used her platform to raise awareness on a level that can only be applauded. While there have been many female pop stars who have tried to emulate the Madonna/Lauper career path, few have managed to give back quite as much as either of them have. Quite simply, they set the template.

In April 1984, Customs and Excise officers raid London's Gay's The Word bookshop and seize all their imported books. This is the start of 'Operation Tiger', which decrees every book imported by the shop to be obscene, thus including works by Oscar Wilde, Armistead Maupin, Tennessee Williams, Kate Millett and Jean-Paul Sartre.

MADONNA

'I made it through the wilderness.'

Madonna Louise Ciccone was always going to be a star – as far as she was concerned anyway. It was just a matter of when. Born in Bay City, Michigan on 16 August 1958, she'd been in New York since 1978 when she dropped out of school to head there to 'make it' – or, at least, get a career in dance. Her beginning could almost be lifted from an early Hollywood musical. She'd not travelled on a plane – or even in a cab – before and arrived in the Big Apple with just $35 and a headful of determination. This was a time when people who couldn't afford much more than a dream went out to pursue it. And if you were able to avoid the lure of drugs and could cope with the unsavouriness and hustle of the city, then your dream felt attainable. Not that it would ever be challenge-free. 'Although I took to New York straight away,' Madonna would recall, 'I was really lonely. I didn't know anyone, I didn't have any money and I didn't have anywhere to stay.

'I was getting lost on the subway trains all the time and things like that. You really have to gear yourself to your work. That's your focal point and that's your security. Slowly I got to know it and became secure, and now it's odd to think how scared I was in the beginning.'

Madonna took dance classes, studying under renowned choreographer Martha Graham, before successfully auditioning and dancing back-up for theatrically fog-horned French disco belt-monger Patrick Hernandez, who was about to hit internationally with the hectic, busy Eurodisco of 'Born to be Alive'.

Madonna had a hunger and an eye for knowing where to be and when. This, combined with her talent and drive, has often seen her labelled as calculating and determined. It is as if these are somehow bad traits to have and that Madonna was some kind of pop praying mantis. But if you're trapped under a wardrobe, you don't just lie there, sigh and think, *This is my home now.* You focus on getting out from under it. It's just that Madonna was a woman, and ambition and drive weren't the done thing, apparently. Fuck that.

At the end of the Hernandez tour, Madonna returned to New York, moved into an abandoned synagogue and set about forming her first band, the Breakfast Club. It was during this time that she briefly worked as a coat-check girl at the Russian Tea Rooms and made her acting debut in the slightly grotty, low-budget soft-porner *A Certain Sacrifice*, a film that unsurprisingly remained unreleased until 1985 when Madonna was deemed successful enough for the producers to finally cash in.

By 1980, her focus was on being a solo turn and in March 1981 she signed to Gotham Records, with Camille Barbone working as her manager for the next twelve months. Madonna then set about doing what any fame-famished artist would do and started touting her tape around various nightclubs and DJs in favour of a spin. Danceteria DJ Mark Kamins finally took interest in both the tape and Madonna, leading to a short romance, and helped arrange a meeting with Seymour Stein, the president of Sire Records. Madonna signed her initial Sire deal for three singles and the option of an album and Kamins produced what would become Madonna's debut single, 'Everybody'.

'I knew that record companies wouldn't listen to my demo tape,' she told *Record Mirror* in early 1984, 'so I started taking it round the clubs and giving it to DJs . . . At that time, I started hanging out in clubs and dancing, and my dream was to make a record that I would want to go into a club and dance to myself.' With the lines 'Let the music take control / Find a groove and let yourself go', Madonna's 'Everybody' took up the baton of disco and used it to encourage a clubland in flux, a clubland that had abandoned the abandon of disco, a clubland that was unsure of how to throw shapes as the new sounds, styles and moods of the new decade began to form.

Released in October 1982, 'Everybody' saw a debut performance by Madonna at the Danceteria, followed by her first solo TV appearance on the US show *Dancin' on Air*. She also travelled to the UK to perform PAs in clubs ahead of the release of follow-up single 'Burnin' Up' in March 1983. It made further considerable gains for Madonna chart-wise back home, equalling the number-three peak in the Billboard Hot Dance Club Songs chart of 'Everybody'.

But popping out a couple of records wasn't enough for Madonna. Oh no, she had bigger plans, as she disclosed to *Smash Hits*. 'I thought, *Who's the most successful person in the music industry and who's his manager? I want him.*' The most successful singer on the planet at that time was Michael Jackson, then managed by Freddy DeMann. And yes, she got him. It increased her pop standing almost instantly.

Manager bagged, deal sorted. Now it was time for that all-important album. Madonna had hired Reggie Lucas to produce but was unimpressed with Lucas's techniques and sought out further help. She met with John 'Jellybean' Benitez, the resident DJ at New York club the Fun House, who agreed to rework some of the tracks. As a bonus, the two of them began dating. Opening in 1979, the Fun House on 526 West 26th Street attracted a younger, straighter clientele of club kids, helped by the presence of DJ 'Jellybean', and would become important in breaking the then underground sounds of New York, such as electro, as well as making hits out of bangers such as Freeez's 'IOU' and 'Walking on Sunshine' by Rockers Revenge. Jellybean debuted Madonna's 'Holiday' at the club, before giving a copy to Larry Levan to play at the Garage, helping it to become a massive anthem in New York's clubland long before it troubled any charts. 'I met Jellybean when my first record came out. After "Everybody" was released, he took me round to all the DJs in the major clubs – the [Paradise] Garage, Fun House, Studio 54[1] – and those places were playing my records.' Benitez remixed the majority of the album, as well as producing her next single. The self-titled debut album *Madonna* was ready to go and was released in July 1983, creeping into the Billboard 200 at 190. It would hang around for a good while before making any impact.

---

[1] Opening in 1977, Studio 54 was located in midtown Manhattan on West 54th Street. Conceived by Steve Rubell and Ian Schrager, it was a temple to excess and operated on an exclusive door policy of only admitting the fabulous. During its heyday, it was THE place to go. Inside, patrons would often enjoy quite a lot of drugs and occasionally shag on the dancefloor. After a series of scandals and bankruptcies, it eventually closed for good in 1986. It's now a theatre.

Meanwhile, for those who didn't want to hang around celebrities, there was the Paradise Garage, opened by proprietor Michael Brody in 1977 in New York's Greenwich Village at 84 King Street. The club was a members-only affair, with a dancefloor that held up to 2,000 people and was presided over by resident DJ Larry Levan. Far more influential as a club than 54 with its focus on an 'everybody is a star' egalitarian nature, it hosted performances from the likes of Diana Ross, Patti Labelle, Chaka Khan, Duran Duran and, indeed, Madonna.

'Holiday' was first released as a single in the US in September 1983, reaching number sixteen towards the end of October. It had started life as a song by Curtis Hudson and Lisa Stevens-Crowder for their own band Pure Energy, who had also been produced by Jellybean, but their label turned it down. Pitched to various other acts, Jellybean introduced Madonna to it towards the end of the recording of her first album. The songwriters Hudson and Stevens-Crowder were initially reluctant for Madonna to record the song. 'We were a little nervous at first,' said Hudson. 'We were thinking of black artists, so it kind of put a whole different spin on it. But once we met Madonna, I knew she was gonna go somewhere. I just didn't know to what level.'

'Holiday' was suggested by Jellybean as a last-minute replacement for another track, a moment captured by him in the *New York Post*. 'I had a demo of "Holiday", so I played it for her, and she loved it.' He'd also been given a one-week deadline by Madonna's label in the February of 1983. 'They said, "If you could have this song done by next Friday, you can make the album." I started on Monday and finished on Friday, and we delivered it.'

There had been several years of disco acts put together to front a producer's productions, but few turns had gone out there to become as relatable to that scene as Madonna. The cult of personality was something that she grasped and ran with. 'I think I'm one of the first disco personalities. A lot of it is rather cold dance music. There's no personality to it, and the people are really forgettable. That's the difference with British music, I think. There's a group and, with it, there's a fashion, there's a look, there's something for people to attach it to. It seems there's more coherence.'

Madonna's first three singles offered dancing ('Everybody'), passion ('Burnin' Up') and escapism ('Holiday'), handily covering the three main immediate interests of anyone on a dancefloor. She was throwing a party, and everyone was invited.

Here, in her first UK interview with Simon Hills, Madonna was nailing her ambition and drive. She'd already filmed a spot in the upcoming film *Vision Quest*, as well as contributing songs to its soundtrack. Asked if she was already overdoing it, Madonna was adamant that 'you can cross over – Judy Garland did it. If Sissy Spacek can be a country singer, why can't I be an actress?

'I don't see it as being so diverse, especially with video becoming so strong. Certain things are central to any performer and one of those elements is being able to watch them. After you've done an album, you often have to wait around for six months until it's promoted, so I might as well act in that time. There aren't any rules that say you can't. Music is very important to me, but the thought that I can only make records for the rest of my life fills me with horror.

'Actually, it had been hard making it as a woman . . . I have had to prove to them wrong, which has meant not only proving myself to my fans but to my record company as well. That is something that happens when you're a girl. It wouldn't have happened to Prince or Michael Jackson.'

This determination was no act, telling *Smash Hits* that 'there's a lot more to me than can possibly be perceived in the beginning'.

Madonna did what she would soon do time and time again – she proved them all wrong. Her determination would, of course, be the making of her. 'Holiday' was released in the UK in December 1983, and entered the charts the following month at number fifty-three, hitting the Top 40 a week later. After a debut performance on *Top of the Pops* on 26 January, the song rose to its peak of number six during an eleven-week stay. As soon as 'Holiday' lost its chart heat, a reissued 'Lucky Star', first issued the previous September, followed in March, rising to a peak of number fourteen. It all looked a little wobbly when the (original) release of 'Borderline' peaked at just fifty-six in the UK in June, but by now, Madonna mania was creeping in.

Madonna was too busy finishing her next long player to be concerned about a potentially waning UK audience. Debuting two new songs from her recently wrapped album at Keith Haring's Party of Life at Paradise Garage that May, she treated the assembled cool arty set to the title track 'Like a Virgin' on a bed draped in white lace, before a quick outfit change into a Haring-designed jacket and skirt for 'Dress You Up'. The crowd remained fairly indifferent to her performance, but in attendance was

Andy Warhol who, despite only catching half her set, told everyone that she was going to be 'the biggest thing ever'.

After flogging an eighteen-month-old album – which, at the end of 1984, had only managed to get to number thirty-five, although it would peak at number six come the summer of 1985 – the moment when everything would coalesce was coming. By the end of 1984, Madonna would deliver that second album, the Nile Rodgers-produced *Like a Virgin*.[2] If she initially looked like a one-hit-wonder disco singer, *Like a Virgin* capitalised on the long-gestating, fan-accumulating success of her breakthrough, launching Madonna into the stratosphere.

In September 1984, she debuted 'Like a Virgin' at the inaugural MTV Video Music Awards, which took place at Radio City Music Hall in New York. She was only nominated in one category – as Best New Artist in a Video for 'Borderline' – but was determined to make an impression. Madonna emerged from a seventeen-foot-tall wedding cake wearing a wedding dress, with a silver belt buckle

---

[2] Madonna's second album would be the chance to lift her out of the disco one-off stranglehold, but her pleas for full creative control weren't being heard by Warners. After appealing to Sire boss Seymour Stein, Madonna was offered the option of any producer she wanted, with Trevor Horn, Jellybean and Nile Rodgers among the choices. She went with Rodgers as she thought he was a genius. When she first met with him and played him her demos, she told him, 'If you don't love these songs, we can't work together.' Rodgers, impressed with Madonna's cojones, responded: 'I don't love them now, but I will when I've finished working on them!'

that read BOY TOY. Coming a bit of a cropper as she descended the cake's steps (when one of her shoes fell off), she styled it out by diving on to the floor and rolling around provocatively, yet when she tried to reclaim her shoe, she ended up flashing her knickers on live television. It was a performance that set the tone for the MTV Awards and would go on to inspire countless other performers in later years. The original idea was for her to serenade a Bengal tiger, but that was scrapped due to the possibility of the tiger breaking loose and munching on half of the audience. Almost overnight, Madonna's profile went stratospheric. She may have entered 1984 as a clubland queen, but as the year closed, she was en route to becoming an icon.

'Like a Virgin' – the single – peaked at number three in the UK in early 1985, having spent a month in the top five by that point, and spent six weeks at number one in the US. The parent album would become her first number one in the Billboard 200 that February and eventually took top-dog status in the UK album chart by September, after 'Into the Groove', 'Crazy for You' and a resurgent 'Holiday' all re-hit the top ten in July and August.

By this point, the extremely canny Madonna had managed to court pop fans who found her relatable. Not for nothing did 1985's The Virgin tour see her playing in giant sheds to crowds of young women who looked like her. Those who sensed the liberation and freedom, and saw dancing as an escape, started copying her style of ten-for-a-pound bangles, bows and crop tops – although maybe not getting as far as being able to afford the Keith Haring-designed skirts or jackets.

So, Madonna. That was her 1984. Not much gay stuff going on there, eh? Well, have a closer look. She wanted to bring some personality into disco. Now, disco itself was a dirty word in the US at that point, mainly due to the whole 'disco sucks' bullshit, which had effectively cancelled out the careers of Chic and the Bee Gees overnight, two of the most prolific and biggest-selling acts of the era. For Madonna to be bandying around that she was disco was almost a political statement in itself. Disco was born of the black and queer communities that would congregate at clubs like Paradise Garage, alongside those who would become the club kids. For all the bacchanal and liberation that Studio 54 signified, it was also famously a bit snooty towards punters if they didn't 'fit in'. Madonna wasn't having any of that. Gay men had found an icon with a story that they could relate to. Here was someone that reflected their outsider-dom.

Madonna had come through the ranks of the club scene, and she'd been connected to the art set of early '80s New York, befriending Keith Haring and acknowledging and appreciating the impact and influence that fed into that. 'Keith's work started in the streets, and the first people who were interested in his art were interested in me. That is, the black and Hispanic community . . . We were two odd birds in the same environment and we were drawn to the same world. Another thing we have in common . . . we have the same taste in men!'

Madonna's affinity with the gay community stems from her ballet teacher Christopher Flynn, who took her under his wing in mid-'70s Michigan and opened her eyes to a world beyond her hometown. Speaking to *Interview* magazine in 2010, she paid tribute to Christopher. 'He was the first man – the first human being – who made me feel good about myself and special. He was the first person who told me that I was beautiful or that I had something to offer the world, and he encouraged me to believe in my dreams, to go to New York.

'He brought me to my first gay club – it was this club in Detroit. I always felt like I was a freak when I was growing up and that there was something wrong with me because I couldn't fit in anywhere. But when he took me to that club, he brought me to a place where I finally felt at home.'

In fact, she was so surrounded by the gay community in her early days in New York that she almost wanted to *be* a member of it. 'I didn't feel like straight men understood me. They just wanted to have sex with me. Gay men understood me, and I felt comfortable around them. There was only that one problem, which is that they didn't want to have sex with me! So . . . conundrum! I was like, "How am I ever going to get a date? Maybe if I cut my hair and I lose a lot of weight, someone will mistake me for a guy and ask me out."'

Madonna's gay audience saw themselves in her: that need to escape to the big city, the emancipation and freedom of the dancefloor, her unashamed approach to sex, and her advocacy for gay rights, especially at a time when AIDS was on the rise. She had surrounded herself almost exclusively with gay men from the outset and fed off them. Her gay fans saw someone who had their backs, someone who told them to be unafraid and to live their true lives. She was, as Boy George once remarked, 'a gay man in a woman's body'.

By the time of Madonna's fourth album, 1989's *Like a Prayer*, her respect and backing of the gays was more noticeable. Each patchouli-scented copy of that album came with a little note inside the sleeve entitled 'The Facts About AIDS'. It was a significant, and somewhat risky, moment. No pop star operating at that level had ventured into the politics of AIDS, but controversy had long become Madonna's calling card – it was to be expected. 'The Facts About AIDS' pulled no punches. It referred to AIDS as 'an equal opportunity disease'. 'People with AIDS – regardless of their sexual orientation – deserve compassion and support, not violence and bigotry,' it announced, before signing off with 'AIDS is no party!'

Madonna was no stranger to AIDS. She lost a number of close friends to the disease throughout the '80s, including her best friend and former roommate, Martin Burgoyne. She'd shared an apartment with Burgoyne on Manhattan's Lower East Side, and he managed her first club tour, as well as drawing the cover image of 1983's 'Burning Up' sleeve. In August 1986, just as Madonna was enjoying global success with her third album *True Blue*, Burgoyne was diagnosed with AIDS-related complex (ARC). Madonna helped care for Burgoyne, paid his medical expenses and leased an apartment for him in Greenwich Village so that he could be closer to the hospital. She was with him when he died of AIDS-related complications that November. He was twenty-three. Not three weeks later, Madonna took part as a model in an all-star AIDS benefit fashion show at Barneys in New York, which benefited the AIDS Research Clinic at St Vincent's Hospital in Manhattan, where Burgoyne had died. In July 1987, as part of her Who's That Girl tour, Madonna performed an AIDS benefit in memory of Burgoyne at Madison Square Garden, raising $400,000 for the American Foundation for AIDS Research (AMFAR).

In February 1990, after being diagnosed himself in 1988, Keith Haring would also die of AIDS-related complications. That October, her mentor from Michigan, Christopher Flynn, passed away from an AIDS-related illness, a few weeks after Madonna had been honoured with the Commitment to Life award for her contribution in raising awareness of the disease by AIDS Project Los Angeles.

In 1991, Madonna was awarded the Award of Courage by AMFAR at a Regent Beverly Wilshire Hotel dinner, where she addressed the rumours that she herself had AIDS. 'When the rumours surfaced that I was HIV-positive, I thought, *Well, someone's really bored today. Let's make up a real juicy story*. I tried to ignore it, but it wouldn't go away. Instead of pointing the finger at people and having witchhunts and ostracising each other for lifestyles and sexual preferences, we should all be uniting to fight this disease . . . but we're not. Because we're afraid. We're scared out of our skins to face the truth that AIDS is not a gay disease, it's a human disease. Now, I'm not HIV-positive, but what if I were? I would be more afraid of how society would treat me for having the disease than the actual disease itself. If this is what I have to deal with for my involvement in fighting this epidemic, then so be it.

'I'm not afraid to be associated with people who are HIV-positive, and I am not afraid to love people who are HIV-positive – because their ordeal is more important than mine, because their courage is larger than mine, because what they're facing is real. And if we can learn to deal with [what's] real, and our fears, then I'm hopeful that we can conquer this disease.'

Musically, while Madonna has always been a dance/club-based pop icon, one of her major nods to the gay underground came with the release in 1990 of 'Vogue'. A housin' stomper that far eclipsed the rest of the attendant *I'm Breathless* album, where fans were treated to both the ecstasy and agony of Madonna that summer when the unspeakable 'Hanky Panky' followed it up. While we could quibble that Malcolm McLaren had got there first a year before with 'Deep in Vogue' and his *Waltz Darling* album, whatever cachet the old punk magpie had, he didn't have the ears of the millions of fans that Madonna did.

She had been inspired by vogue dancers and choreographers José Gutierez Xtravaganza and Luis Xtravaganza from the Harlem House Ball community, the source of the dance form. They introduced vogueing to Madonna at the Sound Factory club in New York. 'Vogue' paid tribute to the ballroom scene in New York where black and Latino gays would gather to serve realness – realness was in essence an aspiration of something that a lot of these unemployed or under-employed and rejected kids could appropriate. Named after *Vogue* magazine, the fashion looks and poses were brought to life in dance in pageants that acted as a safe space away from the hostility that they'd face in everyday life. Predominantly the preserve of drag queens, it later welcomed gay men and trans women as well, who would represent various 'houses' that served as chosen families for many of those involved.

The very idea sounds utterly nuts now, but 'Vogue' itself was never intended to be a single. Warners were keen to issue 'Keep it Together' as a fifth lift from *Like a Prayer*, and so asked Madonna to come up with a new track for the B-side. Shep Pettibone, a longtime collaborator of Madonna who'd been friends with her pre-stardom, sent her a track to which she wrote lyrics. At $5,000, the budget was small. Even during the music industry's most lavish era, the biggest stars were still required to make a tiny amount stretch. Madonna ended up recording the lyrics in a home studio in a mutual friend's basement, where the vocal booth was a cupboard. And, according to Pettibone, it was all done on the first take. The 'rap' segment, where Madonna listed a series of film stars, was thought up in the studio on the spot. When she delivered 'Vogue' to the record company, it was immediately obvious that they had an absolute banger on their hands. To use it as a B-side would be a disgrace.

Now, several years on and 6 million sales later and having reached number one the world over, the impact of 'Vogue', and its David Fincher-directed video, helped edge ballroom culture into the mainstream. And while there were criticisms of appropriation, of feeding off black culture, 'Vogue' confirmed the power of Madonna.

Throughout her career, she's balanced her role as both saviour and victim. There have been controversies and there have been rebirths. If anything, her very existence, and her duality of power and vulnerability, have been her modus operandi. For almost the entirety of her career, Madonna has faced a barrage of noise, insults and criticism, to which she has a measured response. 'I think the most controversial thing I've done is to stick around.'

Over time, Madonna has proved to be an ally to the LGBTQ+ community. Whether it's speaking out against homophobia during concerts in Russia, or appearing at World Prides, or referencing the 2016 Orlando Pulse nightclub massacre in the video for her 2019 song 'God Control', she's been there, right in the thick of it. So, the next time some professional arsehole slags off her cosmetic surgery, her age or her looks, or a fledgling babygay somehow shades the idea that she doesn't speak for them, remember that Madonna has been fighting for their right to be since before they were born. She has provided the soundtrack and presided over the best gay moments of the last four decades. She has been an advocate from the beginning. In a moist-eyed moment during her 2023/24 Celebration tour, she performed 'Live to Tell', floating above the crowd in a glass box around images of people who she – and we – have lost to AIDS. It was a poignant moment, and a reminder of the roots of someone who has now spent a lifetime at superstar level. Someone who can command an eye-watering ticket price (and whose fans seem to be happy paying to be closer to Saturn than the stage, while quietly praying she's remembered to pack some hits). Put together by the AIDS Memorial, it featured Sylvester, Keith Haring, Robert Mapplethorpe and, again, Martin Burgoyne, among numerous others. Still operating at a superstar level of fame that can command an eye-watering ticket price to see live, fans are happy to pay to be closer to Saturn than the stage, quietly praying she's remembered to pack some hits. All hail.

And with that, let's flick back to 1984 Madonna, and see what she claimed to *Smash Hits* was her then-wildest ambition. 'I'd love to be a memorable figure in the history of entertainment in some sexual tragi-comic way. I'd like to leave the impression that Marilyn Monroe did, to be able to arouse so many different feelings in people.'

Safe to say, Madonna's mission to be a star achieved *all* that and more.

In April 1984, the US government announces that researchers have identified the probable cause of AIDS and could be two years away from a cure. The Health and Human Services Secretary, Margaret Heckler, said that the probable cause was a variant of a known human cancer virus called Human T-cell Leukaemia Virus, which attacks human T-cells. This echoed similar findings from France the previous year.

SOFT CELL / MARC ALMOND

'Building your life up and smashing it down.'

As iconic *Top of the Pops* performances go, Soft Cell's debut on the show in August 1981, performing 'Tainted Love', is right up there. It would probably rank highly in some 'We asked 100 gay people' countdown of Most Memorable *Top of the Pops* performances, up there with David Bowie doing 'Starman' in 1973 and Culture Club's 'boy or girl' confuser arrival in 1982.

You know you've pretty much made it when you become the subject of an unsavoury, and very homophobic, urban myth. You can be assured that your newly raised profile, earned after your first major hit and the impact it had, was sufficient enough for you to become the subject of unpleasant school playground bullshit. Such was the case with Marc Almond who, so the schoolkids gossiped, collapsed on stage and was taken to hospital to have his stomach pumped, whereupon doctors discovered he'd swallowed up to two pints of semen. It was vile and absurd, and yet that was the sort of thing gay pop stars had to contend with. How did anyone think up such stuff? Had anyone questioned the sexual antics of the other new names among the chart-topping pantheon of 1981? What was the mythical semen consumption of Aneka? Was Barbara Gaskin known for downing pints of cum? However, neither the iffy cultural appropriation of 'Japanese Boy', nor the hokey am-dram theatrics of 'It's My Party' threatened to destabilise society quite so much as did the spooksome spectre of homosexuality and a man in eyeliner clanking some bangles together.

'My first *Top of the Pops* experience changed my life completely,' Marc would admit. 'I experienced the worst homophobia I've ever experienced at that time. It was a fearful time. I was still living in Leeds in a little house, and I got the press knocking on my door. I got people knocking on my door threatening to bash me all the time, to kill me, because I'd been so uber gay in my *Top of the Pops* appearance.'

Soft Cell formed in 1978 when Marc Almond from Southport met Cheshire-born, Blackpool-raised David Ball at Leeds Polytechnic. Marc had originally studied Performance Art at Southport, making short Warhol-esque films such as *Glamour in Squalor* and *Zazou*, which was described by a reviewer for the *Yorkshire Evening Post* as 'one of the most nihilistic depressing pieces that I have ever had the misfortune to see'. Marc, being Marc, saw this as a compliment.

The two of them actually met on their first day at Leeds. 'I had to find someone who knew where to go,' said Dave. 'I saw this guy in gold-lamé jeans, leopard-skin top, dyed black hair and loads of make-up, and thought he must be in the art department! Marc was actually the first person I spoke to, but it was only in my second year – when I got my first synth – that he introduced himself properly. I knew he did performance art, of course.'

Once the two of them got together, it was clear that they shared a very similar outlook. 'He asked me to help do the music for one of his performances and I was thrilled,' says Dave. 'I was just messing around doing stuff for myself until then – a bit self-indulgent, really – and he heard some of my little songs. He asked if he could have a go at singing some of them and then wanted to do some lyrics. I thought, *Great.* I'm not a singer and I'm not a lyric-writer. It naturally developed from there and, before we knew it, we were doing local gigs.'

Thanks to a loan from Dave's mum, Soft Cell self-released their first single, 'Mutant Moments', in 1980. Spotting Radio 1 DJ John Peel at one of the festivals the duo were playing, Ball handed Peel the only copy he had. Before he knew, Peel had played it three times on his show.

Soft Cell offered sexual nihilism and bleak seediness to the what was, in late 1981, becoming the autumn of the futurists in British music. They were operating in neon-lit darkness alongside other turns who were offering the strange and important sound of the synthesiser, such as the Human League, OMD and Japan. It was a fast ride, as a string of singles, debut album *Non-Stop Erotic Cabaret* and remix set *Non-Stop Ecstatic Dancing* soon followed. Twelve months on from the debut, the follow-up, *The Art of Falling Apart*, arrived, but cracks were already starting to appear with songs that spoke of disintegrating mental states and suggested a general mood of 'we're starting to get on each other's tits'. The relationship between Marc and Dave was at the nexus of the tension of the duo. At one point, it could easily have seen the death of the other.

Without Dave, Marc wouldn't have become Marc, and without Marc, Dave wouldn't have become Dave, but it was a fractious relationship. Their personalities often clashed; they encouraged and annoyed each other in equal measure. But isn't that often the power of great partnerships? Would Marc have been able to express himself in such the same manner had the menace and grubby futurism of Dave not given him that forum? Despite the synth-duo template of the emoting frontperson seemingly doing all the legwork with the boffin prodding an ironing board in the background, more often than not they're far more equal in bringing out each other's personalities.

Soft Cell had been a surge of debauchery and illicitness from the outset. *Non-Stop Erotic Cabaret* had songs about vice, despair, sex and life on the peripheries that spoke to the heart of the nation – or at least the one kid, or maybe two kids, in your school who didn't understand their sexual orientation. There was a seedy menace, a dark underbelly, to the album, full of sex dwarves, thwarted love affairs, tainted loves and emptiness. Yet it wasn't too far from the surface for many people – or enough people to make them pop stars for a good eighteen months, even if they themselves may have found the initial excitement of being two students from Leeds suddenly being chased around Soho by besotted fans a little wearying. In their defence, in less than eighteen months, there'd been both two-and-a-half albums and the pair had enjoyed five top-five hit singles. They were chart darlings and unlikely pin-ups who were a mixture of bewildered, bemused and freaked out. They were also facing constant and increased demands from their record company to keep delivering the goods. It's no wonder a diet of drugs might seem appealing.

Soft Cell, for all their wonder and magic and dark charm, were probably simply not built for prolonged pop stardom. They just wanted to put out a few records and be a mild success and an arty concern. Appearing on the cover of *Smash Hits* wasn't on their to-do list, neither was being screamed at and followed by young fans everywhere when they conjured up their toe-taps. In fact, the whole experience took both them and their unorthodox manager Stevo by surprise. Live dates were either wildly oversubscribed or haphazard, with the duo's early fans finding themselves crowded out by a younger set.

'We were very contained in our little Soft Cell world of sleaziness and neon,' Dave told *Classic Pop* in 2018. 'A lot of people tell me the reason they moved to London was because of Soft Cell. They thought the Soho we were describing in our songs was the whole of what London life would be like.'

'We thought we'd be really lucky if we could maybe get to support the Human League,' claimed Marc. 'There was always the pressure to do another "Tainted Love", which of course we couldn't. We didn't want to write to order, but we should have written more pop songs than we did.' Dave agrees, admitting that they 'let stupid things get in the way of making pop songs, including our own egos. We were clinging onto the idea that we were serious artists – which we were, and that's recognised now, but we never expected to be on *Top of the Pops*. That meant we were always wrestling with ourselves.'

'I set out to be as camp as I could for every *Top of the Pops*,' laughed Marc. 'I was told, "Cut down on all the bracelets and eyeliner", so of course I put more on . . . I was gender-fluid decades before it became fashionable.

'And all the time, Dave was lurking in the background – part-bouncer, part-serial killer. We were influenced by bands we'd seen at seaside casinos as kids – the stony-faced guy playing a Bontempi while some theatrical seaside singer in too much make-up is giving their all. There was something very *League of Gentlemen* about our TV performances.'

By the time of *The Art of Falling Apart*, the frivolity of pop was wearing thin. 'Numbers', said Marc, was 'the most uncommercial song we could release, about sex addiction in the early days of AIDS. We thought pop success was going to be short-lived, so we felt we had to commit commercial suicide. We felt we needed to make a heavier record, to develop as artists and so leave a longer legacy. That [*The Art of Falling Apart*] really is Dave's album – he came into his own with those dark, filmic arrangements. They're such great soundscapes.'

Marc very much played the game during this period, yet you could tell that his experimental urges were creeping in more and more. His replied to *Smash Hits* questions such as 'Do you have a girlfriend?' with responses offering up either Cindy Ecstasy (effectively a rapper and drug dealer who turned Soft Cell onto E when they recorded in New York – not what most mums would call 'marriage material') or reprising the longstanding 'Still haven't met the right girl yet', which would be echoed throughout time by Boyzone's Stephen Gateley and H from Steps in the future.

Much like Freddie Mercury, while Marc was seen as camp, under advice from the label, he was not out. 'I get what Freddie was feeling,' he told the *Independent*. 'I would call it being poisoned by your time. Freddie, I think, loved having this great success that had given him riches beyond his wildest dreams, and it could all end in a moment if anyone thought that he could actually be gay.'

Away from the spotlight though, it was a different matter. 'I went down to Heaven nightclub and Freddie was there. He came over to me and said, "Cheer up, girl! You always look so bloody miserable, dressing in black and writing all these miserable songs. Come with me, girl. We're gonna go for a dance." And he threw me over his shoulder and carried me on to the dancefloor.'

Not ones particularly interested in keeping up a teen-mag presence, before long Marc and Dave were testing the waters outside of the Cell – Dave with his solo album *In Strict Tempo* in November 1983, while Marc and the Mambas – the band he formed with a fluid lineup that would include The The's Matt Johnson and Annie Hogan among others – had already released two albums, 1982's *Untitled* and 1983's *Torment and Toreros*. The latter was seen as a bit self-indulgent. On the album, Marc worked with musicians such as Jim Foetus and Matt Johnson, and covered songs by Scott Walker, Jacques Brel, Syd Barrett and Lou Reed. While in New York, Marc joined the Immaculate Consumptive, a loose assortment of characters formed by Lydia Lunch and Nick Cave. He also became associated with the likes of chart-averse types such as Psychic TV and Einstürzende Neubauten. Both Marc and Dave's albums shared personnel, with some musicians also popping up on The Glove's *Blue Sunshine* – the super-duo of the Banshees' Steve Severin and Robert Smith, who was also currently a Banshee while having a sort-of break from the Cure. Severin and Smith also wrote the song 'Torment' on *Torment and Toreros*. Pop-wise, it was all a little incestuous.

The music industry is littered with 'we should've had some time off'-style regrets. The '80s is no exception, with the likes of Altered Images and Haircut 100 imploding before their time. Exhaustion wasn't seen as anything to worry about – today's understanding and awareness around mental health was a long way off – and, as a result, there was an absurd set of demands placed on chart-friendly acts. They were overworked, juggling pressures to keep the pop fires burning with the coal of top-ten smashes, while looking good on photoshoots and serving fan clubs. Stressed and stretched, bands were thrown into some new world that was far above their initial ambitions.

However, despite having become the act they always wanted to be, and releasing their most extreme and outre album yet, by 1984, Soft Cell were basically done. Marc and Dave called it a day on their highly successful first era, releasing the album *This Last Night . . . In Sodom* and playing farewell shows. The whirlwind of huge success, controversy and non-stop – neither erotic or ecstatic – drug use appeared to be the cause of the split. But there is another explanation: They were simply exhausted with having to be pop stars, and so they parted amicably in order to concentrate on their own projects. There was no real drama to be found. The desire to get out of pop for a bit was high, and yet Soft Cell were still having success in a no-higher-than-number-twenty' type way, releasing singles to keep their label sweet.

This Last Night . . . In Sodom was literally art reflecting a band falling apart. The queasiness of its contents was Ball and Almond basically telling their fans, and each other, to fuck off and die. And if that didn't quite get across, it was soundtracked by sour, brutal and gnarly chaotic pop. In fact, calling it pop would be a fool's errand; machines were pushed to breaking point, there were songs about Hispanic drag queens and about the emptiness of sex and drugs. Lots of drugs. It's completely brilliant in its own way, but was definitely not what anyone who'd stuck a Soft Cell poster-mag on their wall was expecting. '*This Last Night . . . In Sodom* reeks, more than ever, of promises turned bad,' claimed the *NME*, 'of worst anticipations fulfilled up to and including the hilt, and perhaps most of all of a couple of tragic ill-fitting sensibilities who have learned to manipulate their chosen set of tools with callous enterprise.' The review was spot-on. As Dave rightly suggested, 'we had the big-selling pop album, then the "we're serious artists" record and finally the punk album'.

Obviously, Soft Cell didn't manage to kill each other – I checked – and went their separate ways after a pair of farewell shows in Hammersmith. They'd crammed a decade's worth of work into three years. It's no wonder the pair of them were knackered.

As a first-act closer, *This Last Night . . . In Sodom* managed to both amplify the duo's sleaze and reduce their shiny synthpop sheen. As Marc stated in his autobiography: 'Of all the Soft Cell albums, it remains my favourite . . . If I had to link it to a drug, I would call it our amphetamine album.' At moments, it sounds like their *Metal Machine Music*, with Dave pushing his creations almost to distortion, bruising against the deliberately mono recording. A line in 'Mr Self Destruct' – 'Narrow the sorrow, sick of the slick' – sets out the stall for the confrontational nature of the album. The subjects of previous albums – the sex dwarves, the Valium-addicted bored housewives, the tormented lovers – have all turned uglier, gnarlier and filthier. In 'Slave to This', Marc is almost freewheeling with lines like 'Call me Chico, Chico from Puerto Rico / Guilty of another cold-handed sperm murder'. Unsurprisingly, it didn't become a single. Loveless, friendless, emotionless lives of doorway-dwelling habitues, such as 'Little Rough Rhinestone', with the casual violence of glasses into heads, battered people beaten down by exist-ence, or, in the case of 'Meet Murder My Angel', where the ultimate act of love (i.e. murder) is no way back. On its surface, 'The Best Way to Kill' appears to be an attack on their critics, but it can also speak of the repression faced of being yourself where 'It's nice when being yourself behind a locked door / Talk in whispers when you're scared out of your mind by the law'. 'L'Esqualita' sounds like Scott Walker in a skip: 'I'm so sick in my spare time humour-ing thugs / We could go out to dinner but we're always on drugs'. And on it goes. The dark side of the Soho experience – the grime, the blood, the fag-stink of one-night stands and unsatisfactory conquests, the blur of anonymous bodies and dead-eyed encounters – makes *Non-Stop Erotic Cabaret* feel like a day-out at a theme park. It was, as Marc claims, 'a gob of phlegm spat in the face of whoever'. Or, as Dave stated in his memoir, *Electronic Boy*, *This Last Night . . . In Sodom* was the sound of two people who'd taken too much of everything and lost control.'

Soft Cell was never about the joy or magic of dancing, or boy meeting girl, but at this point in their career, they'd doubled down on the themes of self-destruction. They were in tune with the goths, the darkness, the bleakness. And Marc continued to rebel against his pop star life by working with Coil[1], a duo made up of Peter 'Sleazy' Christopherson of Throbbing Gristle and John Balance from Psychic TV.

Once Soft Cell decided to call it a day, Marc's realisation that it was all over took a little time to sink in. 'I was filled with fear, confusion and, yes, regret. Fear for the future and confusion over what I wanted to do next.'

Aware that he'd gone as far as he could down the road of decay and degradation, Marc wasn't entirely sure of

---

[1] Coil's 1984 debut EP *How to Destroy Angels* was subtitled 'Ritual music for the accumulation of male sexual energy'. Marc appeared on their 1985 album *Scatology* under the pseudonym Raoul Revere. The duo would also release a version of 'Tainted Love' that had been rearranged to reflect the AIDS crisis and is considered to be the first AIDS benefit single, donating proceeds to the Terrence Higgins Trust. Marc made a cameo appearance in the not-so-cheery video.

his next move. 'I wanted it to be big, glamorous, trashy, orchestral, acoustic, Broadway musical, pop, underground and electro . . . so it ended up having elements of all those things but not enough of anything.' Released in October 1984, *Vermin in Ermine* was Almond's debut album proper, albeit with the Willing Sinners, who were essentially several of his Mambas. Significantly, and new for Marc, this album had no covers. Every track had been penned by him. 'I wasn't quite sure whether I was pleased with it or not,' he recalled. 'There was a lot I liked about the album, however. It had something of the glamorous trashiness that I'd wanted. I thought I was finally starting to sound like the singer I wanted to be.'

The album did get some favourable reviews, with Chris Roberts at *Melody Maker* saying 'and then there's glitter, Garland, garlands, grace, grime, graphics, gore, Gore, Gomorrah, gold, red and black . . . Be grateful that in 1984 records can still be made by a real man who doesn't eat shit but probably would if it would wind you up. Marc the punk!'

Marc's gay side was starting to seep out. He'd always held it back in Soft Cell in case it became too camp and over the top, only letting it slip out every now and again. 'But by this time,' he observed, 'my lyrics were starting to develop more of a homoerotic edge, and that scared some people away – as did the glitter-jacket image and the flamboyant gestures. But I felt this new direction had more to it.

'I knew that to survive, to have any longevity, I had to constantly reinvent myself, always expressing a new side of my personality, a different image, while constantly remaining true to myself.

'I wanted to take the camp aspect to an extreme, but still retain my fans – a precarious balancing act.'

This new approach was tested when, at the end of 1984, Marc was approached by Bronski Beat to see if he would be amenable to duetting with Jimmy Somerville on a cover of Donna Summer's 'I Feel Love'. Jimmy was such a fan that Bronski had used Soft Cell producer Mike Thorne on their debut album, *The Age of Consent*. Marc was advised by his manager Stevo that it would be a good way of reigniting his career and showing Phonogram that they had been wrong to drop him. 'It would, for me, be certainly the gayest statement I had ever made – more than I felt comfortable with – and it might be seen as some sort of "outing". I wasn't sure whether I wanted that, or if I could handle it.'

After the song became a top-three smash in spring 1985, the ensuing promotional responsibilities happened at a time when Bronski were at each other's throats and Jimmy would leave the group shortly after. 'The newspapers announced that I was to replace him in Bronski Beat,' said Marc. 'I couldn't think of a worse fate.' Marc and Jimmy descended into public feud when Jimmy claimed that 'Marc Almond doesn't do anything for the gay community. He's just a closet case.'

'I responded in an interview, "Jimmy Somerville doesn't think I do anything for the gay community. Well, I would like to do something for it – strangle him."' The pair eventually made up, after appearing at an AIDS charity event a few years later.

Marc Almond's career has seen him tackle chanson, Russian songs and explore European cabaret, as well as the music he'd grown up with. His extensive solo discography veers from collaborations with Coil, Siouxsie Sioux and the playwright Mark Ravenhill, to Jools Holland and opulent pop symphonies with Trevor Horn. And, of course, the chart-topping success with Gene Pitney and 'Something's Gotten Hold of My Heart' in 1989.

He's taken songs by Jacques Brel and Charles Aznavour into the charts, and even reimagined the likes of Madonna and Cher too. He's also keen to celebrate his teenage hero Marc Bolan – the reason why the young Mark changed his name to Marc – and often performs with the tribute turn T. Rextasy. These projects, and so many more across a career of twenty-six solo albums, encapsulate the very definition of versatile. There's also been the triumphant return of Soft Cell after a massive 'farewell' show at London's O2 in 2018, which extended into new music with the comeback album *Happiness Not Included.

Tragedy struck when Marc was involved in a horrific motorcycle accident near St Paul's Cathedral in 2004, which resulted in him being in a coma for several weeks. Following months where he didn't think he'd be able to sing again, Marc tentatively began his comeback and later became a patron of the brain trauma charity Headway. He's always been a survivor, has Marc. He had longevity's number a *long* time ago. Writing for the *NME* in 1984, he said, 'My life is dedicated to creation and destruction, all in one breath. To use my experiences, headlong plunges into Love and Hate to, if not the benefit of others stumbling about in the same murky void, then as an almighty cry: I WAS HERE, HERE IS ME.

'But slit my throat tomorrow and I'd pick up the pen and burn away sheet after sheet of paper. Cut off my fingers and I'd take up tap dancing. Cut off my feet and I'd find an opening in amputee porn. Only at the final cut of all would I shrug my stumps and have to admit: "Well, I'm beat!" Bullshit? Maybe, but frankly, my dears, I don't give a damn.

'I am, will be, must be, the ruler of my own life, of my destiny, the master of my personality and the absolute authority on myself. No one can dictate to me about me and no one can say "Marc Almond is . . ." they can only speculate.'

Marc's life is as storied and as full of the trials and tribulations that befell his heroes. There's been doom and tragedy. Keychains and snowstorms. Torment and toreros. He's gone from cat-food-smearing arty nihilist to an honour-laden national treasure. He's put the hours in, and is way more worthy of the icon/diva title than some. A true artist in every sense of the word.

*In May 1984, after Marilyn is beaten up in a bar in
Australia, the story makes the front page of the* Sun *with a
comment from the local police chief: 'He isn't seriously hurt.
All he needs is a powder puff.'*

PET SHOP BOYS

'Just you wait 'til I get you home.'

In a strange kind of way, we have the Police to thank for
the Pet Shop Boys. Not inasmuch as they helped form
them, more in the fact that, without Neil Tennant having to schlep to New York in 1983 to review one of Sting
and chums' shows for *Smash Hits*, he might not have had
the opportunity to meet up with Bobby Orlando[1], the
producer behind some of Neil's favourite records and
the forefather of the sound that he had in mind for his
pop duo. As Neil would later explain to the *Guardian*,

---

[1]   Bobby Orlando – aka Bobby O – is a New York songwriter, producer and
label impresario who is widely considered as the key innovator of high energy.
Among his numerous production credits are The Flirts' 'Passion', Roni Griffith's '(The Best Part of) Breakin' Up', as well as 'Native Love', 'Shoot Your
Shot' and 'Love Reaction' by Divine, which also featured backing vocals by

111

'our career ambition was to have a record you could only buy on import in the gay record shop on Berwick Street, which we used to hang around in and where I used to buy imports on my *Smash Hits* expenses.'

North Shields-born Neil had grown up in Newcastle and attended St Cuthbert's, an all-boys Catholic school, where he learned cello and guitar. He formed his first band, Dust, a fairly hippy-facing outfit influenced by the Incredible String Band, and also did time as a member of a youth theatre group at the People's Theatre. Moving to London in the early '70s, he spent two years as the production editor for Marvel UK – basically anglicising the dialogue so that it was more suitable for British consumption, and occasionally interviewing musicians for the comic. By 1977, no doubt gee'ed up by punk, he moved

---

a pre-'Male Stripper' Man 2 Man. Bobby was behind the group Oh Romeo, who had a different lead singer for each of their tracks, and also issued a few bangers himself, such as 'I'm So Hot For You', 'She Has a Way' and 'Try It (I'm in Love with a Married Man)'. There were numerous others issued under 'concepts' with names like Barbie & the Kens, Spooge Boy, Joy Toy, Beachfront and Girls Have Fun. A big fan of cowbells, he made Stock Aitken Waterman sound like David Sylvian. To add to his eccentricities, he claimed that 'from 1980 to 1987, I had one goal and one goal only: to be the McDonald's of the record business. I wanted to release more records, like they release hamburgers, than anybody could have. I didn't care if they sold or if they didn't sell. When 1987 came and I had finally reached that goal and my company released over one thousand records, I said, "That's it. No more."' He also wrote a book, *Darwin Destroyed*, which refuted the theory of evolution.

to Macdonald Educational Publishing, where he edited *The Dairy Book of Home Management*, as well as various illustrated books about cookery and learning to play guitar. After that, he was employed at ITV Books, working on the TV tie-ins, such as annuals based on the channel's output. It was after he had commissioned a designer to help out on a book about Madness (the group, that is) that he was offered the chance to join *Smash Hits* as a news editor, working there from 1982 until 1985.

Blackpool-born Chris Lowe played trombone in a school band specialising in showtunes and standard covers, as well as being a piano player as part of an outfit called One Under the Eight. He moved to Liverpool in 1978 to study architecture at the city's university, where he gained a work placement at a practice in London.

That's the background to what is perhaps one of the greatest pop origin stories of all time. In 1981, while individually perusing the wares of an electronics shop on the King's Road in London, Neil – who'd gone there to enquire about his synthesiser – bumped into Chris and the pair began chatting about various things, such as what music they liked and so forth. Realising they had a fair bit in common, mostly that they liked David Bowie, Eurodisco and high energy, they agreed to meet up at Neil's flat to talk further about actually making their own music.

By 1983, Neil was happily ensconced at *Smash Hits*, editing the 'Bitz' news pages and settling in as features editor. He was regularly picking dance bangers such as C.O.D.'s

'In the Bottle' and Rockers Revenge's 'Walking on Sunshine' as his singles of the fortnight. He interviewed the likes of Soft Cell, the Jam and the Alarm, and also put together the iconic 'Happy Christmas from the Stars' flexidisc. Most significantly, he introduced a few choice phrases into the magazine's lexicon – 'The Dumper', 'It's like punk never happened', 'pervy synth duo', 'Puh-*LEASE*' etc. – which readers of a certain vintage still refer to today. Boy George has never quite forgiven him for a shoeing he gave them when Culture Club played at Heaven – to the point that he even mentioned it onstage at the **BRIT** Awards a few years later when presenting Pet Shop Boys with the Best Single gong for 'West End Girls'.

But it was an interview/review of the Police at New York's Shea Stadium that prompted the move towards making Pet Shop Boys something more significant. '*Smash Hits* forced me to go to New York for *one day* to interview the Police, who I'd never *ever* liked, so I thought, "Well, if I've got to go and see the Police play some *horrible* concert and then do a *fantastically* boring interview with Sir Stingford, I'm *also* going to have lunch with Bobby O."' Inspired by the music he was enjoying back home and in the *Smash Hits* office, he tentatively approached Bobby Orlando, whose name was found on most of them. By coincidence, the building where Sting agreed to meet Neil was also where Bobby Orlando had his offices.

Meeting Bobby at New York eatery Applejack on Broadway, Neil had a cassette of some songs that he and Chris

114

had worked on. Over a meal of cheeseburgers and carrot cake, Neil made the decision to jack in the writing and give 'being a popstar' a go. Reflecting on this momentous occasion to *Smash Hits* in 1988, when Pet Shop Boys had very much made it, Neil recalled asking Bobby Orlando. 'I said, "Have you ever worked with any English groups?" He said, "No." I said, "Why not?" He said, "Well, no one's ever asked me." So I said, "*Actually, I'm* in a group. There's just two of us." So Bobby O said, just like that, "Let's make a record. We'll make a record. It'll be *fabulous*."'

And fabulous it was. Kind of. Among the songs on that tape were 'Bubadubadubadum', 'In the Club or in the Queue', and 'Oh, Dear', which they'd demoed with Ray Roberts in London between 1982 and 1983.

It was also around this time that they decided that West End wasn't much of a happener as a band name and rechristened themselves Pet Shop Boys – mostly because they had friends who ran a pet shop and because they thought it was something a 'British hip hop group' might call themselves, although there was also an idea that the name stemmed from a far more unsavoury practice.[2]

---

[2] 'Pet Shop Boys' was said to be American slang for homosexuals who gained sexual kicks from putting hamsters up their arse. Now, as Iggy Pop once put it, 'I'm just a modern guy', but even in my broad knowledge of niche sexual endeavours, such a thing would not only be unhygienic, but also harrowing for any hamsters involved. Like, how do you even begin to think of going there? Let's pop that one down as a homophobic urban myth.

The duo recorded thirteen songs with Bobby Orlando, with a view to those becoming their first album, but their newly acquired manager Tom Watkins talked them out of it. Only four of those tracks would be officially released in their original Bobby O incarnation – 'West End Girls', 'A Man Could Get Arrested', 'Pet Shop Boys' and 'One More Chance – while the rest of them, including 'Opportunities (Let's Make Lots of Money)', 'Two Divided By Zero', 'Rent', 'It's a Sin' and 'To Speak is a Sin', would crop up as reworked versions on subsequent releases.

So, newly christened and with a handful of songs to boot, Pet Shop Boys returned to the UK ready to become pop stars. The first release of 'West End Girls' was on 9 April 1984 through Bobby Orlando's label Bobcat Records, which was then distributed by CBS/Columbia. Unfortunately, it was only available in the UK as an import, which was perhaps not quite what the boys themselves had in mind. Bobby Orlando made his presence felt on the cowbell-heavy, none-more-1984 track, which did become a club hit in the US and a minor hit in France and Belgium, while reaching a not-exactly-encouraging 133 in the UK.

By the time of their second single with Bobby Orlando, 'One More Chance', the duo made their first-ever stage appearance at the Fridge nightclub in Brixton, singing and playing over tapes. By March 1985, they terminated their contract with Orlando and signed with EMI. Neil had become frustrated with his increasing eccentricities and believed they needed a proper manager. But as part of the split, Bobby Orlando demanded a percentage from future records. It was a canny move. From then on in, Bobby Orlando was quids in.

After hiring new manager Tom Watkins[3] and his newly formed Massive Management company, the duo also signed a deal with Dave Ambrose at EMI (Ambrose had signed Duran Duran, Sex Pistols and Talk Talk. He knew his stuff). Ambrose sent them into the studio to rerecord 'West End Girls' with producer Stephen Hague. At this point, Neil left *Smash Hits* and, at his leaving party, was given a mocked-up cover with the headline 'How I Left Britain's Brightest Magazine To Form My Tragic Pop Group, Went Down The Dumper And Asked For My Job Back'. Little did they know but Pet Shop Boys would grace the magazine's cover within the year. Incidentally, Neil didn't need to ask for his job back, but did return to guest-edit an edition in 1987 on a day-off while recording *Actually*.

---

[3] Tom Watkins would become a huge figure in British pop over the next decade, helping to launch Bros and East 17 among others, as well as co-writing most of Bros' hits. In 1981, he also set up the graphic design agency XL Design, initially designing record sleeves for Wham!'s 'Wham! Rap' and taking on ZTT Records in 1983 as a client. They were responsible for designing the sleeves and ads for Frankie Goes to Hollywood's first four singles and album, designing the interior of SARM West recording studios, and having a hand in the artwork for Art of Noise, Grace Jones, Kim Wilde, OMD, Nik Kershaw and Duran Duran. Mark Farrow, Pet Shop Boys' long-time designer, joined XL, which later became Three Associates. Watkins' 2016 autobiography, *Let's Make Lots of Money: Secrets of a Rich, Fat, Gay, Lucky Bastard*, is a rollicking read. He died in February 2020.

Released on 28 October 1985, the second version of 'West End Girls' fared slightly better. Creeping in at an inauspicious number eighty, the single finally hit the top ten in December, dethroning Shakin' Stevens' festive nuisance 'Merry Christmas Everyone' to become the first new number one of 1986. Hurrah! Over the next year or so, 'West End Girls' would go top ten in eighteen countries, reaching the top spot in Canada, Finland, Hong Kong, Israel, New Zealand, Norway and the US.

Speaking to the *Guardian* in 2020, after 'West End Girls' had been voted The Greatest UK Number One, Neil reflected on its success. 'I can see that "West End Girls" is quite a lot of records in one record. It's a dance record. It was actually written to be a rap record, back in the day. It's a moody soundscape. It's about the city at night. It's about boys and girls meeting to have fun and presumably to bond. It's about sex. It's paranoid. At the same time, its message is sort of like "Dancing in the Streets" – it's about escape into the city at night, which is emblematic of pleasure.'

'West End Girls' kicked off one of the most fantastic careers in pop. Pet Shop Boys are the architects of their own universe, and their intention was always to make amazing records. Building an aesthetic that allowed for the listener's interpretation rather than spelling everything out.

It's been present through their choice of collaborators, too. The artist and filmmaker Derek Jarman had already made a name for himself with films such as *Sebastiane* and

Jubilee. Sebastiane depicted the martyrdom of Saint Sebastian, was entirely in Latin, and filled the screen with male nudes. Sitting just on the right side of pornography, it was one of the first films to present positive images of homosexuality, while *Jubilee* saw Elizabeth I transported to a modern-day England depicted as a brutal wasteland, its cast including Jayne County, Jordan, Adam and the Ants and Toyah, along with cameos from Siouxsie Sioux and the Slits. Jarman pretty much pioneered a unique, queer and English form of arthouse cinema. And he wasn't averse to making quick money from directing videos for the Smiths ('The Queen is Dead' and 'Ask'), Marianne Faithfull ('Broken English'), Marc Almond ('Tenderness is a Weakness') and, curiously, Wang Chung's 'Dance Hall Days'.

Jarman's association with Pet Shop Boys saw him approach the mainstream with his work on the videos for 'It's a Sin' – you can't get more mainstream than three weeks at number one – and 'Rent'[4]. He also created the

---

[4] Neil Tennant has said that the inspiration for 'Rent' came from rent boys, 'but the lyrics' narrative is given by what I imagined to be the mistress of a New York politician and the refrain is wistful and romantic'. The term 'rent boy' was famously used by Charles Thomas Swinscow, who admitted in 1895 to having worked as one in a London male brothel, which led to the Cleveland Street Scandal, an investigation that precipitated a public outcry and which was used in the prosecution of Oscar Wilde that year on charges of gross indecency. In December 1984, the BBC documentary series *40 Minutes* showed the short film 'Rent Boys', which focused on the phenomenon of young male prostitutes in Manchester and Birmingham.

projections for their 1989 tour, which were full of his oeuvre: oversaturated images of theatrical decadence, the grim melancholic beauty of a pre-gentrified London, and homoerotic symbolism. This was all at a time when Clause 28[5] and AIDS – two causes that Jarman campaigned and raised awareness of – sought to dampen and deny gay people any voice or equality.

'It's a Sin' began what Neil refers to as the duo's 'imperial phase', a couple of years when they could do no wrong chart-wise, only coming an apparent cropper when 'Domino Dancing' failed to get to number one. This

---

[5] Clause (or Section) 28 was a legislative designation brought in by the Tories to prohibit the 'promotion of homosexuality' that came into effect in 1988. Named after Section 28 of the Local Government Act 1988, which added Section 2A to the Local Government Act 1986, the amendment stated that a local authority 'shall not intentionally promote homosexuality or publish material with the intention of promoting homosexuality' or 'promote the teaching in any maintained school of the acceptability of homosexuality as a pretended family relationship'. The Tories used gay rights as a battleground during the 1987 general election, under the premise of protecting the family, with chief dog-whistler Margaret Thatcher telling her party conference that 'children who need to be taught to respect traditional moral values are being taught that they have an inalienable right to be gay'. It was pure homophobia, but a Tory-facing press ran with it. The sheer fear of falling foul of the law and the threat of prosecution saw LGBTQ+ societies disband, and while there were no successful prosecutions under the law, there were legal attempts to use it to stop the funding of LGBTQ+ and HIV/AIDS prevention initiatives. It was disbanded in 2000, but the ugly fact that it was created in the first place shows just how vile things got for gay people in the '80s.

imperial phase included collaborations with gay icons Dusty Springfield and Liza Minnelli, and the featuring of Ian McKellen in the 'Heart' video. These hook-ups were an indication of where the pair's interests lay. They also secured the extremely important Christmas number-one slot with their poppers-aloft cover of 'Always on My Mind'.

There was also the poignancy of songs such as 'It Couldn't Happen Here', which stemmed from a conversation Neil had with a friend who expressed a belief that the AIDS epidemic wouldn't have much of an impact in Britain. Neil noted that 'AIDS entered my life in 1986. A very good friend of mine, whom I grew up with in Newcastle, was diagnosed with AIDS in that year, and he died two and a half years later. The song "It Couldn't Happen Here" on *Actually* was specifically about the experience of finding out his diagnosis.' There's also 'Your Funny Uncle', which was inspired by the funeral of a friend who had died of an AIDS-related illness, where Neil notices the deceased's uncle observing the gay friends in attendance that his nephew had. 'All the details are true: the cars in slow formation, and so on. He did have an uncle, who had been in the army all of his life and suddenly found himself at the funeral of his evidently gay nephew who'd died of AIDS. I think it must have been quite a difficult situation for him, but he was really nice and dignified, and spoke to all of his nephew's friends. I had to give a reading, and the bit I read was from the *Book of Revelation* . . . At the end, it says there's somewhere where there's no pain or fear, and

I found it a really moving piece of prose, and attached it to the end of the song.'

The same friend's death who inspired 'Your Funny Uncle' was also the subject of what would perhaps become Pet Shop Boys' greatest song.

By the time of 1990's *Behaviour*, Neil and Chris would have come up with, for want of a better word, their funeral song. Songs popular at funerals have come in many forms, and for many years the standard was Frank Sinatra's 'My Way' – the basic get-out clause (the brassneck 'I may have been an absolute shit when I was alive but I did it my way') for people who'd behaved like wankers. 'Being Boring' was one of the first songs to tackle the perspective of loss and the movement of time for gay people.

'Being Boring' has its roots in two things: an accusation of being boring by a Japanese fan, but also a Zelda Fitzgerald quote, as Neil confirmed in the Pet Shop Boys biography *Literally*. 'Obviously it was inspired by the fact that we're supposed to be boring or something, and I thought what a good song title it would be. Then I remembered that, when I was eighteen or nineteen, all my friends in Newcastle had a party and the invitations quoted this famous Zelda Fitzgerald quote from the 1920s: "We were never bored, because we were never boring." I spoke to a friend, Dave Rimmer, recently and told him about this song and he said, "I've got the invitation in front of me." It was quite a big do at the time – it was called "The Great Urban Dionysia Party".

The first verse is about finding the invitation. It then says, "We were never feeling bored, because we were never being boring." The second verse is about leaving Newcastle to go to college in London. And someone had said to us, "The trouble with you lot is you'll have experienced everything by the time you're eighteen – you'll have nothing left to experience." And the third verse is me, now, just thinking where the people are who I was with then. So it's quite a sad song, but quite jolly too.'

Neil went into more detail in the booklet for *Behaviour: Further Listening*, the reissue of the *Behaviour* album. 'It's just the sadness of having a close friend die, because I always thought he'd be somewhere there with me. When we were teenagers, we would always discuss that we weren't going to settle for boring lives, we were always going to do something different. And then when it came down to it, I did become a pop star and, at exactly that time, he became very ill.'

Derek Jarman was also the unlikely catalyst behind the duo's decision to tackle 'Go West'. Originally released as a single by Village People in 1979, the song was written by Jacques Morali, Henri Belolo and lead singer Victor Willis, based around the famous 'Go west, young man' quote from American newspaper editor Horace Greeley in 1865. The song's melody resembled the State Anthem of the Soviet Union, composed by Alexander Alexandrov and adopted in 1944 before being relinquished in 1991 after the dissolution of the Soviet Union. The Village People's original was a butch and cheery ode encouraging men to head to San Francisco. Pet Shop Boys took the song and amplified both the East and West elements, as well as enhancing the original's chord progression from Pachelbel's *Canon*. The oomph of the new version was weighed out by the melancholic delivery by Neil and the almost industrial-strength doof in a very post-Soviet and post-AIDS twinning to make it almost unbearably moving.

It was in 1994, in an interview with the then recently launched *Attitude* magazine, that Neil revealed his sexuality – which, for many fans, put everything into perspective. He had originally told the *NME* in 1986 that 'we've never said anything about our sex lives to the newspapers or to magazines, and we don't intend to'.

Talking to interviewer Paul Burston, Neil felt relaxed enough to open up. 'The thing is, we were kind of stitched up by the *NME* on that one. They did an interview with us, and then they went on and on about hamsters. They never actually asked us, "Are you gay?" And then Jimmy Somerville was quoted everywhere, slagging us off. His view is that the entire point of being a pop star is to be a positive role model. I reject any notion of being a positive role model to anyone. I personally find that an arrogant way to think of oneself . . .

'The Pet Shop Boys came along to make fabulous records. We didn't come along to be politicians, or to be positive role models. Having said all that, we have supported the fight for gay rights.

'And what's more, I do think that we have contributed, through our music and also through our videos and the general way we've presented things, rather a lot to what you might call "gay culture". I could spend several pages discussing the notion of "gay culture", but for the sake of argument, I would just say that we have contributed a lot. And the simple reason for this is that I have written songs from my own point of view . . .

'What I'm actually saying is, I am gay, and I have written songs from that point of view. So, I mean, I'm being surprisingly honestly with you here, but those are the facts of the matter.'

Explaining his decision to the *Guardian* in 2018, he said, 'In the '80s – and the '90s, for that matter – it was such a big deal, being gay. You knew your audience had a lot of women or girls in it, so you wanted to include everyone. I still sort of think that when I'm writing, to be honest. Also, I don't write about my life in the direct way that most, if not all, artists do nowadays . . . It isn't anything to do with pronouns. It's to do with poetry really.'

The key thing is that Pet Shop Boys operated in an environment where 'gay' pop music was seen as either glittery, camp and celebratory (Erasure), sleazy and occasionally traumatic (Soft Cell) or fiercely political (Bronski Beat). Pet Shop Boys managed to straddle and combine all of these strands to be something relatable. Their music has also had a grounding in reality and history. That it all began – and nearly ended – with the release of 'West End Girls' in 1984 and a desire to make music with a producer behind some of the gayest music of the early '80s, showed that their instincts have always been right.

In response to hysterical reporting, in May 1984, the National Union of Journalists published the leaflet 'AIDS and the Media' with information to members regarding the reporting of AIDS. These included such points as 'AIDS has nothing to do with wildfires or icebergs' and 'AIDS is not a "plague"', while also condemning journalistic invasions of privacy, such as when 'one Sunday newspaper got hold of the name and address of a gay man with AIDS, interviewed his neighbours and threatened to print a photo of his house if he did not cooperate'.

BRONSKI BEAT

'The love that you need will never be found at home.'

The regional homosexual, for want of a better phrase, was one that could explain the plight that many young gay men and women found themselves in back in the wretched old days, trapped in increasingly suffocating surroundings in fear of getting a pasting or rejection from their families. In both fact and fiction, there have been people wanting to escape the confines of narrow minds and narrower scenes of – *if any* – ill-attended gay nights in backstreet pubs, in search of a better existence as a part of life. And so was the case with Bronski Beat. Jimmy

Somerville, Larry Steinbachek and Steve Bronski were effectively three Dick Whittingtons of cock fun, fleeing their hometowns towards London in need of excitement and a more tolerant lifestyle.

The key thing about Bronski Beat is that they looked like the boys next door. People could relate to them because, well, they looked relatable. Gay acts were predominantly about swish and sauce and femininity, either in the overt butch mandrag of cloney macho masculinity or the female-adjacent flourish. Bronski Beat looked like your brothers or funny uncles. Sure, there were traits of what was gay signifying – the MA1 jackets, Levi's 501s and Doc Martens are practically a uniform in some areas of the scene – but, to all intents and purposes, there was nothing outwardly homosexual. The worst that anyone could throw at them – and, oh boy, they did – was that Jimmy Somerville looked like a potato. More importantly, the Bronskis were an act that weren't afraid to be political, outspoken and a bunch of queens all at the same time. 'We talk about everything,' Steve said to *Gay Times*, 'but gay politics affects us directly, so we talk about that more than anything else.'

Jimmy had moved down to London, escaping Glasgow and a homelife that had seen his mother send him to a psychiatrist after several suicide attempts. 'I first realised I was gay when I was very small, about ten years old, and I decided it was really me when I was about fourteen. I had a hard time at school because I was obviously gay and there was no one to talk to about it, no one to confide in.

128

'Even now, in the problem pages, you get replies saying things like, "You may not be gay. It could be a *phase* you're going through." Well, my "phase" has lasted for eight years now and it doesn't seem to be going away!

'I retaliated. I grew my hair really long and had it permed, and ran around town with boys that I met. I became a real screamer!'

He had been involved with a documentary film entitled *Framed Youth: The Revenge of the Teenage Perverts*, which had been made by the London Lesbian and Gay Youth Video Project. Jimmy (initially styled 'Jimi') certainly multitasked his talents – as a participant and an editor, as well as providing a song for the soundtrack, 'Screaming'. The film was basically a 'young adults' type affair about gay issues, and featured gay people going up to straight people in the streets and asking what they thought about homosexual rights and the like. Seeking straight people's views on homosexuality could have gone several ways, but the film was one of the first to show gay people in a completely normal light. The question 'Could you tell me what a lesbian is, please?' garnered such varied answers as 'I would call them a sex maniac' or 'It's two wimmin, innit?', while 'What would you do if you found out your sister was a lesbian?' was greeted with the response of 'Kill 'er'. The film won Best British Documentary at the Grierson Awards in 1984 and would eventually gain a wider audience (after a fashion) when screened on Channel 4 in 1986. Viewed from the distance of forty years, it's almost quaint, yet still mildly horrifying, that in the collective span and history of LGBTQ+ rights, it's almost yesterday. Other contributors of note to the film included Mark Ashton and Richard Coles, two people who would later feature significantly in the story of Jimmy Somerville.

Jimmy's performance of 'Screaming' so impressed his then-new flatmates Larry and Steve, who'd already been tinkering about with synths in their Brixton abode, that it was suggested that they got together to make some music. Also sharing the flat was Gill Whisson, who would go on to design sleeves for the band. And, in a coincidental gay pop crossover, Jimmy had originally lived in a west London flat which had also housed future Pet Shop Boy, Chris Lowe. The Brixton house the soon-to-be trio lived in had the reasonably unlistenable Sex Gang Children in the flat below, and a performance artist named Regine in the flat above.

In the film, Jimmy is also seen discussing his home life, growing up in Ruchill near Glasgow, and how relations were with his parents. The three Bronskis gelled and shared the opinion that many gay performers, of the few that were visible at least, were fairly inoffensive and so, instead, they wanted to bring a more political edge. Making their debut at the festival September in the Pink, a GLC-funded event at Heaven nightclub, as the newly named Bronski Beat – an apparent pun on Roxy Music, and a slightly better name than the originally mooted God Forbid – they performed a short set alongside turns such as Passing Faze and Abandon

Your Tutu. There was also a fashion show, DJs and short films by John Maybury and Isaac Julien.

Bronski Beat had become such a hot ticket that they were signed by London Records after only nine shows. This was a remarkable feat back in the early '80s for any act, especially one that was as 'out' as Bronski Beat were. Part of that rapid ascent was a meeting with Colin Bell at September in the Pink. Bell was part of the committee that put the festival together and was also the A&R at London Records. Somerville later recalled to the *Guardian* that Bell 'knew that we didn't have to be sold, that it would market itself on the gay angle if we were unapologetic enough about it'.

It was around this time that the trio also met with ZTT. However, that wasn't productive. Jimmy recalled to the *Guardian* that 'someone involved with them told us to get T-shirts printed with "Cum" and "Queer" and "Bent" on them. Well, I don't think so!' Colin had some form in knowing what he was doing. He'd been head of publicity at Polygram before then, helping the careers of ABC, Tears for Fears, Dexys Midnight Runners, Dire Straits and Soft Cell during an especially rosy period for the company. As part of his label management role at London, he was involved in all aspects of not just Bronski Beat's and the Communards' careers, but also the those of Bananarama and Fine Young Cannibals. He would also play a key role in bringing early house music releases to the label (and the UK in general), graduating to managing director, overseeing dance label **FFRR** and eventually the careers of All Saints, Shakespears Sister and East 17.

'Colin understood that, by just being ourselves, it might make it to a wider audience, but I don't think anyone had any idea how wide that might be. It was all down to the power of the song.

'I was never really aware of my voice until friends from the video project mentioned it to me,' Jimmy told *No1* magazine. 'Even now, I've only been singing for about twelve months, and I'm still not used to it myself! Sometimes I even frighten myself with it. I think *Is it really me making those sounds?* It's weird!'

Ahead of its release in May 1984, Bronski Beat took the acetate of the 12-inch of 'Smalltown Boy' down to Heaven and handed it to DJ Ian Levine. When he played it, it was like a bomb going off. The reaction was such that Levine would play the track twice more that night.

The band weren't terribly keen on being mentioned in the same breath as Frankie Goes to Hollywood all the time. This was more a matter of circumstance and the fact that they'd arrived a few months after 'Relax', no doubt making it handier for the press to lump them together. The pop music press – and, indeed, the wider tabloids – had been unaccustomed to two ostensibly 'gay' acts coming through as they both had. When asked about both the Frankies and Culture Club, they shirtily informed *Smash Hits* that being gay was not about 'ribbons and frocks' or 'shocking and outraging'. As Larry told *Record Mirror:* 'Even before we formed a band, dressing up in that way wasn't part of our culture anyway . . . We're not deliberately non-glam, we're just not glam people, we're just us' – although Jimmy countered it with 'I might buy some dreadlocks and frocks . . . No, but seriously, imagine me in leather. No thanks.'

'We're just like all the other millions of gays in this country,' added Steve. 'It's just a few that dress up and everybody seems to think gays are all like that. It's about time people found out what other people are doing.'

'We're just wild queens,' confirmed Jimmy, 'not wee skinheads. Most gays we meet really support us, but we meet some bitchy queens who are just waiting for us to sell out, to go for the soft option because it's safer.'

The ultimate goal of Bronski Beat, was, as Jimmy revealed to *Gay Times*, to 'put our point across in a fun way, through dance music, with a simple setup, without ramming a message down people's throats. It's just honest and emotional because the pain and violence come from the heart.'

The band's social awareness – for want of a better phrase, dear God – included such innovations as the telephone number of the London Gay Switchboard being etched into the inner groove of the 12-inch vinyl version of 'Smalltown Boy'. This was the sort of thing you might find on independent releases where records released in small runs could get away with making a statement, rather than on a major-label release. It also didn't go unnoticed that the imprint the band released their music on via London was called Forbidden Fruit.

Bronski Beat often felt compromised by their new status as pop stars – and by how they felt they were beginning to be held up as this slightly risqué, issues-based group appearing on TV pop shows and in magazines, when they ideally wanted to express their more political stance. Yet somehow, in retrospect, that was the perfect position to be in: a Trojan horse barging into the pop landscape and offering something with a little more substance than the likes of Howard Jones' bland platitudes.

The Bronskis wanted to make a stance, that ultimately it was all about the music. They did think Frankie's records were brilliant, but got annoyed when Holly and Paul claimed that songs like 'Two Tribes' weren't political. As Jimmy told *Smash Hits*: 'You have to make a stance, not only about being gay. We just want to wake people up to what's happening . . . Like that song "Hard Rain". It's about nuclear weapons, the fate of the world. That's more important than anything!

'I don't really expect everyone to understand what we're singing about. All I'd ask for is people to be neither condemning or patronising about it. I think that everyone can identify with the emotions we sing about whether they're straight or gay. Maybe we can help some of them through the bad times.'

'Smalltown Boy' did very good business around Europe. A UK number three, and number one in the Netherlands and Belgium, come February 1985 it would be topping the US Hot Dance Club Play charts, having already crept into the Billboard Hot 100 on Christmas week in 1984, hitting a peak of number forty-eight come March.

Reflecting on 'Smalltown Boy' to the *Guardian* in 2012, Jimmy explained how he was 'still incredibly proud of the video. It's a simple wee story, but for 1984, it was quite radical. I don't think for a second it's in the class of Ken Loach or Mike Leigh, but it borrowed a little bit from that thinking. It was an amazing time because gay men and lesbians had just found their voice and we could introduce the idea that homosexuality wasn't just about what you did behind closed doors. It wasn't about "the twilight world of the homosexual", or whatever the press used to call it; it was about gay people doing their food shopping in Sainsbury's. It's ridiculous to think about this now, but that hadn't been addressed in pop music before. These were fairly intimidating times as well. You'd get abuse from the police and the public on Pride marches. Now they're a nice family day out.'

The trio were also soon courted by Elton John, who signed them to a publishing deal with his company – although Elton's status led to them being aghast when he sent a limousine to pick them up from their Camberwell flat. 'We were mortified! All the local kids were staring so we dived into the car . . . But Elton's a great guy. When he met us, he gave us all a big kiss – in front of his wife!' Ahem.

The follow-up single, 'Why?', arrived on 14 September 1984. It was a much more urgent and somewhat furious shard of high-energy pop, as the trio fully intended showing their teeth after the melancholic 'Smalltown Boy'. 'We thought it would be good to give them an angry song this time,' Steve told *Record Mirror*. Jimmy agreed. '"Smalltown Boy" was too nicey nicey. Everybody loves it.

'"Why?" is a continuation of the "Smalltown Boy" story where the boy leaves home because of the pressures. "Why?" is about coming to the big city but, at the same time, it's not all fun and games; there's just as much pressure. It's about the idea that someone can't love someone else without reverting to physical violence because they won't accept it. It's about constantly having to fight for love, because that's what we have to do, try to change the law, people's attitudes. It's a constant struggle to fight for your right to love and that's a right that everybody should have – to love who they want.

'People don't seem to realise how stifling and dangerous things are now. You can't even hold hands on the street without being arrested.'

The song was dedicated to gay playwright Drew Griffiths, who had been murdered in June 1984 by a man whom he'd picked up in London's Elephant and Castle.[1] 'He'd been stabbed through the heart eighteen times,' explained Jimmy. It was also written for a friend of the

---

[1] Drew had a difficult life. He was ostracised by his family at the age of fourteen when they sent him for gay aversion therapy. Moving to London in 1973 from Urmston in Lancashire, Drew was one of the co-founders of the gay

band, named Martin, who had fled the country due to his sexuality and his relationship with a much younger man whose parents objected to the relationship and went about demonising Martin in every way they could.

Speaking to *Melody Maker* at the time, Jimmy was seething. 'Oh yeah, it's angry all right. Those are the stages I went through and still feel. After the isolation you're made to feel like dirt, deviant and unclean. You realise you're not alone and that's when the anger sets in . . . I think "Why?" is going to be the decision maker for us. It's like, how much are people prepared to accept about what we have to say?'

The debut album, *The Age of Consent*, arrived a few weeks later on 15 October. It was recorded in both London and New York; the sessions in the latter made for an eventful fortnight that saw Jimmy attacked on the subway and Steve and Larry availing themselves of some of the seedier bars of the city. It was a bit much even for them.

The album's title was suggested by Jimmy during the recording at The Garden studios in London. Larry and

---

theatre group Gay Sweatshop and was a key figure in opening up the group to more than just gay men. His lifestyle led to him contracting hepatitis B and his attachment to drink saw him becoming increasingly haphazard; he set fire to his house, ran up huge debts and fled to Paris to live as a tramp. After recovery, he would write for radio and television, but the stress found him soon setting fire to furniture again. In 2016, the Metropolitan Police were urged to reinvestigate Drew's murder. However, the following year, they announced they would no longer be actively investigating his death, but the case would continue to be subject to periodic review.

Steve agreed immediately. It was also Jimmy's idea to include the little-known information about the different international ages of consent for males to engage in gay sex, legally, on the inner sleeve of the album. This was an eye-opener in itself. The age of consent in the UK was still twenty-one, based on legislation from 1967, while across Europe it was anything between fourteen and sixteen. It wasn't until the Criminal Justice and Public Order Act 1994 that it was reduced to eighteen. The Sexual Offences (Amendment) Act 2000 finally reduced it to sixteen in England, Wales and Scotland, matching the law for heterosexual couples.

The Age of Consent sold extremely well for an album steeped in gay anthems, becoming a number-four hit in the UK and spending more than a year in the album charts. Containing the previous singles and three cover versions – George & Ira Gershwin's 'It Ain't Necessarily So', Donna Summer's 'I Feel Love' and John Leyton's 'Johnny Remember Me' – among six more of the trio's compositions. It was an instant classic, its entire existence was one of both celebration and education, with the pink triangle artwork[2] emphasising where the album's intentions stood.

---

[2] The history of the pink triangle is a little grim. It was first worn as a cloth badge in Nazi concentration camps to identify a prisoner as a male homosexual, and later bisexual men and transgender women. It was reclaimed as a symbol of gay liberation, initially as a memorial to those who'd been ostracised and killed by the Nazi movement, and then a positive symbol of community identity as the '80s arrived. In the early part of the decade, AIDS Coalition

Even 'I Feel Love' was politically charged as during a performance in 1983, Donna Summer had proclaimed 'I have seen the evils of homosexuality . . . AIDS is the result of your sins' – a remark that she has since apologised for. 'Donna Summer can eat shit,' Jimmy and Steve told *Gay Times* . . . 'Now it's gonna be OUR record.'

When issued as a single close to Christmas, 'It Ain't Necessarily So' featured a photo referencing *The Wizard of Oz*, albeit with a satanic wolf head replacing Dorothy's. The 'friends of Dorothy' image seemingly passed fans by. But even in the context of a cheery cover of a standard, and following the first two singles, it still felt a tad subversive.

On 10 December, the band headlined 'Pits and Perverts', that concert at the Electric Ballroom in London to raise funds for the Lesbians and Gays Support the Miners campaign – and an event that was featured in the 2014 film *Pride*.[3] The 'Pits and Perverts' benefit raised £5,650

---

to Unleash Power (ACT UP) used it to highlight the increase of AIDS deaths with the slogan Silence = Death. The triangle has since been used universally and in a variety of forms on monuments and memorials honouring gay and lesbian people.

[3] When researching the story behind LGSM, writer Stephen Beresford found a very amateur homemade documentary from 1985 called *All Out! Dancing in Dulais*, which was created by LGSM for the miners. It follows the story of how lesbians and gays befriended the small Welsh village by taking a punt and travelling there to give money directly to the striking families. It showcases the bonds that were formed between the two communities.

[4] In those twelve months, Arthur Scargill of the NUM led the fight against these closures against prime minister Margaret Thatcher, who wanted to

(the equivalent of £22,397 in 2024) for striking miners and their families in South Wales. While Bronski Beat were the headline act at the event, the night was most notable for a speech given by a member from the National Union of Mineworkers (NUM) to the 1,500-strong audience, 'You have worn our badge, "Coal not Dole", and you know what harassment means, as we do. Now we will pin your badge on us; we will support you. It won't change overnight, but now 140,000 miners know that there are other causes and other problems. We know about blacks and gays and nuclear disarmament, and will never be the same.' The miner's strike began in March 1984 as industrial action against the closure of collieries and finished almost exactly a year later.[4] Somerville was best friends with Mark Ashton, the activist and co-founder of Lesbians and Gays Support the Miners (LGSM), who was the key character in the film.

---

reduce the power of trade unions. It has been estimated that the number of person days lost to the action was 26 million, making it the largest protest since the General Strike of 1926. Thatcher used everything she could – heavy-handed police and an anti-working-class right-wing press – to demonise Scargill and the striking miners. It ended with the NUM's defeat and a weakening of the trade union movement. LGSM groups were also formed in ten other areas across the UK, among them Manchester, Brighton, Southampton and Lothian. A Dublin LGSM group was also formed. Lesbians Against Pit Closures (LAPC) was instituted in November 1984 and focused on raising money at women's venues in London, with the money raised donated to the Rhodesia Women's Action Group in Worksop in Nottinghamshire. LGSM gave practical support to LAPC.

Ashton died from an AIDS-related illness in 1987. Despite the fact that his songs feature in the film, Somerville claimed that he couldn't bear to watch it at the cinema as it would 'make him bawl his eyes out'.

Jimmy left Bronski Beat in April 1985 after the release of a duet with Marc Almond on a re-recorded 'I Feel Love'/'Johnny Remember Me'. Tensions between the three Bronskis had become such that Jimmy's urge to carry on in a more political vein was at odds with the pop that Larry and Steve were keen on pursuing. Even though a post-*Age Of Consent* song had been recorded, 'Run From Love' (which ended up as part of the band's *Hundreds and Thousands* remix album), Jimmy went off to form the Communards with Richard Coles. Things were already looking slightly shaky for the trio in February when Jimmy was arrested in a gents toilet in Hyde Park for 'offences against the public's morals'. It was felt that Jimmy's arrest might be a little *too* gay for such a politically charged trio.

Larry and Steve recruited a new singer, John Foster, who debuted on that November's 'Hit That Perfect Beat'. Although it became the band's third top-three single, things rapidly tailed off as they'd not hit those heights again, with Foster departing himself in 1987 and later replaced by Jonathan Hellyer.

However, things didn't remain quite so rancorous between Jimmy, Steve and Larry. They reformed for a one-off International AIDS Day concert in November 1987, supporting New Order at Brixton Academy. Bronski Beat as an entity eventually folded before the '80s were up – as did, after two well-received albums and the biggest-selling single of 1986 in 'Don't Leave Me This Way', the Communards. Jimmy had been through two bands in the space of little more than five years. And, by 1989, he'd begun his solo career with his debut single 'Comment te dire adieu'.

The Communards were progressively more political and vocal about gay rights, including touring as part of the Red Wedge set-up. They appeared in Labour Party political broadcasts and became more vocal about AIDS in the pages of *Smash Hits*, *Record Mirror* and *No1*, as well as discussing the oncoming bullshit that was Section 28. Alongside the hit cover versions, there were the duo's self-penned songs, such as 'For a Friend'. This was written about Mark Ashton, who had died only twelve days after being diagnosed with HIV in early 1987. All the band's proceeds were given to Mark Ashton's AIDS charity, but the record company refused to donate their profits. The duo appeared on *Breakfast Time* on BBC One to discuss Radio 1's reluctance to playlist the song, which Jimmy put down to the fact that it was about a man dying of AIDS.

Following the demise of the Communards, Jimmy and Richard had a falling-out. Jimmy discovered that Richard had lied to him about having HIV when in fact he didn't, plus Richard had become increasingly distracted by the perils of pop fame, such as doing loads of drugs and losing his mind slightly – to the point where he eventually became a reverend and an unlikely national treasure as a bonus. While the pair have since reconciled, it is understandable that Jimmy would be hurt.

Jimmy strutted into solo stardom with his debut album *Read My Lips*, which contained a cover of Sylvester's '(You Make Me Feel) Mighty Real', with the video of the title track featuring various ACT-UP (AIDS Coalition to Unleash Power) slogans throughout.

Sadly, a Bronski Beat reunion of the original trio is now unable to happen. Larry, who post-Bronski moved to Amsterdam in 1994 and continued to make music and worked on various stage musicals, died in December 2016 after a battle with cancer. Steve Bronski, who'd relocated to Thailand for a while and who had revived the band with various replacements up until he had a stroke in 2018, died from smoke inhalation in a fire at his home in Soho in December 2021.

Paying tribute to Larry, Jimmy posted a link to 'Screaming' on his social media, saying, 'We were young, brave and determined. Too OUT to stay in! Thank you for that moment, Larry.' And as for Steve, Jimmy noted that 'working with him on songs, and the one song that changed our lives and touched so many other lives, was a fun and exciting time. Thanks for the melody, Steve.'

Jimmy continues to work and perform, occasionally on the – very lucrative – retro festival circuit. He's done bits of acting, including appearing in the film *Orlando* in 1992. But he's not interested in being Jimmy Bronski/Communards for the rest of his life, and lives quietly in Brighton.

While new music is a rarity, he's well aware of the significance and impact he's had on people's lives. 'I don't care what anybody wants to say about my career, either before or after that. I am immensely proud of the fact that we were responsible for the one song that encompasses sexuality and politics in that time and place. It is absolutely my proudest moment, because the song is so raw and honest, even people who didn't like gay people couldn't disagree with it. It just struck a chord. Even though it is specifically about a gay man's experience of growing up in shitty suburbia and leaving home, it could be about anyone's.'

'We were just three openly gay men writing songs about our lives,' Steve Bronski reflected to *Classic Pop* in 2019. 'A lot of people in our community just happened to relate to our songs, which was amazing. I believe certain music and songs are timeless, and the fact that 'Smalltown Boy' and 'Why?' are seen as relevant today would say that they meant something to somebody and maybe helped them.'

* * *

Looking back at Bronski Beat, and at *The Age of Consent* in particular, it's still somewhat revolutionary that a trio of normal-looking gay lads could have had such an impact. It was as if the political was as key as the music. With a buffet of gay rights, miners and nuclear war, they couldn't have been more 1984.

'Smalltown Boy' has had a lasting quality, almost transitioning into a modern standard with a variety of cover versions making it still pertinent to modern ways, and managing to speak and relate to new listeners in a way that their contemporaries never did.

As for the age of consent, while progress has been made, there are still a number of countries in the world where it is still illegal to be gay. Some of those that have come out of the dark ages include Cyprus and the Republic of Ireland (where the age of consent is now seventeen), Russia (sixteen) and Romania (fifteen). Spain's previous age of twenty-three (or 'punishable by the law either as a case of "public scandal" or "corruption of minors" defined as persons under 23') is now sixteen.

While it's fair to say that things are better in Europe, it's still only in the last twenty years that there has been certain equality with heterosexuals, with laws being passed to allow gays to marry or serve in the armed forces. Progress has been slow and, my word, there's a lot more to be made across the world, but in general there's a forward motion towards equality.

Homophobic attacks, sadly, are still with us. While much of this could be down to more reports of such things due to the nature of the closet in 1984, hate crimes in the UK have soared in recent years, with transphobic hate crimes on the rise, too. Reports of systemic homophobia and failings among certain areas of the police force also mean that many people are afraid to come forward. Parallels with the fearmongering and abuse that gay people endured during the early years of the AIDS crisis were reflected in pandemic-related attacks and quack theories that somehow LGBTQ+ people were responsible for COVID. For every two steps forward for the LGBTQ+ movement, it seems, the worst of humanity will always be there, continually walking backwards.

Bronski Beat made the personal political and opened many an eye to the plight of gay people around the planet. And they did it with pop music. 'Smalltown Boy' is not only a gay classic, it's a heart-breaking tale that you can dance to. In the early '80s, for any gay man, the dancefloor was the place to be.

Following years of denial about his sexuality, in June 1984,
the actor Rock Hudson is diagnosed with AIDS. When he
dies in the October of the following year, he leaves $250,000
to help set up the American Foundation for AIDS Research,
with Elizabeth Taylor serving as the organisation's
founding national chairman.

HIGH ENERGY

'Your love is lifting me.'

High energy. A music that's seldom celebrated. It's trashy, tinny, shallow and clattering. It's the sound of music at its most basic. Electronic blues. A true metal machine music. It adheres to the structure of rock and features the dynamics of rock, and yet is culturally absent, blank. It's the nadir as far as critical wisdom is concerned. It's occasionally a shorthand for homophobic approaches to what gay people like. It's surface, bass-less and bereft of depth.

It's also yearning and wonder. The sound of desire and need and urgency. It is non-judgmental, egalitarian and shorn of nostalgia. The propulsive clank and clatter, winding up into an intense and pulsating crescendo of oncoming lust and ecstasy. The sound of poppers. The scent of sweat and bodies. Stickiness and desire. It can go deep, taking you deeper than you'd dare yourself, speaking the unspoken – the gap between 'the here' and 'the where you long to be'.

So, there you go – the two schools of thought depending on which side you're on. Whether it's empty trash or modern soul, it packs gay – and straight – dancefloors the world over. It's been the lingua franca of gay disco since the late '70s and early '80s with its lyrical content full of suggestion, sexual meaning and base desires, or sadness, sentimentality and tragedy.

High energy is disco stripped of all the superfluousness. The strings, the trills, the thrills and the fancies which defined the almost carefree decadency of the late '70s were eschewed in favour of a mechanical man-machine music. It became the default music for gay nightclubs and sex bars, as it replicated the cyborg-esque existence of those who headed out for hedonism and pleasure, an increasingly anonymous music soundtracking an anonymous existence of sexual encounters with anyone and everyone. That this music's rise coincided with the rise of the clone – identikit images of macho stereotypes sometimes at complete odds with the man beneath the moustache and muscle – was to be expected. In some nightclubs, such as New York's The Anvil and The Mineshaft, the DJ was replaced with pre-made tapes. In these small clubs, the removal of the DJ booth freed up much-needed floorspace to accommodate the influx of men who were intent on mechanically grinding their amyl-fuelled bits to the amyl-fuelled hits. This was the era where men had come out of the bathhouses and into the gyms. Weightlifting and locker-room fantasies appeared to be the primary motive now. The bumming was still real, even if the music didn't feel like it was.

There is some argument about high energy's ancestry, but one of the two key high-profile touchstones can be traced back to the early electronic music created by Giorgio Moroder and his work with Donna Summer. Having stretched an orgasm out across one side of an album with 'Love to Love You Baby', the pair then proceeded to invent the future with 'I Feel Love'. Indeed, the concept of the accompanying album *I Remember Yesterday* was to have each track evoke a different musical decade. The title track looked to the '40s, 'Love's Unkind' appropriated the '50s and so on. For 'I Feel Love', the team aimed to create THE FUTURE, employing a Moog synthesiser.

'I Feel Love' foxed and upset people. It divided the original soul and funk turns who found it too alienating and European. Many deemed it an insult that Donna Summer should be presented as a disembodied voice over dehumanising electronics. Any sort of feel or boogie was erased in favour of surface and effect. But it was perfectly structured to become the true music of gay men because the culture at that point was about gratification, soulless hook-ups and a clone-y blankness of being the music of a sex robot. Cock. Bumming. Men. They were the mirror representation of each other.

In 1978, an underground remix of Donna Summer's 'I Feel Love' by Patrick Cowley was constructed using loops and overdubbed elements of the original into a beyond-human-endurance near-sixteen-minute remix, which he distributed through the Disconet Remix Service. Moroder wasn't entirely flattered, it has to be said. However, patrons of the dancefloors were and, by 1982, demand had got such that Casablanca picked the remix up for an official release. An extremely edited-down single version hit the airwaves again, propelling the song back into the UK charts in December 1982, a month after Cowley died. He had managed to turbo-boost the song into new realms of future. The original eight-minute version had long been a DJ's friend, allowing them to have a wee break when 'dropped' at an opportune moment. Cowley's version allowed DJs to now not only have a wee, but also nip out for a couple of fags, hit the bar and maybe even fill up on supplies from the buffet.

The song was also catnip for gay nightclubs. Even now, nearly fifty years later, its ability to ram a floor is undiminished. At some point, the future will actually catch up with it, but that future still feels like one that is some way off. It's also worth pointing out that in 1995, Faithless and Masters At Work remixed it and it made the Top Ten. And yet despite their game efforts, it wasn't a patch on the original. It wasn't even in the same postcode, frankly.

It was a bit like trying to update a cheesecake by adding gravy to it.

The other key hit following on from 'I Feel Love' was Sylvester's '(You Make Me Feel) Mighty Real' in 1978. Produced by Patrick Cowley[1], it sounded like a throbbing rush. It was a record that felt like each element was designed to enhance each part of the body, while Sylvester swooped, swooned and diva-ed ecstatically over the top.

However, it was not all plain sailing, with disco sunk by the iceberg of the US Disco Sucks movement. Steve Dahl had been working as a DJ for ABC-owned radio station WDAI, but was fired on Christmas Eve 1978 as part of the station's switch from rock to disco. Playing up at the injustice of his dismissal, Dahl created an anti-disco movement, which he claimed was 'dedicated to the eradication of the dreaded musical disease known as DISCO'. His influence spread to the point where there were reports of fights breaking out at disco events across the country.

---

[1] Cowley's own solo career yielded such supreme bumming-adjacent pumpers as 'Menergy' and 'Megatron Man'. He wrote 'Right on Target' for handsome clone Paul Parker and collaborated as equals with Sylvester on his own 'Do Ya Wanna Funk?' In a short space of time, Cowley managed to run with the Moroder blueprint while creating a nice sideline in soundtracking shonky gay porn films with numbers such as 'Lumberjacks in Heat', '5oz of Funk' and 'Pigfoot', most of which have been lovingly reissued by the Dark Entries label. Lord knows what he would've gone on to do had he lived longer. 'Menergy', 'Mighty Real' and his remix of 'I Feel Love' were intense and urgent pulses from an arena that he'd barely skirted the dimensions of.

In July 1979, as part of the entertainment between a double-header of baseball games featuring the Chicago White Sox and the Detroit Tigers at Comiskey Park, Dahl invited baseball fans to bring along disco records that he would detonate. Disco Demolition Night, as it was billed, would also offer a discount to anyone who turned up with a disco record.

The White Sox expected an uptick in attendees, looking at maybe another 5,000 on top of their usual crowd of 20,000. Instead, a whopping 50,000 people turned up to participate and witness the *Fahrenheit 451*-esque spectacle whipped up by Dahl. Some accounts speak of many more trying to get into the packed stadium. Tellingly, the crowd didn't just bring disco records, but almost anything recorded by black artists, including releases on Stax and Motown and many other pre-disco era records – indicating that they were either a bit thick or, you know, racist. Any records that the grounds' staff didn't collect were thrown on to the pitch from the stands. Following the explosion, people stormed the pitch chanting 'Disco sucks!', celebrating this supposed annihilation of the genre they loathed. Things got so out of hand that riot police were called, and the second game was abandoned.

Almost overnight, disco became a dirty, shameful word, something shallow and hedonistic that was associated with gays and blacks and weaker people, rather than the supposed more 'authentic' and 'real' posturing of rock. It basically destroyed everything in one fell swoop. As part of the fallout, Chic went from the biggest act in the US to barely nothing, KC & the Sunshine Band's label TK filed for bankruptcy a year or so later, and the Bee Gees, who'd spent most of the last few years at the top thanks to the huge popularity of *Saturday Night Fever*, fell from grace pretty much instantly.

The irony of this is that, by killing off disco because of its associations of gayness, it created a vacuum into which 'I Feel Love' and 'Mighty Real' were let loose from the shackles of disco and were free to shape a whole new phenomenon: high energy. The spirit of disco would eventually have the last laugh, as high energy, if anything, was even *gayer*.

Fast forward to 1984 and the musical avatar of the high energy movement, as far as chart success is concerned, was 'High Energy' by Evelyn Thomas. Initially discovered by Ian Levine[2] back in 1975 when he was scouting for gospel/ soul singers to promote in the UK, Evelyn recorded the

---

[2] Ian Levine was Heaven's first resident DJ and advised the club on its set-up. His interest in music started at the age of thirteen when he began building a collection of Motown records. He would attend many Northern soul nights and, when he left school, became a DJ at Blackpool Mecca. By 1974, he had travelled to the US to produce acts such as the Exciters, Barbara Pennington and Evelyn Thomas. He set up the label Record Shack to issue singles like Miquel Brown's 'So Many Men, So Little Time' and Earlene Bentley's 'The Boys Come to Town'. He then formed Motorcity Records, while also mixing and producing a host of acts, such as Hazell Dean, Take That, Bucks Fizz, Amanda Lear and Bananarama.

songs 'Weak Spot' and its follow-up 'Doomsday', which charted in the UK. After signing with Casablanca for her 1978 album *I Wanna Make it on My Own*, she soon found that Casablanca weren't that arsed in doing anything with the album and left her to her word. It was all a bit of a mess until she reconnected with Ian Levine for 'High Energy'.

'High Energy' was relentless, pounding, the sound of a gay club backroom at full flight. Bassline-wise, it was also not entirely different from Frankie Goes to Hollywood's 'Relax'. The trick was to feel the hit of amyl that would tune in with Evelyn's high notes. There wasn't much to it really. It's high energy at its most basic and primal. No counter melodies, no bonus accessories, just the sound of a clattering pound over competing sequences. The chorus kicks in like an ecstatic chariot, where both the listener and music are in union, riding on the mechanic doof. Evelyn is your inner voice. She's the encouragement on your ride. 'High Energy' spoke to dancefloors internationally, spending eleven weeks atop the Record Mirror Hi-NRG club chart, and reaching its peak of number five in the UK charts in June the same week that 'Two Tribes' entered at number one and 'Smalltown Boy' crashed the top five in one of the gayest charts of all time.

What 'High Energy' – and, indeed, other high energy numbers such as Hazell Dean's strident 'Searchin'', Miquel Brown's diet-of-penis 'So Many Men, So Little Time', Divine's boisterous 'You Think You're a Man', Earlene Bentley's clattering 'Caught in the Act' and numerous others provided – was escape. They channelled the desires and longing of men wishing to abscond from the traumatic outside world via the dancefloor by form of an epiphanic emancipation, with divas be-lunging the wants and dreams and hidden fantasies of their audience who could only dream of such a cock-heavy lifestyle. Fun, frantic, heavy and doofular, this music spoke to its audience.

Also around this time a combination of Boystown, Italo Disco and gay disco floor-fillers were being compiled into weekly charts. In July 1982, *Record Mirror* started publishing the Boystown Chart based on the notion that 'so many records have been hitting the Breakers purely on the strength of play in gay discos that it seems timely to list the specifically gay club hits on their own'. Topped by the then-unstoppable 'Can't Take My Eyes Off You' by Boys Town Gang, it saw the likes of Goombay Dance Band's 'Rain' alongside the Flirts' Electroclash-inventing 'Passion', Soft Cell's 'Torch' and, somewhat improbably, 'Da Da Da' by Trio among a very random Top 20. Within weeks, it would see Patrick Cowley/Sylvester's 'Do Ya Wanna Funk?' and tracks by Bobby Orlando, Lime, Sharon Redd, Klein & MBO and Capricorn alongside singles like Afrika Bambaataa's 'Planet Rock' and Yazoo's 'Situation' in there. It was almost Balearic compared to the influx of high energy bangers that would be coming down the line in the next few years.

In the UK, along with a succession of clubs introducing gay nights into their weekly line-up rather than them reduced to the backrooms of pubs with a DJ spinning 'YMCA', the surge in high energy and female-trauma disco saw a series of labels forming specifically to license the latest sounds from the scene.

The sales information for the Hi-NRG/Disco chart, and the rise of club records and underground dance tracks into the main chart, had much to do with how the sales figures were collated and where the shops were. If a specialist dance shop was selling 500 copies of a record without being required to submit sales figures to the chart compilers, it was the ten copies sold in a chart-return shop that mattered more. Martin Wedge, who worked in record shops during this period, explains: 'Both the BMRB and Gallup had a weighting system in place to even out regional sales patterns. Overall, the chart did reflect what was selling other than these occasional situations. Gallup especially were very proactive at policing the chart. They had a lot of data coming in from the data port terminals and they had non-chart back-up panels to check for sales irregularities. The BMRB did the same but their manual diary system was obviously less responsive.'

This would explain why bangers such as Shannon's superb 'Let the Music Play', Laura Branigan's minxy pounder 'Self Control', Eartha Kitt's purrsome 'Where is My Man?', Gloria Gaynor's flouncy 'I Am What I Am', the Weather Girls' hen-night anthem 'It's Raining Men' and more started to make inroads into the proper charts. The gays helped create the foundations for these hits and, once mainstream radio got hold of them, crossover success was assured.

By the mid-'80s, high energy had fully parked its tanks on pop's lawn. What started out as a subgenre that took from disco, Northern soul, Eurodisco, futurism, pop and soul was to become the sound of almost every nightclub for the rest of the decade and beyond.

Over in Chicago, dance music's next revolution was in its infancy. Having brought a drum machine in 1982 in order to oomph up disco classics for dancefloor usage, Frankie Knuckles, along with Jamie Principle, was creating the future. Both 'Your Love' and 'Baby Wants to Ride' were composed in 1984, and although it would be another couple of years before anyone outside of Chicago's clubs would get to hear them, this blueprint of what would become known as house music would transform clubland during the rest of the decade.

Principle had originally composed 'Your Love' based on a poem he'd written for his first love, and inspired Knuckles' first beat-heavy original, which was first available as a dubplate and reel-to-reel tape before its first official release in 1986. There was an inherent queerness in the heterosexual Principle as the male diva, excelling at the role that had primarily been the domain of the female. New Yorker Knuckles and Principle had emerged from a Chicago scene that revolved around mostly gay and black nightclubs. 'It was hard being accepted by straight people,' Principle explained to the *Guardian* in 2016. 'I've always been an affectionate person, regardless if it's male or female. For me to be in a culture that would let me do that and not have me be afraid of who I am was beautiful, and it made me start to have a sense of self.'

You can hear high energy's DNA in post-1984 crossover tracks such as Man 2 Man Meets Man Parrish's 'Male Stripper', Colonel Abrams' 'Trapped' and Farley 'Jackmaster' Funk's 'Love Can't Turn Around' among many others. You can follow its influence in the lineage down to the key songs: without 'I Feel Love', you'd probably not have got 'Mighty Real'. Without 'Mighty Real', you'd probably not have got 'Blue Monday'. Without 'Blue Monday', you probably wouldn't have got 'Love Reaction'. Without 'Love Reaction', you'd probably not have got 'Searchin''. Without 'Searchin'', you'd probably not have got 'You Spin Me Round (Like a Record)'. Without 'You Spin Me Round (Like a Record)', you'd probably not have got 'Venus'. You get the idea.

High energy was also the base ingredient that Stock Aitken Waterman took from the underground and enjoyed the most top-of-the-charts traction with. It can be heard in the productions and re-swizzles of Shep Pettibone, John Luongo, Phil Harding and more. It is the forefather of the communality of acid house and rave, the peaks, the builds and the rushes of everything that you've heard on a dancefloor and lost your shit to during the last forty years.

The lure and thrill of high energy is best exemplified by noted pop scholar Neil Tennant when he once declared that 'the one thing the public does like, by the way, and always will like is high energy records. That's why "It's A Sin" was number one. In my opinion, high energy is genuine pop music – it's contemporary, of its time, it's not the slightest bit retrospective, it doesn't worry about being tasteful, funky or trendy and it says something to people. Like "I Heard a Rumour"; the attitude is great. It would be true to say that when I saw Bananarama on *Top of the Pops* doing that, I would have given *anything* to be one of them.'

High energy, then. It will make you dance, it will make you sweat and it will make you want to be one of Bananarama. The *ultimate* goal of all pop music, surely.

In July 1984, President Ronald Reagan announces, in a statement to the Presidential Biblical Scoreboard *magazine, that his administration would resist any government endorsement of homosexuality. It would be another year before he publicly acknowledges AIDS.*

DIVINE

'I always gave you so much more than you deserve.'

Divine's legacy is a peculiar one. Obviously, he was a drag trailblazer and worthy of all the 'iconics' the modern set would want to throw at him, but there was always something more and *extra* about what he achieved in his short life.

From a CV that seemed to focus on the 'eats shit in a film', it is perhaps his role in John Waters' *Hairspray* that has had a longer-term impact on culture. Playing Edna Turnblad in the film, Divine set a new standard. While technically it was a role that could be played by anyone, something about Divine's performance led it to becoming a stand-out template.

Born Harris Glenn Milstead on 19 October 1945, in Baltimore, Maryland, Divine was an only child whose parents lavished anything and everything on him. Glenn was bullied as a child, mainly due to his weight and his effeminacy, and after leaving school he worked as a florist. His parents were concerned he might be gay and took it upon themselves to send him to a psychiatrist to help 'cure' him.

Glenn's early dalliances with dressing-up involved dragging-up as Santa Claus for his parents' day-care group, and in 1963, he studied at the Marinella Beauty School, gaining work as a hairdresser focusing on the bee-hive styles of the era. A bit of a spoilt brat, all told, he stayed at home living with his parents, who somehow kept funding his increasingly lavish lifestyle which enabled him to host parties where he'd dress up as his idol, Elizabeth Taylor.

Speaking to *Record Mirror*, Divine described his early life. 'I would pull faces while the teacher wasn't looking and clown around. But Maryland was a very boring place to be, and I so desperately wanted to be a movie star. I thought to myself that I would never make it because I wasn't good looking in a conventional way. Then my friends suggested that I was very funny and entertaining and I should do something different.

'So, I began dressing up. I could never see anything wrong with doing it, although in those days a lot of people were very suspicious. Some people wear a white collar or overalls when they go to work. I used to happen to wear a nice dress.' What Divine had was perspective – a refreshing 'Oh, do fuck off' to his haters. 'There's a lot more to worry about than a man who wears a dress and puts on make-up. There's pollution in the rivers, muggers on the streets and we could blow ourselves up tomorrow. I'm harmless compared with all that.

'If people find this shocking then they *need* to be shocked.'

In 1965, he connected with fellow Baltimore resident John Waters. Being the same age, they set about taking advantage of the countercultural aspects of the era: hanging with hippies, smoking pot and generally creating a new family from their fellow travellers in far-outness. It was Waters who would christen Milstead 'Divine', taken from a character in Jean Genet's novel *Our Lady of the Flowers*. Divine's subtitle, as it were, became 'the most beautiful woman in the world, almost'.

'John said that I was Divine, so that became my name and the character I played.' Waters also had ambition to become a filmmaker, although a lack of funds – and, it would seem, taste – saw him determined to make some of the trashiest movies ever made, such as his debut *Hag in a Black Leather Jacket* and the follow-up, *Roman Candles*, which starred Divine in his first role.

'Divine got shaped with each movie, starting with *Eat Your Make-Up* – the look progressed, it was always over the top – *Glamour Gone Berserk*, very cartoonish. John said that Divine should be like Snow White's wicked stepmother, Cinderella's sisters, the wicked witch from *The Wizard of Oz* and Jayne Mansfield or Diana Dors – ballsy women, sexy, blonde, sleazy, but glam.'

Divine was effectively Waters' muse, yet he had deliberately kept his involvement in these films a secret from his parents for fear of feeling their religious wrath. They did buy him a beauty salon in order to encourage him to settle down into conventional life. Unsurprisingly, he refused to cooperate and his mum ended up managing the place.

By 1970, he was done with 'running' the salon and opened up a second-hand clothing shop – Divine Trash – in Provincetown, Massachusetts. When it dawned on him that the shop wasn't a goer financially, he sold all the stock, as well as the furniture from his rented apartment (leading to a warrant for his arrest from his landlady), before heading to the gay mecca of San Francisco in order to be a full-time homosexual.

In 1970's *Multiple Maniacs*, Divine played Lady Divine, the owner of an exhibit, The Cavalcade of Perversion, which murders its visitors, and at the climax of the film is raped by a giant lobster. Understandably, Waters was a little worried that the film might end up being confiscated due to its, um, 'plot' and ironically chose to screen the film in churches and other non-commercial venues. The film was the first of Waters to gain widespread . . . let's call it 'acclaim' . . . and saw critics singling out Divine as something of a new superstar.

It was, however, their next movie with which both Waters and Divine made a true impact. *Pink Flamingos* starred the latter as Babs Johnson, seemingly the filthiest woman alive. The scene that topped it off – and somehow became a defining moment in American cinematic history – was when Divine ate dog shit. Waters had billed it as an exercise in poor taste – no kidding – and its notoriety kickstarted both his and Divine's career. Divine had mixed feelings about the whole affair, to the point where he was getting increasingly fed up with dog shit being the thing that anyone wanted to talk about. But he also knew the value of controversy, and what would create box-office gold. 'I don't like films like *Star Wars*, with all those machines zapping over the place. Carrie Fisher is so sexless. People want to see tits.'

Divine had already become something of a cause celebre of the underclass. Budget-free and tasteless, it was inevitable that his 'brand' should be extended into popular music. Divine had already issued the rocky 'Born to Be Cheap', but his work with Bobby Orlando took everything up another level. The collaborations 'Native Love', 'Shoot Your Shot', 'Shake It Up' and 'Love Reaction' would send shockwaves throughout international clubland, taking Divine into the charts around Europe and, primarily, the US Club lists.

'Love Reaction' would also bear some resemblance to New Order's 'Blue Monday'[1]. I say 'bear some

---

[1] 'Blue Monday' was a collage of many inspirations – Kraftwerk's 'Uranium', Donna Summer's 'Our Love', Klein and MBO's 'Dirty Talk', Sylvester's 'Mighty Real' and even Ennio Morricone's 'For a Few Dollars More'. It just didn't have space to incorporate 'Spys' and 'Passion' too. During an interview

resemblance' – it's practically a photocopy with Divine bellowing over it. In fact, it got to a point where 'Love Reaction' was raised in a copyright case, suggesting that it was a complete rip-off of 'Blue Monday', and yet Orlando reckoned that 'Blue Monday' was a rip-off of both his toe-taps, 'Spys' and 'Passion'.

Come 1984 and 'You Think You're a Man' was yet another significant leap forward for not just Divine, but also the then new production trio Stock, Aitken and Waterman (SAW). While 'Love Reaction' (which reached number sixty-five) and 'Shake It Up' (eighty-two) had been minor UK hits, in July 'You Think You're a Man' took both Divine and SAW into the UK Top 20 for the first time. Divine had just signed to the London label Proto, run by Barry Evangeli, a flatmate of Pete Waterman. The two had arranged a deal for SAW's first release by Agents Aren't Aeroplanes,[2] and also had Hazell Dean

---

on Radio Clyde, Divine admitted that it was 'a complete rip-off of "Blue Monday"', even when prior to that he claimed he'd heard it on the radio. 'It came on and I thought for sure it was "Love Reaction",' until he learned of the origins. Conversely, New Order even interpolated 'Love Reaction' into live versions of 'Blue Monday', possibly in a piss-taking gesture.

[2] Made with a pair of Essex ladies – sisters Julie and Diana Seabrook – Agents Aren't Aeroplanes' 'The Upstroke' was a novelty cash-in on the burgeoning success of Frankie Goes to Hollywood's 'Relax', even down to the cover art. Recorded in February 1984, just as 'Relax' had started its reign at the top, it was released on Proto Records, run by Barry Evangeli, which had already issued gay club-directed tracks such as the yet-to-be-a-major-hit 'Searchin'' by Hazell Dean.

on their books. Divine's manager was looking around for producers to work on 'You Think You're a Man', written by Geoff Deane[3], who up until then had been the face of Modern Romance. Having first considered Ian Levine, he opted for the fresh trio on account of their studio being the most hi-tech.

'We had a thought that most of the emerging subculture of upbeat club dance music was being made on the cheap,' Mike Stock recalled. 'Some of the songs in the genre were not very good. The important aspect was the beat and tempo. We thought we could take it up a notch by introducing a proper song and recording in better quality. We mixed in a 12-inch format to help the DJs and went to the market with extended versions.' Geoff Deane was the writer of "You Think You're a Man", which we recorded and which became our first proper chart hit. The high camp and outrageousness of Divine caused a big enough stir in both the clubs and the mainstream.'

'I knew the Divine record would be our big break,' claimed Waterman. 'I don't know how. I just knew. He'd been big on the gay disco scene for a couple of years, but if we could take him into the pop charts, it would be a real coup.

---

[3] Geoff Deane had hoped Gloria Gaynor might be interested, but after she said no, he recorded a version with Sam Brown who was at that point, despite her young age at the time, better known as a top session singer and for being entertainer Joe Brown's daughter. She'd get her moment in pop a few years later with the top-four success of her moody smoocher 'Stop'.

'So, we went down the studio to record the single and Mike and Matt actually taught him how to sing properly. He did the song with proper singing on it then got a cab to the airport to fly back to America. Barry came down to the studio to hear the track, but when we played it to him, he was horrified. "Why's he singing?" he asked. "I don't want singing. I want shouting." So we rang the airport and got them to send Divine straight back. He came in, did the whole thing shouting rather than singing, in one take, and headed off back to the airport.'

When Waterman briefed the record's promoter, he insisted that he focused on getting it into the pop outlets. 'A lot of people around me didn't think that was a great idea.

'The song was almost immediately number one in all the gay charts and everyone was really pleased and surprised. I wasn't. I mean, it was obvious it was going to be a big gay hit. A huge transvestite singing "You Think You're a Man"? I wasn't expecting a medal.'

Having entered the Top 40 at number thirty-eight, a week later the single had risen to twenty-six, which is when *Top of the Pops* came a-calling. Divine was invited onto the show which was broadcast on 19 July 1984. Divine was no stranger to British TV, having appeared on *The Tube* a few months earlier, where Muriel Gray interviewed him out of drag. Gray seemed a little spiky around the concept of Divine, even challenging him about his 'outrageous image'. In his defence, Divine pointed to Boy George and

Marilyn, saying that it was nothing new. However, Gray responded they were asexual and attractive compared to Divine's grotesqueness. 'It's the glamour that doesn't exist anymore that was around in the ,'50s,' he replied. 'but because of my size, there's a comedy aspect.'

Top of the Pops' producers had a bit of a nervo when first encountering Divine, bearing in mind the BBC were on the backfoot regarding anything too controversial post-'Relax' (although Frankie Goes to Hollywood had been welcomed back to perform 'Two Tribes' on the same show). It was also totally live rather than pre-recorded, so no wonder the BBC were concerned Divine could easily go off-script and been even more outrageous than planned.

Even though he kept to the script, it didn't go down too well with the viewers – at least the type of viewers who feel compelled to lift up a phone, dial up the BBC and complain. The next day, the tabloids were full of moral outrage about Divine's appearance and, being the squeaky-clean moral guardians[4] they were, comforted their readers with some tits on the next page.

---

[4] The tabloids certainly had their hands full with moral outrage in 1984, with the miners, Greenham Common protestors, unions, gay people, AIDS and a fat man in a dress to clutch their pearls at. With the increasing prevalence of video recorders in homes, a whole host of films that bypassed the British Board of Film Censors (now British Board of Film Classification) were proving popular as video rental shops became THE place for bored teenagers to hang out and score the likes of straight-to-video films such as *Driller Killer*, *The Evil Dead*, *Cannibal Holocaust* and *I Spit on Your Grave*. Moral crusader Mary

'I'm more shocked than all the people who phoned the BBC,' Divine quipped. 'My performance was toned down and I kept to all the rules. God knows what would have happened if I'd done my real show. I'm surprised so many people in Britain, which I consider my second home, have such closed minds . . . I'm very hurt.'

It didn't necessarily hurt the record though, as 'You Think You're a Man' peaked at a not-shabby number sixteen, spending two months in the Top 40.

The follow-up, 'I'm So Beautiful', was also written by the SAW team, but didn't have the same impact, stalling at number fifty-two in October. Not that that was seen as any massive inconvenience to Divine at the time, as he'd already had enough success on the club scene to put on a show. It just lacked the impact of 'the hit', feeling like Divine was just ad-libbing over some high energy off-cuts in the studio. He'd make one more trip to the Top 40 in April 1985 with a version of the Four Seasons' standard 'Walk Like a Man' that reached number twenty-three, before repeating the high-energy cover trick with Sam Cooke's 'Twistin' the Night Away', which rose no higher than number forty-seven and was followed by his final

---

Whitehouse believed that these films would destabilise society, and the term 'video nasty' was soon being used by hysterical tabloids. Seventy-two films were initially added to the director of public prosecutions' list of banned films, giving them a cachet among thrill-seeking teens. Whitehouse, along with Tory MP Graham Bright, introduced a private member's bill for tighter controls, which became the Video Recordings Act of 1984.

chart entry, 'Hard Magic', in November. He also enjoyed a star turn at London's now new and improved annual Gay Pride.[5]

1985 also saw Divine return to acting. He appeared in hokey Western *Lust in the Dust* – his first film without John Waters' involvement – and he took a small role as a gangster in *Trouble in Mind*, which was specifically written for him. It was a non-drag role, and Divine was keen to show his versatility rather than be dwarfed by the limitations of the stereotype.

Divine's next role – or next *two* roles, actually – followed his reunion with John Waters in 1988's *Hairspray*, in which

---

[5] By 1984, the annual Gay Pride march through London – the only one in the country at that point – was facing disinterest with attendance numbers declining on from previous years. You could hardly blame them: previous Prides involved police arresting men in drag on charges of 'possessing offensive weapons'; the event was moved to Huddersfield to show solidarity with club owners who'd faced police harassment in 1981; and after horizontal rain at the 1982 march and a general air of disorganisation, attendance was down to fewer than 2,000 people in 1983.

Things came to a head at the 1984 event where there was a lack of police support, combined with organisational difficulties at the final meeting spot at the University of London Union, where nobody knew what was going on and there was an absence of a women-only space. A month later, after assessing the debacle, a shake-up of the organising committee was the catalyst to make sure that Pride 1985 would be VERY different. And it most certainly was, attracting more than 11,000 punters, with turns such as Divine and Tom Robinson providing entertainment. It marked a rebirth of the event that would grow over the next few decades into one of the biggest Pride celebrations in the world.

he was cast as both Edna Turnblad ('What drag queen would allow herself to look like this? I look like half the women from Baltimore') and as Arvin Hodgepile, the racist television station owner. As one of Walters' more accessible films, *Hairspray* looked set to deliver Divine the breakout role he had hoped for, and indeed reviews focused on his characters, as well as on the film's lead Ricki Lake, who played his daughter Tracy Turnblad.

As a result of this higher profile, he was in demand as a regular guest on chat shows. Even his mother had become a subject of interest, proud at the star that her once-wayward son had become.

Finally, Divine had made it.

But there was to be no happy ending. On 7 March 1988, three weeks after the nationwide release of *Hairspray*, Divine was found dead at the Regency Plaza Suites Hotel in Los Angeles. He had spent the day rehearsing a role in TV show *Married . . . with Children* and, after a meal with friends, returned to his room. Shortly before midnight, he died in his sleep of heart failure. His body was discovered by his manager Bernard Jay, and his friends stayed with his corpse until it could be removed without any press taking photos. He was buried in his hometown of Maryland in a grave alongside his grandmother. John Waters was one of the chief mourners. In the weeks afterwards, the IRS confiscated many of Divine's belongings to auction off in order to settle debts with unpaid taxes.

In an interview in 2019, John Waters spoke about Divine, measuring where he sat on the modern spectrum of gender and sexuality. 'People [think] Divine – they always think wrong – was trans. Divine never dressed as a woman, except when he was working. He had no desire to be a woman . . . He didn't want to pass as a woman; he wanted to pass as a monster. He was thought up to scare hippies. And that's what he wanted to do. He wanted to be Godzilla. Well, he wanted to be Elizabeth Taylor and Godzilla put together.'

Divine's influence is still felt today. An inspiration on both ANOHNI, who recorded the song 'Divine', and Roisin Murphy, who re-enacted the attack by Lobstora from *Multiple Maniacs* in her video for 'Movie Star', he was also a key influence on the character of Ursula the Sea Witch in *The Little Mermaid*. The aesthetic of Divine, the monstrous clown, the outrageous fucks-free delusion, is one that has since been inspirational to a generation of drag artists, the unconventional beauties who'll serve trash realness rather than doll themselves up as the supermodel.

A musical based on *Hairspray* opened in 2002 on Broadway, and a London run followed soon after. In both, the character of Edna Turnblad was played by a man – testimony to the ground-breaking brilliance of Divine's original characterisation. A film based on the musical was made in 2007 starring John Travolta, once again bringing the genius of Divine's role to a much wider audience, and making more than $200 million in the process. John Walters had made the original movie for £2 million.

Divine just wanted to be an entertainer and one can only imagine how big a star he would have been had he lived. The possibilities of where he'd have gone and what he would've done are easy to imagine, as the potential was all there. You can trace lines back to his influence in all the drag queen clowns, super bitches and loveable monsters that surround culture today.

As he himself rhetorically asked, 'Why settle for being an ordinary guy when you can be a superstar?'

In September 1984, Conservative-led Rugby Borough Council declared that it would actively exclude LGBT people from its equal opportunities policies. The Sun *ran an editorial saying, 'Let's ALL follow Rugby in fighting back' against what it described as 'the sick nonsense' of gay rights.*

HAZELL DEAN

'I'm searching for my destiny.'

Hazell Dean's career wears all the hallmarks of British entertainment. It has all the non-starts, thwarted opportunities and dues paid of anyone who gamely rose through the working men's club circuit, holiday parks and function entertainment. Hazell was originally a guitarist who would perform with various jazz turns in and around her home turf of Great Baddow near Chelmsford in Essex. At the age of eighteen, she pivoted to lungsmithery honing her craft singing in big bands and, in 1976, taking part in *A Song for Europe* with a ballad called 'I Couldn't Live Without You for a Day'. The panel opted for Brotherhood of Man's 'Save Your Kisses for Me' instead, leaving Hazell in eighth place. It wasn't all bad news, though. She signed a deal with Decca off the back of her appearance. However, each subsequent single she released failed to chart.

In 1981, she recorded her debut album, *The Sound of Bacharach & David*, which was made as a promo release exclusively for radio stations. It was a clever way to secure airtime for Hazell and raise her profile. Many radio stations couldn't afford to cough up the royalties to spin the Bacharach & David originals sung by the likes of Sandie Shaw and Dionne Warwick, but they could afford our Hazell. Ironically, in 2024, an original copy of Hazell's now-much-sought debut goes for upwards of £400.

Hazell tried the *A Song for Europe* route again in 1984, this time going one place better with 'Stay in My Life'. But any dismay she may have felt at not being deemed as good as eventual winners Belle and the Devotions was short-lived. Fast becoming the queen of the last laugh, she could take comfort in the fact that her single 'Searchin' (I Gotta Find a Man)' recorded a year earlier in 1983 was hurtling towards the charts thanks to being reissued. Having initially done serious business in the gay clubs, the reissue peaked at number six. After years of grafting at the showbiz coalface, Hazell Dean had finally arrived.

'Searchin'' dropped onto Hazell's doormat when songwriter/producer Ian Anthony Stephens came a-knocking. Her versions of 'Our Day Will Come' and 'Got You Where I Want You Baby', released by Decca, had been successful on the Northern soul scene where he worked as a DJ. Impressed by her voice, Hazell was who he had in mind when he wrote the song. 'He sent me the track after he'd tracked me down through various publishing companies,' Hazell told the *Daily Record*, 'and when I heard it, it just sounded so fresh and new and different. It felt like I'd found the sound I'd been looking for. It was the little place where it worked for me and completely changed the direction of my career.'

Almost overnight, 'Searchin'' turned her into the Queen of High Energy. 'High energy dance music wasn't really on my radar at that time. I had always wanted to be a singer-songwriter, strumming a guitar. I was happy singing ballads, but 'Searchin'' was such a special song, it literally burst into my life and changed my career path.'

The success of "Searchin", as Hazell explained to *Smash Hits* in 1984, was down to simplicity. 'A lot of people look down on high energy, maybe because it's not stating something deep or political or whatever. But my record's a good disco record and a good pop record and, at the end of the day, that's what it's all about. Good songs.'

However, it was when Hazell made her live gay-club debut at London's Heaven that she was anointed into the pantheon of gay disco diva. 'It was incredible,' she later told *Classic Pop* . 'I knew the gay audience really liked "Searchin'" and obviously lyrically it was very appealing to the gay male audience. To be stood backstage, and hearing a crowd of a thousand pumped, sweaty, beautiful boys chanting my name was amazing. What's not to love?'

It was an epiphany for this self-confessed 'girl next door'. Her life offstage, she admitted, consisted of 'simple things – going shopping, going down the beach . . . I generally like pottering around my flat organising things.'

Hazell's role in the burgeoning high energy movement is unquestioned. 'Obviously, I was very aware of those tracks and artists. I bumped into many of them when we were doing PAs here in the UK and across Europe and the USA. It was the music I heard when I was working in the clubs, but not what I was listening to in my own home. That said, the transition of many of those tracks from gay clubs to mainstream charts was very exciting, and I am proud to have been the first British artist to have crossed over to the mainstream in the UK and pioneering the high energy sound globally.'

Hazell was soon trotting up and down the circuit, both locally and internationally, to perform her hit, which was perfect for the gay scene, a song she would define as being 'very up, very frantic with a real powerful singer, a heavy tempo and based in the northern soul of the '60s'. The only issue, at that point, was that there was no follow-up in the pipeline. 'Searchin'' was very much a one-off. It took a chance meeting with Stock Aitken Waterman, at her then label Proto, for her to see that any further success was possible. 'Pete Waterman, who I already knew, approached me. I was in the charts with 'Searchin'' and he asked me what the plans for a follow-up were. I didn't have a follow-up ready, so Pete invited me to meet two guys he had just started to work with, Matt and Mike. They were hungry for their first chart hit. I was riding high in the charts without a follow-up. It was perfect timing for me and them.'

As Mike Stock recalled to the *A Journey Through Stock Aitken Waterman* podcast, 'I remember her saying at times this was so important to her . . . that dreadful follow-up situation – how do you follow up a hit?' Impressed by what she heard when the SAW team played her the yet-to-be-released Divine thumper 'You Think You're a Man', they got to work on a number called 'Dance Your Love Away', a song which had already been recorded and released by American singer Michael Prince.

'I heard "You Think You're a Man" and I loved it. Incidentally, my longtime Dean & Ware production partner, Pete Ware, also worked at PWL with Matt and Mike, and was Divine's musical director until his death. Divine was a very charming man . . . out of drag!'

Unimpressed with the lyric, SAW reworked 'Dance Your Love Away' into 'Whatever I Do (Wherever I Go)'. It was the follow-up that was required and opened its chart account at number thirty-five that July, rising to number four and giving Hazell, and SAW, a first top-five hit.

The idea that SAW would go on to be the key sound of the rest of the decade wasn't something Hazell ever considered. 'I was too busy working and travelling the world, in what we call my "Hazell Dean bubble". Does anyone really recognise a phenomenon when they are in the middle of it? The guys worked hard. Pete put his home on the line to finance projects. They deserved the success they had. It was their passion. There are lots of rumours about what it was like in The Hit Factory, lots of urban myths, and lots of totally fabricated stories. Only those who were there at the time will ever know the truth.'

In another first for SAW, the trio then embarked on working on Hazell's second album, *Heart First*. Billed by them as the first high energy album, it came out at the end of October, but failed to chart. While everyone involved seemed quite happy with it at the time of recording, it wasn't a full-on SAW-fest: Stock and Aitken wrote four tracks, while Hazell dipped into her singer-songwriter background to co-pen another three. The album's failure to chart was put down to poor promotion and bad timing[1]. Proto and SAW were both operating on next-to-no budget, and the record had to compete with oxygen-hogging headline releases by Frankie, U2, Wham! and Bronski Beat.

Smash Hits gave *Heart First* a mere 4/10, claiming that 'you'd find better on an old Cilla Black record, I fear. Sounds like a rush-job.' The score put it on a par with others albums reviewed, including those by Limahl, the Stranglers and Neil from *The Young Ones' Heavy Concept*

---

[1] It wasn't helped by the non-Top 40 action of *Heart First*'s third single 'Back in My Arms (Once Again)' either, which Morrissey reviewed in *Smash Hits* and declared a 'sillified charade from a creature who could never be suspected of having too much talent . . . Vilest single of the fortnight.'

Album – although these all scored one point more than poor old Gary Numan's admittedly hard work *Berserker* long player. Not that Hazell really had an opportunity to think about the critical reaction, as she was now busy becoming successful in the US. 'They embraced the little English girl and made me very welcome. Divine's manager, Bernard Jay, looked after business for me in the USA. I have very happy memories. I was there when voguing started. I performed at the legendary Studio 54. Dusty Springfield and Grace Jones came to see me in LA. It was a crazy time.'

Hazell left Proto in 1985 when the slightly-less-on-a-shoestring-y EMI swept into action and offered her a deal. However, the next few singles failed to make much impact in the UK. 'They Say It's Gonna Rain' fared well in Europe and gave Hazell, possibly thanks to its interpolation of a Zulu chant, a number-one single in South Africa. 'I was number one for eighteen weeks, I believe. I did not visit the country during that time, as morally I could not justify performing in an apartheid country. Nelson Mandela was still in prison. I believe in equality and could not perform in a country that sanctioned racial segregation and political and economic discrimination against non-whites. I have performed there since, notably on the "Rewind" tour, where I had a special Zulu drum introduction for my show. The stadium audiences went crazy!'

Hazell's return to the upper reaches of the UK charts came with the SAW-produced garland that was 'Who's

Leaving Who'. Originally recorded as a strident Laura-Branigan-esque strut by Canadian country songstress Anne Murray a year or so earlier, the song was reworked by SAW into a storming Eurobanger for Hazell, giving her a number-four smash in April 1988. The hard-driving, competitive nature of The Hit Factory soon gave the impression that SAW was operating a conveyor-belt system, with various acts recording the same song. 'Pete obviously had the successful formula of Motown in mind. He wanted it to be a family. I was there at the start and I remain friends with Pete to this day. I should be the Diana Ross to his Berry Gordy!

'Yes, the boys recorded some tracks with several artists, and there were some that I heard after their release and wished had been offered to me, but that's just the way they worked. It's no big deal.'

Hazell Dean's career has been a true lesson in allyship, and while chart success may be a distant memory, she's been there at the frontline ever since that debut at Heaven. 'From the moment I walked on stage at Heaven with those boys chanting my name, there has been love from the LGBTQ+ community. I have performed at Prides all over the world. I witnessed the total devastation of the early days of the AIDS epidemic. I have seen so many changes over the years, and I have stayed loyal to the fanbase who kickstarted my career.

'The rise in hate crime against the LGBT community, and particularly the aggression aimed at our trans sisters and brothers, means it is now more important than ever to stand together at Pride events to fight hate and prejudice. I have only one message to share at every Pride. TURN IT INTO LOVE!'

Hazell is still recording but, after thirty-eight years, she announced her live retirement in 2021. Giving her last live performance at Pride in Hastings that August, she bowed out as the unrivalled Queen of High Energy and a formidable ally to the LGBTQ+ community.

'AIDS STUDIES HINT SALIVA MAY
TRANSMIT INFECTION'
According to Californian pathologist Dr Murray Gardner, 'It
probably takes multiple exposures to contaminated saliva. It
probably will not occur overnight and probably will not result
from a single drink or kiss. But with enough virus exposure,
you increase the chances of infection. Without a question, it is
a public health matter of great concern.'
– *New York Times*, 9 October 1984

THE SMITHS

'I am human and I need to be loved just like everybody else does.'

With a scathing wit and dismissive of all that didn't interest
or excite, Morrissey and the Smiths barged into showbiz and
offered an alternative – a refreshing counterpoint to what
was seen as the excesses and vacuity of pop music. They
were a breath of fresh air against the soggy futurists, and
a swift two fingers towards society as a whole. The Smiths
were important in puncturing through with an alternative,
with Morrissey informing *Smash Hits* that 'our basic message
is you don't have to be cool'. They wooed outsiders, kids

who felt isolated and strange, and gave them a voice. 'I really do think what we do is of tremendous value,' parped Morrissey. 'I think people do need a different voice and we supply it. The face of pop music has become a little too grim, too clean and safe and tidy. I couldn't imagine how things would be if we weren't here.'

It was all there, a character to whom the disaffected could clasp to their lonely bosom. He spent much of his time 'reading books and hiding from the human race' and was from the outset, a bit of a gloomster even at school: 'I can't remember ever actually smiling.' His interests lay in icons such as James Dean and Oscar Wilde; he felt the latter was 'impossible to read a single line without swimming in tears. A day rarely passes when I don't listen to *The Importance of Being Earnest*. I have it on tape.'

Having set himself up as the very opposite of the directional fun and joy that Wham! was then offering, and a vehement enemy of the synthesiser, Morrissey's backstory of a life on the dole chimed with disaffected youth. He met guitarist and co-writer Johnny Marr when the latter first pressed his nose against Morrissey's window in May 1982. 'Quite literally. It left a terrible smudge. I think he'd been eating chocolate or something. He seemed terribly sure of what he wanted to do, which I liked. He said "Let's do it and do it now." So we did it. Then.'

Once the pair had gathered enough songs to think about forming a band, Marr went out and recruited drummer

Mike Joyce and bassist Andy Rourke. Prior to that set-up, and as proof that no one arrives as fully formed as they first appear, the Smiths' first-ever gig was at Manchester's Ritz on 4 October 1982 as an unlikely support to fashion-y funksters Blue Rondo à la Turk. The event was actually a fashion show; Marr had strong-armed the promoters to get them onto the bill. The band's line-up wasn't finalised past Morrissey and Marr, with Mike Joyce only coming onboard last minute after hearing the demo tape that featured them backed by drummer Simon Wolstencroft and bassist Dale Hibbert, whom Marr had wooed away from his band the Adorables to join the Smiths. And, after introducing them on stage, Morrissey's chum James Maker joined in on tambourine.

It wasn't perhaps their finest moment as Joyce's snare drum broke, but with 'The Hand That Rocks the Cradle', 'Suffer Little Children' and 'Handsome Devil', alongside a cover of the Cookies' 'I Want a Boy for My Birthday', their stall had been laid out and the march towards greatness began. There would, though, be casualties almost immediately. Hibbert's time as a Smith was brief, having discovered his services were no longer required when Marr's schoolfriend Andy Rourke turned up. According to Hibbert, 'Johnny and Steven told me they had plans to launch themselves as a "gay band".'

'A lot of my mates were gay guys who liked rock music,' said Johnny. 'I liked the idea of us being a band that were saying things for the gay community.'

Morrissey took it further, telling *Rolling Stone* in 1984 that he was a 'prophet for the fourth gender'. He was extolling a life of celibacy, but nodding to the urges of both male and female and a disruption to traditional norms. Somewhat presciently pre-empting the landscape of discussions in 2024, and a departure from a set menu towards a buffet-style approach to sexuality, Morrissey declared that 'the sexes have been too easily defined. People are so rigidly locked into these two little categories. I don't know anybody who is absolutely, exclusively heterosexual. It limits people's potential in so many areas. I think we should slap down these barriers.'

Having remarked how they found it easy to garner a certain amount of attention, the quartet released their debut single, 'Hand in Glove', in May 1983, as part of a one-single deal with Rough Trade. However, once momentum kicked in, and the single sat steadfast in the independent charts, the deal was expanded into a proper contract.

Their second single, 'This Charming Man', followed at the end of October and launched them into the proper charts. It led to their memorable debut on *Top of the Pops*, whereupon Morrissey, festooned in beads and wearing what's best described as a blouse, stormed into the nation's living rooms, athletically a-twirling gladioli. The confidence and cocksureness of their performance, and its after-effects, impacted an audience at a level considered akin to a 'Starman' moment.

A scholar of what makes pop music tick, Morrissey knew the cultural weight of providing the performance that would be spoken about in the playground the next day, rather than, say, those of Paul Young or Thompson Twins. Morrissey looked fully formed, anemically erotic and in command of this national television debut. As Marr told the *Guardian* in 2011, 'everyone remembers the flowers Morrissey took on to the show. I'd been very aware of how powerful *Top of the Pops* could be visually from my childhood watching T. Rex. We'd first used gladioli onstage at the Hacienda about a year before, to counteract the all-encompassing austere aesthetic of Factory Records. People assumed it was an Oscar Wilde homage, but that was a bonus. The flowers made the stage very treacherous if you were wearing moccasins, but they became emblematic, iconic. Morrissey was using those gladioli in a way that was far from fey, almost brandishing them. Morrissey provided flamboyance, the rest of us wore sweaters and provided a streetwise, gang aspect.' To dismiss Morrissey as a bit of a weed is a fool's errand; there was a masculinity that suggested beneath the cardigan was someone who'd be quite handy in a fight.

The Smiths were very much at the vanguard of what would become known as indie. Alternative music was in full bloom, with post-punks, new wavers and experimental types, with many guitar-based acts, such as Echo & the Bunnymen, in that transition having banished their independent shackles almost instantly for life on a major label. Indie, at that point, didn't really exist as a term. Independent was effectively Cocteau Twins, Depeche Mode and New Order by nature of them being on independent labels – 4AD, Mute and Factory respectively. The independent charts were full of goths, old punks and novelty stuff that wouldn't have got through past reception at a major label[1], but the *sound* of indie – the jangly gang with guitars and DIY aesthetic – had its Year Zero with the Smiths.

They certainly put in the hours. In the wake of the January 1984 release of 'What Difference Does It Make?' came the singles 'Heaven Knows I'm Miserable Now' and 'William, It Was Really Nothing'. Morrissey explained that 'William . . .' came about after 'it occurred to me that, within popular music, if ever there were any records that discussed marriage, they were always from the female's standpoint – female singers singing to women – whenever there were any songs saying "do not marry, stay single, self-preservation, etc". I thought it was about time there was a male voice speaking directly to another male saying that marriage was a waste of time . . . That, in fact, it was "absolutely nothing".' The song was written about Morrissey's short friendship with Billy Mackenzie, the mercurially operatic vocalist with the Associates. (The Associates responded with 'Stephen, You're Really Something' a few years later.)[2].

---

[1] The first independently released single to top the UK chart was actually gloopy smoocher 'Save Your Love' by Renee & Renato in 1982. Fancy that!

[2] Billy Mackenzie is an interesting case. Much like Morrissey, his sexuality was a guarded secret, although if pushed, he considered himself bisexual, revealing his orientation in an interview with *Time Out* in 1994 ('I'm just waiting for the day when we're all what we were intended to be . . . hermaphrodites'). A true flamboyant one-off who spent record company money on chocolate guitars and feeding his beloved pet whippets with caviar, he died in 1997 after an overdose of paracetamol and prescription drugs in the garden shed of his father's house in Auchterhouse in Angus, brought on by depression over his mother's death.

They came with a wealth of classic B-sides, including 'Please, Please, Please, Let Me Get What I Want' and 'How Soon is Now', which could easily have stood their ground in the charts in their own right (which 'How Soon is Now' subsequently did). As well as the debut album, in November Rough Trade released a collection of mostly BBC session tracks called *Hatful of Hollow*, which many fans prefer as the 'true' sound of the band to the over-production of their debut.

Then there were the sleeves. Rough Trade production manager Jo Slee, along with layout designer Caryn Gough, worked extensively with Morrissey to bring his visions to life. Slee would take Morrissey's ideas, doodles and photocopies, clearing copyright and working with him to create the band's cover art. Speaking to *Q* magazine on the release of *Peepholism*, her book about the cover art of both the Smiths and Morrissey, Slee explained that 'his use of visuals can sometimes be obscure, sometimes comic, sometimes convoluted, but impossible to sum up in one sentence'. Morrissey had already raised eyebrows with the use of an image on the sleeve of 'Hand in Glove' by Jim French, from Margaret Walters' history, *The Nude Male*, telling *HIM* magazine that 'it could be taken as a blunt, underhand statement against sexism, yet in using that picture I am being sexist. It's time the male body was exploited. Men need a better sense of their own bodies. Naked males should be splashed around the Co-op, you know.' In his memoir *Autobiography*, he reflected on the Smiths' artwork as a ploy to 'to take images that were the opposite of glamour and to pump enough heart and desire into them to show ordinariness as an instrument of power – or, possibly, glamour.' The cover of 'What Difference Does it Make' featured an image of Terence Stamp, taken on the set of the 1965 film *The Collector*, which was issued but quickly withdrawn and re-shot with Morrissey recreating the pose. Stamp had initially refused to be on the sleeve, which alerted Slee to the nature of personal permission alongside commercial copyright. Stamp eventually gave his permission after a word from his mate Sandie Shaw, and the original image was reinstated. Morrissey said he chose images where people looked 'sensitive and inverted, like Terence Stamp. The bedsit person with the ragged cardigan on. I like that, people who look like they're failing. I'm really fascinated by failure . . . in other people, of course.' The bedsit-dwelling cover star of the original 1984 release of 'William, It Was Really Nothing' was actually taken from an advert for ADS (Analog & Digital Systems Inc.) from circa 1981, that read 'Will you still respect your speakers in the morning?' In this context, though, it looked like a despairing young man in his pants. However, ADS threatened legal action citing 'deceptive trade practices', and the single was reissued a few years later with an image of Billie Whitelaw on the sleeve instead.

The photo of Viv Nicholson on the sleeve of 'Heaven Knows I'm Miserable Now' was one of several Moz-driven homages to her. Nicholson had won the jackpot on the Littlewoods football pools, a whopping £152,300 (the equivalent of £4.2 million in 2024). She was seen as a working-class woman made good, although her infamous catchphrase 'Spend, spend, spend' would come back to haunt her as she blew the lot in four years. The image of her looking a bit grim in a deserted northern street sug-gested a folk hero in Morrissey's world. Nicholson would also go on to feature, in a shot where she's standing by a colliery in Castleford, on the German release of 'Barba-rism Begins at Home'. Morrissey had also taken the line in 'Still Ill' – 'Under the iron bridge we kissed / And although I ended up with sore lips . . .' – from her autobiography. In using this image, Morrissey reclaimed her agency from the noise that surrounded her when she first came to 'fame'. She would become one of many women who featured on Smiths sleeves, alongside Yootha Joyce, Rita Tushingham, Pat Phoenix and Shelagh Delaney among others – strong women with fierce working-class backgrounds who'd been through some shit but still retained their dignity.

The image of Joe Dallesandro on the Smiths' debut album, taken from Andy Warhol's *Flesh*, directed by Paul Morrissey, shows Joe as 'the hustler'. To avoid further controversy, the image was cropped. In the full image, the hustler is midway through wanking off another chap.

The male on the sleeve of *Hatful of Hollow* was the otherwise unknown Fabrice Colette, in a shot taken by Gilles Decroix. The image originally appeared in the July 1983 issue of French magazine *Libération*, which com-memorated the 20th anniversary of the death of author

Jean Cocteau and showed Colette's tattoo – taken from a drawing in Cocteau's book *Le Livre Blanc* (The White Book) – on his shoulder.

This combination of strong female characters and apparently 'failed', mostly naked men gave the Smiths an additional visual language that added a further dimension to their appeal. While the music drew you in, the artwork intrigued. Who was that on the cover? What had they done? Where did they sit in the Smiths' universe? Whether or not they were specifically chosen as gay or queer-facing images, or just from Morrissey's internal scrapbook of interests – 'The songs, and the album title, and the sleeve, and whatever else you might wish to investigate, are simply . . . me' – they drew Smiths fans into a world of references and influences that you wouldn't get from Nik Kershaw or Matt Bianco.

The Smiths' 'message', according to Morrissey in *Smash Hits*, was 'that people should discard any notions of in-ness or coolness and simply relax and be themselves, whatever that may be. Ninety per cent of immediate daily anxieties are futile worries.' This was something that was taken to heart, even if, as time wore on, Smiths fans had begun to copy the stylings of Morrissey, be it wearing National Health specs, growing quiffs, shopping at Evans outsize ladies retailers or clasping flowers at any given opportunity.

Again, it's hard to stress quite what an impact the Smiths had. One only has to look at their second studio album, 1985's *Meat is Murder*, and its title track, which turned swathes of people – some notable, like Thom Yorke – into vegetarians seemingly overnight, putting what was once deemed an alternative lifestyle into the mainstream.[3]

Many gay fans saw Morrissey's sexual ambiguity as a sign that he was definitely 'other'. While rumours persisted throughout his career, no thanks to his lyrics and choices of cover art, there was definitely a queer aesthetic running throughout. But it wasn't until the 2013 publication of *Autobiography* that he detailed his first serious relationship with a man, describing the moment in the mid-'90s when he and photographer Jake Walters became a thing as 'the eternal "I" became "we"'. That appeared to have confirmed what lifelong observers had possibly thought: that this loner, with his lack of interest in girls as a teenage boy, was in fact gay, something that seemed to align with his outlook. But all was not quite square. He addressed that remark in his book by claiming to his fansite that 'unfortunately, I am not homosexual. In technical fact, I am humansexual. I am attracted to humans. But, of course, not many.' As if to redress the balance, he also claimed that he had considered having a child with a woman, Tina Dehghani, who became a 'lifetime constant'. He wrote that 'Tina and I discuss the unthinkable act of producing a

---

[3] Vegetarianism wasn't a new fad by any means and dated back to Roman times. It's just that nobody had quite the platform that the Smiths had at that point, and soon the pop kids were bypassing bacon in favour of aubergines. Paul McCartney had been advocating vegetarianism since 1975.

mewling miniature monster. Had I ever previously known such a thought?'

What ultimately made the Smiths and Morrissey so special and appealing to their gay fans was their butch femininity, that combination of the homoerotic and muscular. Morrissey's wit and wordplay had opened him up (ahem) to the gay experience. His fondness for the works of Shelagh Delaney, Oscar Wilde and Truman Capote combined to give a very arch representation of his view, where both tragedy and comedy exist in tandem. This gave rise to lyrics, such as these hugely identifiable lines in 'How Soon is Now': 'I am human and I need to be loved / Just like everybody else does'.

The Smiths also offered a third way to straight fans, those who weren't necessarily into sports or who were quietly navigating their own path, being bookish and/or sensitive. The Smiths showed that you were fine as you were. Visually, they were aligned to the key aesthetic of rock 'n' roll of looking like a gang that you wanted to be part of. These disparate collections of people, often decried as outsiders, represented and attracted you, reflected your interests and offered further reading – and it was something that fans could and would buy into.

'The great thing about boys in my generation is that they liked bands that didn't give a shit if some people thought they were gay,' Johnny Marr told *Spin*. 'Whether they were or not was almost fuel to the fire. I'm sure that was true for those British guys of that generation: Ian McCulloch and the rest of the Bunnymen, Depeche Mode, Martin Gore and Dave Gahan and those guys, or Robert Smith. That was something that guys in our audience, straight or not, clicked with.'

The truth was that the Smiths offered something for everyone. Their intention to be a gay band may not have seen them in the trenches alongside Bronski Beat, but a vague association didn't hurt. There was an overt campness to Morrissey, a fey dandyism more attuned to Joe Orton and Quentin Crisp, and a turn of phrase that could be as cutting as any of the vintage *Coronation Street* matriarchs. They certainly ignited a few fires in the minds and loins of their fanbase. Yet their crowds were a free-for-all of nervous petals in cardigans mixing with footie fans. This combination undermined the 'welcome-all' notion that people only became accepting of each other once they necked a few Es a few years later. The Smiths also offered a cleverness and occasional hilarity that was inherently northern. And it was a *passion* to be a Smiths fan, cocking a snoot at any sneery fool who dumped them into the category of depression and miserablism.

In 2024, the Smiths remain as important as ever, albeit with caveats. While there have been discussions about reforming in some fashion, the likelihood of that happening is, frankly, nil. There are those who've sided with either Morrissey or Marr following their split in 1987, and there have been ongoing undercurrents of tension between them ever since, exacerbated by rancorous exchanges. There are also those who can no longer countenance listening to them, and there are the diehards who continue as normal, batting away any inkling of problematic outbursts from Morrissey.

The glimmers of love between the ex-members were evident when Andy Rourke died in May 2023. Marr had announced it on his socials, with a longer tribute on Instagram, saying: 'Andy and I met as schoolboys in 1975. We were best friends, going everywhere together. When we were fifteen, I moved into his house with him and his three brothers, and I soon came to realise that my mate was one of those rare people that absolutely no one doesn't like . . . Throughout our teens, we played in various bands around south Manchester before making our reputations with the Smiths from 1982 to 1987, and it was on those Smiths records that Andy reinvented what it is to be a bass guitar player. I was present at every one of Andy's bass takes on every Smiths session. Sometimes I was there as the producer and sometimes just as his proud mate and cheerleader. Watching him play those dazzling basslines was an absolute privilege and genuinely something to behold. But one time which always comes to mind was when I sat next to him at the mixing desk, watching him play his bass on the song 'The Queen is Dead'. It was so impressive that I said to myself "I'll never forget this moment."'

Andy will always be remembered as a kind and beautiful soul by everyone who knew him, and as a supremely gifted musician by people who love music. 'Sometimes one of the most radical things you can do is to speak clearly,' said Morrissey. 'When someone dies, out come the usual blandishments . . . as if their death is there to be used. I'm not prepared to do this with Andy. I just hope . . . wherever Andy has gone . . . that he's OK. He will never die as long as his music is heard. He didn't ever know his own power, and nothing that he played had been played by someone else. His distinction was so terrific and unconventional, and he proved it could be done. He was also very, very funny and very happy, and post-Smiths, he kept a steady identity – never any manufactured moves. I suppose, at the end of it all, we hope to feel that we were valued. Andy need not worry about that.'

Time can be a great healer. One day, a new generation will be listening to Morrissey and the Smiths with no idea of the dramas that surrounded them in later years and that coloured their diehard fans' opinions of them. Morrissey's plain-speaking has seen him curdle into saying some fairly unpleasant things and bemoaning the fact that no label will sign him, like some Norma Desmond character that's been down one too many YouTube holes.

That's the thing with making an impact so great that fans clasp a band to their bosom with such passion and devotion. The almost life-changing investment made can often lead to feelings of betrayal when paths and outlooks grow wide apart. But for any pop turn to have made *such* an impact in the first place meant that they must have been very special indeed. Remember them this way.

In November 1984, police raided Manchester's Napoleon's
club under the pretext that the manager was 'permitting
licentious dancing'. Chief Constable James Anderton denied
a 'drive against gays' after he was accused by the Gay
Activists Alliance of closing in on the gay scene 'in pursuit
of his crusade for moral purity'.

ELTON JOHN

'There are times when we all need to share a little pain.'

When musicians talk about wanting to achieve 'longevity as an artist', delivering chart-topping singles decade
after decade, they probably think of Paul McCartney or
Madonna. They might even think of Cliff Richard. The
wise ones, however, try to emulate the career trajectory of
Elton John.

Let's examine the evidence. Elton's first top-ten hit,
'Your Song', reached its peak in February 1971, when
George Harrison was the first Beatle to score a solo number
one, Marc Bolan was making his way towards the nation's
bedroom walls, and David Bowie was still considered a
one-hit wonder. Elton's own first number one, 'Don't Go

Breaking My Heart', dethroned 'The Roussos Phenomenon' by Demis Roussos in July 1976. And in 2021, some forty-five years later, he enjoyed three consecutive chart-toppers in the space of three months aided by Dua Lipa, Ed Sheeran and the undiscussable LadBaby.

Elton enjoyed a pretty good 1983. His album *Too Low for Zero* had been his biggest seller in years, aided by the inclusion of two smash hits in the form of 'I'm Still Standing' and 'I Guess That's Why They Call it the Blues'. It may have helped that it was his first album co-written with Bernie Taupin since 1976's *Blue Moves*, as well as also reuniting him with his classic band line-up from the early '70s: Dee Murray, Nigel Olsson and Davey Johnstone, plus Ray Cooper. This created his most cohesive collection for years, while also allowing Elton to navigate the transition from the '70s into the '80s.

So where was Elton in 1984? Well, 1984 couldn't have gone any better for him. Basking in the success of *Too Low for Zero*, he embarked on a world tour, had another album in the can, would headline Wembley Stadium that summer and his beloved Watford FC reached the FA Cup final for the first time in their history.[1]

---

[1] When Elton bought Watford in 1976, becoming the first pop star to buy a football club, everyone thought he'd gone barmy. But he was deadly serious, and critics underestimated his bond with the club, which dated back to childhood. One of his first moves was to install Graham Taylor as manager, and together they steered the club from the Fourth Division to the First, finishing second behind league champions Liverpool at the end of the '82-'83 season.

That June, 'Sad Songs (Say So Much)', the first single off his new album, *Breaking Hearts*, peaking at number seven in a 'quite gay' Top Ten where Frankie Goes to Hollywood were at both number one with 'Two Tribes' and number five with a resurgent 'Relax'. Wham!'s 'Wake Me Up Before You Go-Go' was at number two, Bronski Beat's 'Smalltown Boy' at three, and Evelyn Thomas's 'High Energy' was at number nine. That week, at least, he was quite literally in among the gays. Sort of. He must have felt really welcome in such company, especially having just married – oh, hang on – a *lady*.

Yes, in 1984, one of the most vocal and inspirational musicians at the forefront of equality and gay rights, someone whose AIDS Foundation would go on to raise millions, and become one half of the UK's first high-profile same-sex marriage, married a woman. Several people seemed a little surprised, not least the press, who found it very peculiar.

'It was Valentine's Day, and Elton John was making one last attempt at being heterosexual,' reported the *Daily Australian*, rather cattily. It was definitely surprising for anyone

---

And, in May 1984, Watford reached their first FA Cup final, only to lose to Everton 2-0. Elton stepped down as chairman of Watford in 2002, but still serves as honorary life-president of the now-Championship club. After Taylor died in 2017, Elton posted a tribute. 'When we started working together in 1977, I had huge ambitions and hopes for my childhood club, but Graham's understanding of the game and leadership achieved something beyond even my wildest dreams. He was a true genius.'

who'd been following Elton's career and life up until then. He had previously cancelled a wedding with his fiancé Linda Hannon in 1970 and shared a five-year romance with his manager John Reid.

Elton had recorded *Breaking Hearts* at AIR Studios in Montserrat with producer Chris Thomas, aided once again by German recording engineer Renate Blauel. She'd been present at the recording of the previous album and had a reputation for being very thorough and reliable. Elton had come to rely on her presence when he'd re-record vocal takes, as was the requisite back then for *Top of the Pops* performances. Indeed, Elton didn't initially want to go to Montserrat unless Renate was going out there, too. Ahead of *Too Low For Zero*'s Australian tour, Elton and Renate went out to dinner on 10 February 1984. On their return to the hotel, the rest of the band were in the bar. Guitarist Dee Murray recalled seeing the pair in the doorway, holding hands, when Elton said 'Guess what, man? I'm engaged.' It was a whirlwind engagement, with the couple tying the knot four days later in Sydney in a ceremony attended by the likes of Olivia Newton-John and John McEnroe. Another of the guests, Barry Humphries, remarked that 'halfway through the ceremony, the minister was saying a prayer and behind him, a cockroach crawled up the wall. I don't know if it was a good or bad omen.' Even Elton's great chum Rod Stewart was a little thrown by the news, sending a telegram that declared 'You may still be standing, but we're all on the fucking floor.'

Elton had hinted at finding a wife as far back as 1976 in his infamous *Rolling Stone* interview, in which he came out as bisexual. 'I'd rather fall in love with a woman eventually because I think a woman probably lasts much longer than a man. But I really don't know . . . I haven't met anybody that I would like to settle down with – of either sex.' The interview was notable for Elton's candid revelations. 'I crave to be loved . . . My life in the last six years has been a Disney film and now I have to have a person in my life. I have to . . . Let me be brutally honest about myself. I get depressed easily. Very bad moods. I don't think anyone knows the real me. I don't even think I do.

'I don't know what I want to be exactly. I'm just going through a stage where any sign of affection would be welcome on a sexual level.'

The truth was, despite the triumphs, Elton was not in a good place in 1984. Cocaine had been a constant, and when he wasn't hoofing wheelbarrows of that, he was drinking. Despite this diet, he had made an impression on the reserved and quiet Blauel, and a chemistry had developed. Towards the end of 1983, he was introducing Blauel to friends as his girlfriend. Barry Humphries recalled that 'she was very attractive and nice. We talked mostly about art at lunch, and not much about music.

'I thought, He's chosen this path. I hope it brings him great happiness. I think it probably did for a while.'

The marriage initially seemed to have the desired effect on Elton, although his tour schedule meant they were unable to enjoy a honeymoon. Elton was fiercely protective of his wife, informing the *Daily Express* that he had to 'be the one who helps her and eases her into things. She isn't used to the razzmatazz.'

Unfortunately, the marriage didn't work. Elton's schedule dictated that the two of them were apart for long periods, and rumours began to circulate in the lesser press that he was still sleeping with men. Behind closed doors at Woodside, his home in Windsor, the two were sleeping in separate bedrooms. During the making of the biopic *Rocketman*, Elton told the director, Dexter Fletcher, that he had been 'looking around and this person was there for me. And I thought, *Oh I haven't tried being married to a woman. Maybe that's what I need.*'

Elton has lamented this period in his life. 'I wanted more than anything to be a good husband, but I denied who I really was, which caused my wife sadness, and caused me huge guilt and regret. I was not a well budgie. I was married and it was just one bag of coke after another.'

'Even though I knew I was gay,' he told the *Los Angeles Times* in 1992, 'I thought this woman was attractive and that being married would cure me of everything wrong in my life . . . When you take that amount [of drugs and alcohol], you can't have any relationship.

'A drug addict thinks like this: I've had enough boyfriends and that's not made me happy, so I'll have a wife. That will change everything. And I loved Renate. She's a great girl. I really, really loved her. But, you know, it is one of the things I regret most in my life, hurting her.'

Cracks opened up further when, on 25 February 1987, the *Sun* published a story based on the insights of one 'Graham X', who let it be known that Elton was up to all sorts. The next day's paper featured further revelations. Elton denied both stories and issued two libel writs against the paper. On the third day, the headline ran 'You're A Liar, Elton' and, over the next few months, the wretched rag continued publishing stories. After the paper printed something borderline insane about Elton having had his pet Rottweiler's barks removed, it was the final straw. When this lawsuit became the first to go to trial, Elton proved that his dogs weren't actually Rottweilers and were perfectly capable of barking. The case fell apart when it was discovered that 'Graham X' had nothing to do with Elton, but had been coaxed along by the *Sun*, who'd also paid him handsomely for his bullshit. The paper was successfully sued and forced to print 'SORRY ELTON' on its front page. 'They can call me a fat, old, talentless poof,' Elton said, 'but they mustn't tell lies about me.'

As the end of 1988 approached, it was revealed that Elton and Renate had divorced. According to those 'sources' again, the couple had had their ups and downs, mainly due to Elton's touring and recording schedule. The pair insisted they were parting amicably and hoped to remain the best of friends. Elton then went back into the studio to throw himself into working on his next album. If anything, his marriage and eventual break-up with Blauel can be seen as the catalyst for him to begin recovery and treatment for his excesses, to set him on the road to recovery and acceptance.[2]

In an interview in 2010, Elton admitted that his prolific cocaine usage wasn't the only problem. 'I'd stay up, I'd smoke joints, I'd drink a bottle of Johnnie Walker and then I'd stay up for three days and then I'd go to sleep for a day and half, get up, and because I was so hungry, because I hadn't eaten anything, I'd binge and have like three bacon sandwiches, a pot of ice cream and then I'd throw it up, because I became bulimic, and then go and do the whole thing all over again. And I'm not being flippant when I say that, when I look back, I shudder at the behaviour and what I was doing to myself.' In 2012, Elton also discussed his denial when friends were dying of AIDS. 'I was having people die right, left and centre around me, friends. And yet I didn't stop the life that I had, which is the terrible thing about addiction. When you take a drug and you take a drink and you mix those two together, you

---

[2] Elton's issues with addiction and bulimia echo those of many other gay men, who are three times more likely to experience depression compared with the general adult population. Potential causes of these include relationship problems, accepting one's homosexuality, experiencing homophobia, institutional discrimination, and alienation from gay communities. According to Loren A Olson's article 'Infidelity and Forgiveness: The Complexities of Coming Out in a Straight Relationship', 'the decision to remain in the closet is impacted more by the fear of loss rather than the prospect of potential gain'. Strikingly, it wasn't until 1973 that homosexuality was declassified as a mental illness. And it took the World Health Organization a further nineteen years to conclude the same in its International Classification of Diseases.

think you're invincible. I came out of this HIV-negative. I was the luckiest man in the world.'

* * *

The first sign of the AIDS-campaigning champion Elton of the future came in 1985 when he released a single as part of a collaboration with Dionne Warwick, Gladys Knight and Stevie Wonder – a cover of the Burt Bacharach/ Carole Bayer Sager song 'That's What Friends are For'. Elton would return to raising money for AIDS research in 1987 when he appeared at a World AIDS Day concert at Wembley Arena. He co-hosted the benefit with George Michael, with the likes of Kim Wilde, the Communards, Holly Johnson and Boy George on the bill.

In the background, the allegations, the constant crap and the aggro from the tabloids was taking its toll. Elton was starting to drink heavily and was, on many occasions, too depressed to get out of bed. And when he did break cover for appearances, he looked terrible. There was a reckoning heading his way and, along with his divorce, Elton set about auctioning off all his stage gear and ephemera. So began the long road towards getting sober. 'It was more that I wanted a new start. I wanted to completely remodel and redecorate Woodside. I didn't want to live in a berserk pop star's house anymore. I wanted somewhere that felt like a home.'

On his road to sobriety and as part of getting his shit together, Elton volunteered for a charity called Operation Open Hand. This brought him into direct contact with AIDS patients from all over Atlanta. It was motivation enough. In 1992, he established the Elton John AIDS Foundation.

On the foundation's website, Elton notes that he has 'lost many dear friends to this terrible disease. In the mid-1980s, I began channelling my grief into efforts to help raise money for the pioneering charitable organisations that formed during those dark, grim years to fund AIDS research and provide vital services to people with HIV/AIDS.'

There are two AIDS-related deaths that Elton often cites. The most famous, of course, is that of his close friend Freddie Mercury, who died of AIDS-related bronchial pneumonia in 1991. But the first was Ryan White whom Elton first met in 1985.[3]

---

[3] White was a young man from Indiana who was infected with HIV as a result of a blood transfusion during a lung biopsy in 1984 and given six months to live. Following his diagnosis and a brief illness, he wanted to return to school, but his fellow students and their parents had other ideas. Put simply, he was barred. One hundred and seventeen parents and fifty teachers signed a petition encouraging school leaders to ban White from school. The principal and school board succumbed to this pressure, forcing White's family to file a lawsuit to overturn the decision. When White was finally allowed back to school, half of the students stayed away, many residents on his paper round cancelled their deliveries, and he faced homophobic abuse whenever he was seen on the street. The publicity surrounding his story – and an increase in news stories about AIDS in general – thrust him onto the news agenda. Indirectly, Ryan became the poster child for AIDS awareness in the US. White disliked the media spotlight, and the pressure it put on his parents, saying that he would happily trade it all to be free of the disease. Following his death in 1990, numerous fundraising events were set up in his honour, and his mother went on to establish the Ryan White Foundation to help other families in similar positions. In 1993, the gay rights and AIDS activist Larry Kramer declared that 'little Ryan White probably did more to change the face of this illness and to move people than anyone. And he continues to be a presence through his mom, Jeanne White. She has an incredibly moving presence as she speaks around the world.'

The Elton John AIDS Foundation has raised in excess of $565 million (£446 million) since 1992, and funded programmes across the world, with its profile on the celebrity circuit raised by the annual Elton John AIDS Foundation Academy Award Party. Significantly, the foundation is among the top ten philanthropic funders of HIV/AIDS grants worldwide, the second largest HIV-related philanthropic funder of LGBTQ+ communities, and the top philanthropic funder in Eastern Europe and Central Asia.

Elton has also long been known for giving away large amounts of his personal wealth to charity. Inspired by how he felt after Ryan White's death, he decided to start donating royalties from each single he'd release to four British AIDS charities, starting with 1990's 'Sacrifice', which became Elton's first solo number one. Previously released as the flip of his 1989 single 'Healing Hands', it gained traction after DJ Steve Wright started playing it. Topping the charts wasn't too bad for a song he'd initially not wanted on the album. By 2004, the donation of his royalties had resulted more than $43 million being given to organisations around the world, making him the most philanthropic person in music for that year. It's a title he's retained annually ever since.

It was also at the beginning of the '90s that Elton met the Canadian filmmaker and then-advertising executive David Furnish, who'd been brought along to a dinner party at Woodside in an attempt to help Elton to meet new people. David was initially wary and shy when he met Elton, as the latter recalled in his memoir, *Me*. 'I later discovered that he'd heard a lot of gossip on the London gay scene about the inadvisability of having anything whatsoever to do with Elton John, unless you had a burning desire to be showered with gifts, forced to put your life on hold in order to be whisked away on tour, then summarily dumped – usually by his personal assistant – when he met someone else, or lost his temper with you during a post-cocaine comedown, or announced he was getting married to a woman.'

As their relationship grew, obstacles began to emerge. David's situation was one that many gay men have faced. 'I left Canada,' he told the *Observer* in 2001. 'I left my family behind, because I was ashamed. I ran away.' After David informed his family that he was in fact gay and was going out with one of the planet's most famous people, Elton proposed to him. And, on 21 December 2005, the first day that such a thing could be performed in England, they entered into a civil partnership. After same-sex marriage became legal in England and Wales in 2014, they upgraded to full marriage on the ninth anniversary of their civil partnership. In December 2010, the couple welcomed their first child, born via surrogacy, Zachary Jackson Levon Furnish-John, and, in 2013, their second – from the same surrogate – Elijah Joseph Daniel Furnish-John.

Elton John's life has been a spectacular run through all the glitz, glamour and success a single human being can handle, with the level of drug and drink intake that could lay waste to a small country. He's hung with music and showbiz royalty and legends, had audiences with world leaders, met kings and a *lot* of queens, and yet could also probably give you detail on what Hell actually looks like from the inside. He has consistently been a force for good and his impact on raising AIDS awareness, fighting for tolerance and acceptance, and using his status in order to raise as much money as possible for research, is something truly outstanding, inspiring and beautiful. Everyone should be more Elton.

*In November 1984, Chris Smith, newly elected to the House
of Commons, declares: 'My name is Chris Smith. I'm the
Labour MP for Islington South and Finsbury, and I'm gay.'
The announcement makes him the first openly out homosexual
politician in the Commons. In 2005, he was the first
politician to disclose he was HIV positive.*

DAVID BOWIE

'They always let you down when you need 'em.'

Undoubtedly, David Bowie's combination of sex, glamour, sleaze and transformation shaped a generation of musicians.

People like Boy George: 'For me, Bowie was the beginning of me going, "Oh my god, I'm not alone." It didn't matter whether he was gay, straight or bisexual, he was a massive role model.'

People like Holly Johnson: 'It really sparked my imagination, and for a whole generation of people. Angie and David were the It couple for us. I'd heard the word "queer", but I'd never heard the word "bisexual" – or even an artist claiming they were. That was a huge moment for me.'

People like Marc Almond: 'I went to see Bowie in concert in Liverpool when I was about fifteen or sixteen with
my mates . . . It was a glam-rock epiphany.'

People like Neil Tennant: 'The Ziggy Stardust tour
came to [Newcastle] City Hall in June 1972 and he was
electrifying. It was the best concert I've ever been to.
David Bowie transformed the way I felt about pop music.'

And even people like Madonna: 'Here's this beautiful,
androgynous man, just being so perverse . . . I came home
a changed woman.'

Bowie had gone from aspiring mime artist, jobbing
blueser/mod and president of The Society for the Prevention of Cruelty to Long-Haired Men to astral, space-
facing troubadour with the release of his first proper hit
'Space Oddity' in 1969. Then he painted a gold circle on
his forehead, blew everyone's minds when he said he was
bisexual and draped his arm around his guitarist on telly.
A large percentage of those watching that epiphanic *Top of
the Pops* performance went straight out to form bands. He
then famously told everyone 'That's it! I'm off' when he
played Hammersmith. He discovered plastic soul and did
so many drugs at one point that he'd taken to hiding his
piss in the fridge, away from witches (the goon). He'd fallen
to Earth, invented the idea of going to Berlin and 'was
only waving' when he arrived at Victoria Station that time
during the '70s.

He'd even considered writing a musical about George
Orwell's *1984*, only to be denied by Orwell's widow. He

turned these ideas, including a song called '1984', into his *Diamond Dogs* album, as well as performing his own musical extravaganza at Soho's Marquee Club in October 1973, cheekily called *The 1980 Floor Show*. It would also be the last sighting of Ziggy Stardust. That's how 1984 David Bowie was.

It was looking like Bowie business-as-usual as he kicked off the '80s by telling Robert Fripp to shut up and bestowed his blessing on the futurists. He only started making money when he hooked up with Nile Rodgers in 1983 to make his biggest-selling album *Let's Dance*. He'd been listening to James Brown and Albert King, and wanted his new music to be big, brash and jazzy. Taking inspiration from R&B and vintage rock 'n' roll, he showed Nile a photo of Little Richard getting into a Cadillac, and said, 'That's what I want my album to sound like.'

However, in 1984, Bowie came a cropper. Four words: *Jazzin' For Blue Jean*. Bowie played dual roles in the twenty-one-minute, Julien Temple-directed film to promote the single 'Blue Jean' – those of both Vic and the rock star Screaming Lord Byron. In it, the hapless Vic tries to woo a woman (played by Louise Scott) by claiming he knew Byron, and takes her to one of his shows, only for Byron to eventually meet Vic and the woman, and clear off with her at the end. As Vic, Bowie wears a 'Relax' T-shirt and, at one point as Byron, a turban. The film took cheeky pot shots at his career and had some shonky *Minder*-esque London boozer locations that looked like they'd been filmed with all the panache of an instant coffee advert. It even featured a future member of Right Said Fred in Byron's band. It really had it all.

It's as if the two sides of Bowie are sent up : as Vic, the 'I'm just a normal bloke' side is desperate to please, but to no avail as his date has no time for Vic once she is wooed and entranced by the educated, sophisticated and other-worldly Byron. As she departs with Byron, Vic chases after them, shouting, 'I'm speechless! You conniving randy bogus oriental old queen! Your record sleeves are better than your songs!' The film then breaks the fourth wall with Bowie claiming Julien Temple has changed the ending of the video. It's quite strange. And not in a great way. Bizarrely, *Jazzin' For Blue Jean* won a Grammy for Best Short Form Video. It was the only award Bowie received from the Grammy panel during his lifetime. The clowns.

With this, and Paul McCartney's musical-drama *Give My Regards to Broad Street*, it really was the autumn for legends showing themselves up something rotten in order to 'get down with the kids'. In a year dominated by the Hollywood-level production of the John Landis-directed video for Michael Jackson's 'Thriller' from the tail end of the previous year, the kids were proving strangely resistant to a couple of old blokes slapsticking it around London. (Bowie was thirty-six. McCartney was forty-two. Old.)

The Eddie Cochran-inspired 'Blue Jean' was, as Bowie claimed a few years later, a bit of sexist rock 'n' roll about picking up birds. It was ersatz rock for the MTV age, an arena populated by many of his 'children', and unlikely to ever be confused with 'Drive-In Saturday', 'Life on Mars' or even 'The Laughing Gnome'. It is quite possibly no one's favourite Bowie song. In fact, if you were on a date with someone who declared it as their favourite-ever David Bowie song, you'd suddenly remember you'd left the iron on and be tapping your location into your Uber app before they finished the sentence.

Released that September, Bowie's sixteenth album *Tonight* was his first since *Pin-Ups* to feature barely any songs written by him. He attributed this to his label wanting a new album rather than his proposed live souvenir of his colossally successful Serious Moonlight tour from the year before.

Bowie himself said that *Tonight* 'didn't have any concept behind it. It was just a collection of songs. It sounded sort of jumbled, it didn't hold together well at all . . . though, if you take a song out of context and play it, it sounds pretty good. But if you play it as an album, it doesn't work, and that was unfortunate.' Critics were less kind and gave it the sort of shoeing that Bowie had never before experienced. For many, the stand-out track was the Bowie-written 'Loving the Alien'. The co-writes with Iggy Pop, recently flush after Bowie had covered 'China Girl' on *Let's Dance* the year before, amounted to 'Tumble and Twirl' and 'Dancing With the Big Boys'. There were also covers of Pop's 'Tonight' (with a then-freshly rejuvenated Tina Turner), 'Neighbourhood Threat' from *Lust for Life* and 'Don't Look Down' from *New Values*.

Iggy must have initially thought his boat had come in and was probably idly looking in estate agents' windows, pondering how many extra bedrooms he could handle. Alas, it wasn't to be. Bowie's intergalactic pansexual chameleonic ways of a mere decade ago suddenly felt as far away as the invention of air travel. Although it entered the album chart at number one, its absence on anyone's Christmas list saw it fall out just fifteen weeks later – a mere shadow of the entire year that *Let's Dance* had spent on the chart.

If Bowie wasn't fond of *Tonight*, it was the follow-up, 1987's *Never Let Me Down*, that he considered as his nadir, later referring to this period as his 'Phil Collins years'. 'It was such an awful album,' he told *Rolling Stone*. 'I really shouldn't have even bothered going into the studio to record it. In fact, when I play it, I wonder if I did sometimes.

'It didn't make me feel good. I felt dissatisfied with everything I was doing and, eventually, it started showing in my work. The next two albums after *Let's Dance* showed that my lack of interest in my own work was really becoming transparent.'

Fortunately, despite the *Tonight* debacle, 1984 was as good a time as any to get into David Bowie, with pretty much all of his catalogue available on mid-price around the £2.99 mark. Imagine handing over £20 and snapping up, for instance, *Hunky Dory*, *Low*, *Ziggy Stardust*, *Young Americans*, *Heroes* and *Station to Station* and STILL having enough change for a slap-up chip supper?

Also, his first label, Deram, had 'enterprisingly' issued
Love You Till Tuesday, the soundtrack to the 1969 promotional showcase of short films he'd made in his pre-fame
era, which also made its debut on video. It was not to be
confused with his self-titled debut, although he did share
several tracks from his Anthony Newley-esque kinky cock-
ney baroque phase. Deram had pulled this stunt before,
when 1967's 'The Laughing Gnome' was reissued as
a cash-in during 1973's peak Ziggymania. It was as if
'The Laughing Gnome' would follow him around like
an embarrassment for eternity. The label behaved like a
suspect uncle trotting out cheesy school photos whenever
Bowie got too big for his boots, making sure that behind
every sharp turn in Bowie's fantastic voyage, there'd be a
faint echo of a 'ha ha ha' and a 'hee hee hee'.

The rest of Bowie's '80s were at best patchy. It was as if
after a decade or so of being the ahead-of-his-time pansexual avatar, he was now playing catch-up with everyone.
There was the triumphant Live Aid appearance (although
the no-fucks-given insertion of the relatively obscure non-hit
'TVC15' into his set was a WTF moment), and there would
be the wonderfully elegant masterpiece that was 'Absolute
Beginners' (the song, that is. The film was . . . well . . .).

But 1984. What should have been the most David Bowie
year of ALL the years was the time he seemingly lost his
lustre and went a bit boring and slightly shit. Perhaps he
was happy to be on the backfoot for a change, to put his
feet up for a year or two and let his 'children' run things for

a bit. Pop was having a queer moment, but the man who'd been at the forefront of illuminating a less heterosexual way of existing looked like he was regretting ever saying anything in the first place.

*   *   *

David Bowie dying was something that no one seemed to have made plans for – no one apart from himself, that is. *Blackstar* had been released on Friday, 8 January to universally good reviews. But then, two days later, Bowie died. The curtain came down in an awesome, spectacular way.

The sheer level of grief and public mourning was overwhelming – and rightly so. Aside from the musicians who paid tribute, and the thinkpieces and obituaries that struggled to encapsulate everything, there were the fans who Bowie had turned on in the first place. Several generations of people who felt his impact first-hand, and sensed him as a conduit to unleash their true selves in music, art, fashion and sexuality, were bereft. His spirit had fed into culture like few artists had ever achieved before, and there was a sense of a cosmic unravelling that this energy was no longer here.

Yet, if anything, he *is* still here. Bowie and his characters and images and ideas continue to connect and intersect culturally. His legacy will be something that each subsequent generation will explore and find things to inspire them. There was far more to him than *Jazzin' for Blue Jean*.

'Given an inch, the homosexuals demand all. Granted legality, they have advanced boldly, noisily, immodestly, without shame, flaunting and organising themselves, proselytising vigorously, demanding ever-fresh "rights", privileges, hand-outs, immunities, special representation.'
– Colin Welch, *Spectator*, November 1984

CULTURE CLUB / BOY GEORGE

'It matters what you say, it matters what you do.'

Up until 1984, the biggest names in pop music, and those who had poster supremacy, were Spandau Ballet and Duran Duran. The two acts were remarkably similar in outlook. Both had emerged through the New Romantic club scene: Duran in their native Birmingham had become the 'house band' at the club Barbarella's, while the Spands were practically formed at London's Blitz.

Each initial line-up featured five young men as equally interested in hair and clothes as they were in musicianship. Actually, the primary goal initially was looking good. What also made them stand out was that there was a democracy as to who was cover-friendly. *Smash Hits* chose to introduce Spandau Ballet via the medium of hunksome bass player

Martin Kemp on the cover in December 1980. Duran Duran's front-page debut, three months later, involved a photo of keyboardist Nick Rhodes and drummer Roger Taylor. Both bands were pin-up friendly, which for two acts steeped in artier influences such as Roxy Music and David Bowie, took them by surprise. 'We were an art band in my mind,' John Taylor would tell *Record Collector.* 'Suddenly, we'd got a teen following that I did not see coming at all. We thought, *This is different.*'

Each member could tot up the number of banners being held up by fans at gigs to ascertain which of them were the most fanciable. According to the *Smash Hits* Readers' Poll in 1981, Simon Le Bon was the voters' favourite Duran ahead of John Taylor. He was still top Duran dog in 1982; number one overall, in fact, while John, Nick and Roger were well placed within the top ten. The Spands' Tony Hadley and Martin and Gary Kemp had to make do with positions between eleven and twenty. Duran Duran were victors across all categories by nature of just existing.

Yet the other big act of that period and regular runner-up behind the Duran/Spand stranglehold was Culture Club. Seemingly coming out of nowhere, they barged directly onto pop's top table, usurping Duran and Spandau to the number-one spot.

The appeal of Boy George, Jon Moss, Roy Hay and Mikey Craig seemed like the ideal pop utopia. They played on their melting pot of colour, sexualities and beliefs. Formed in 1981, Culture Club's focal point was their lead singer Boy George. George had seen David Bowie on his Ziggy tour, circumnavigated his way through punk, had been a key devotee of the Blitz club scene and featured on the fringes and sidenotes of many other acts' antics.

Known for his outlandish dress sense and ability to stand out from the rest of the fashion-facing club set, George knew how to turn heads. Despite it being a very competitive and bitchy scene, everyone who encountered him knew that he would eventually become a star. But none of them, not even George, was quite prepared for *how* big a star he was to become.

In one of Culture Club's earliest pre-fame interviews, at the grand old age of twenty, George claimed that Culture Club made 'pop songs and music for housewives. We don't want to become one of those "video bands" who spend all their time in the studio and not enough time on the road.' Even then, despite his playing with genderbending, he preferred to keep people guessing as regards his sexuality. 'I suppose you could say I'm multi-sexual . . . I'm not one of those people who could go on a march in support of gay rights. I don't want to get involved in a tribe. I'm an individual and I want everyone to take me as I am.'

They faltered with their first singles: 'White Boy' has no chart credits to its name, and although follow-up 'I'm Afraid of Me' did manage to break into the Top 100, it was literally at number 100. Their increasingly nervous record company, Virgin, were looking at their spend and gave Culture Club one more opportunity to see if they could actually sell some records. According to George, it was their last chance at securing an album deal, and so they released the mid-tempo, reggae-lite 'Do You Really Want to Hurt Me'. Initially picked up by Radio 2, it made a modest debut at number sixty-six, which was already a far better return than the previous singles had managed. It broke into the Top 40 the following week at thirty-eight.

Not that George was terribly keen on it being released as a single in the first place. While it had a reggae flavour, it wasn't as authentic as perhaps he'd hoped. This was a good few years before pop reggae would start to be the avenue along which genuine reggae acts, such as Aswad, would finally break through. The reviews weren't that great, either; *Smash Hits* called it 'weak, watered-down, fourth-division reggae . . . awful'. About a month or so later, the makers of this 'fourth-division reggae' would be helping to sell several thousand more copies of the magazine, popping up on the front cover more often than any of their rivals.

Also, as is often the unlikely factor in these things, the band were offered a last-minute chance to appear on *Top of the Pops* after Shakin' Stevens had pulled out. With less than twenty-four hours to prepare for their performance on the John Peel-presented edition on 23 September 1982, it was an instant sensation.

Top of the Pops was a huge deal. British television was still limited to just three channels, at least for another month or so, before Channel 4 turned up, and so the reaction from the press the next day was unheard of for a new band appearing on the show. 'Is it a boy or a girl?' was the tenet of the press headlines. The *Sun* was especially intrigued. By the end of the month, by which time 'Do You Really Want to Hurt Me' had settled into the top spot, the newspaper was running an exclusive interview with George. Journalist Judy Wade opened with 'He is Number 1 in the charts and they call him the Gender Bender . . . He is the sensational singer who looks like a girl, sounds like a fella and behaves like something strangely inbetween.' By the fourth paragraph, George had upended Wade's agenda with a revelation: 'I suppose I am actually bisexual. Or multi-sexual – because there's a lot to discover in life, y'know.' Inevitably, the *Sun*, being the bastion of class, discretion and dignity, had also tracked down George's mum for a quote.

In the real world, outside of any confected outrage from middle England and its tabloids, the reaction to George was far more accommodating than the papers suggested. People started approaching him in the street to say how much they liked the band and his look. 'I get fans of both sexes. Actually, I get more girls after me than the four straight guys in my band put together,' he claimed. 'I'm working so hard at my career that I'm too exhausted by the time I fall into bed for any of that. I lost my virginity with a girl when I was sixteen, but sex has never been an obsession with me. It's just like eating a bag of crisps. Quite nice but nothing marvellous. Sex is not simply black and white. There's a lot of grey.'

This was revolutionary. Sure, there'd been a mild tabloid kerfuffle, and lots of very unsavoury rumours about Marc Almond, when Soft Cell had made their *Top of the Pops* debut the year before, but that was more to do with his seemingly unsettling pervery, rather than any bending of genders. Culture Club were instantly a talking point across the nation. It was almost a Bowie-draping-his-arm-around-Mick-Ronson moment, with *Top of the Pops* retaining the power to apparently subvert, galvanise and inspire the country's school playgrounds. By the end of 1982, when 'Do You Really Want to Hurt Me' entered the Billboard Hot 100, eventually peaking at number two the following February, Culture Club had gone from the pop fringes to superstars.

'Although I famously said at the time that I'd rather have a cup of tea than sex,' George told the *Guardian* in 2008, 'my sex life was actually really rampant. But I'd been brought up to think it was dirty and wrong, and not to be made public. So, you're dealing with a lot of things – not just other people's opinions, but your own insecurities as well. In a way, nothing's changed. Things might have changed on the surface, but everyone's still as uptight.'

There was also another factor in the band's set-up that underpinned the internal tension present throughout their career – George and drummer Jon Moss were engaged in a secretive on-off affair. While this may have made for some of the band's greatest songs, it also caused their biggest fights. Behind hotel room and studio doors, George and Jon would take things out on each other, with Mikey and Roy often caught in the crossfire. Speaking to the *Guardian* in 2015 about 'Do You Really Want to Hurt Me', Jon said, 'I imagine the song is about me. I think most of the songs are. I was a muse for Boy George, for better or worse. There was a lot of subjectivity in his writing – "Oh, everything's happening to me. Oh, you didn't call me" – a lot of assuming other people don't have their own problems.'

However, George put the record straight on that. 'Jon wasn't my muse. I wrote it about another former partner, Kirk Brandon. But when you write songs about other people, they're really about yourself anyway. A lot of those early songs, like "Time" and "Victims", were all "woe is me". I did play the victim. That was the role I took on: "Oh, why are you doing this to me?" Back in the day, I spent so much time trying to change the people I was in love with – and not trying to change myself.'

Now that the band were able to make an album, they recorded their debut *Kissing To Be Clever*, and released it that October. Although not an instant chart-topper, it rose to number five in the UK and spent fifty-nine weeks in the Top 100. Anglophile American fans into the music of the British invasion took it to a not-too-shabby number fourteen, where it wandered around the Billboard 200 for a full eighty-eight weeks.

Within a twelve-month period, Boy George and Culture Club had become inescapable, a Ronnie-Corbett-dressed-up-as-Boy-George level of unavoidable. However, if 1982 had seen a mania develop, by 1983 the world was theirs. Come September, things were about to go even *barmier*.

Entering the UK singles chart at number three, 'Karma Chameleon' rose to the top the following week and stayed there for six weeks. It would become the biggest-selling single of 1983, eventually shifting 1.52 million copies. In the US, it climbed to the top in early 1984 and spent three weeks at the summit. The accompanying album *Colour by Numbers* would shift 10 million copies globally and top the charts around the planet.

When he won the award for Best Single in the annual *Smash Hits* Readers' Poll at the end of 1983, George admitted he was 'glad people liked this record because when we released it, we were very worried because it was a change of direction . . . We're very happy about this because I think, of all the things you can possibly win, the best single is the most important because your whole job is making music and if you can make something that really is worthwhile – and that will go down in history – I think I'd rather do that than be the Best Dressed or whatever.'

George began the year as the co-cover star, alongside Annie Lennox, of *Newsweek*'s 'Britain Rocks America – Again' special. The magazine followed the Culture Club phenomenon as they toured the States, tracing the evolution of British pop in only the way Americans can. It looked at the new British invasion and how twenty years ago 'were the days of the Dave Clark Five, the Swinging Blue Jeans and Herman's Hermits – clean-cut, cute and, in retrospect, innocent bands. These are the days of Public Image Ltd, ABC and New Order – savvy and sometimes sinister names that conjure up a strange new world of pop music.'

At the 1984 Grammy Awards, when picking up the award for Best New Artist in an acceptance speech filmed in the UK, George said, 'Thank you, America. You've got taste, style and you know a good drag queen when you see one', blowing a cheeky kiss to the camera. On a night that had already featured Annie Lennox dressed as a man[1], he

---

[1] The US also lost its mind at the sight of Annie Lennox dressed as a man for Eurythmics' appearance at the Grammys. While she wasn't averse to dressing up, her androgyny was very much a constructed image and feminist statement. And she wasn't keen on being lumped in with any genderfuckery either, telling *Pride Source*'s Chris Azzopardi in 2014 that 'I really felt it was diminishing in a way. I wasn't bending gender; I was making a statement in a kind of subtle way . . . I was saying, "Look, as a woman I can be equal to a man", and in this partnership with the Eurythmics, where I was in a partnership with a man, the two of us felt so connected that my gender didn't matter.' Looking back, it seems so tame, but the Grammys performance of 'Sweet Dreams (Are Made of This)', on 28 February 1984, was considered subversive. That it took another twenty-seven years for Lady Gaga to pull a similar stunt at the 2011 ceremony, dressed as her alter-ego Jo Calderone, shows how easy it is to still alarm an American audience. Gaga may not have admitted it, but Lennox sensed it was a homage. It was a far cry from the time that MTV pulled the video for 'Love is a Stranger' off air because they thought the lead singer was a transvestite. There was also nothing particularly sexual about Lennox's look; it was more of allure and character play.

wasn't quite prepared for the storm those words caused in the States. 'I didn't really consider what it meant for anyone else,' he told *Variety* in 2018, 'as I was in England . . . But people were freaking out when I said that. Look, sometimes the world just isn't ready – for a word, for a shift of the moral compass. I'm glad I said it now. I just wish I had said it with a bit more intention at the time.'

World tours, universal adoration and legions of fans copying George's 'look' was one thing. But behind the scenes things weren't as rosy. The fame and toll of travelling non-stop around the planet was starting to work the band's last nerve. Things slid into autopilot, and the urge to write new songs took a backseat as resentment grew internally. Roy and Mikey were a little miffed that their input and contribution to the Culture Club behemoth wasn't being noticed due to overriding press fascination with the colour of George's hair or the length of his hem, the likes of which caused headlines every other day.

In a somewhat forward-facing feature for *Smash Hits* during the summer of 1984 entitled 'May the Best Man Win', George was asked his opinion on some of his fellow androgynous voyagers. With quotes from Marilyn, Pete Burns and DJ Tasty Tim, it remains one of the cattiest, bitchiest pieces ever to appear in a teen magazine. The key lesson readers learned from these man-woman confusers was that they were all jealous of each other's success and that each one had been doing it *way* before the other. The only one to get off lightly was Tasty Tim, who seemed quite nice by comparison.

Marilyn had come through the Blitz scene almost con-currently with George, with whom he'd been a flatmate and good friend. However, throughout the height of Culture Club's success, the two were the best of frenemies, regularly exchanging salty, bitchy barbs. Marilyn – born Peter Robinson – was seen as a one-trick pony who had dressed up as Marilyn Monroe on a couple of occasions. He then followed George into pop music when a call went up around the music industry for the next big gender-bender. Releasing a handful of surprisingly good singles such as 'Calling Your Name' and 'Cry and Be Free' at the end of 1983, he was an in-case-of-emergency Boy George for kids TV, someone pretty much constantly 'in reception' between 1983 and 1984. He'd also popped up in Eurythmics' video for 'Who's That Girl', alongside a succession of fellow pop stars. He was famous for being famous.[2]

---

[2] Marilyn's existence reads like a courtroom artist's sketch of George's career, half-irritated that his legacy would feature George's name in it for eternity ('I think I'm famous for being somebody's friend') and yet somehow grateful that anyone would remember him at all. In 1985, after his music career sputtered to a halt, Marilyn cut off his hair and tried to make a comeback, but to no avail. He and George actually worked together on a comeback of sorts in 2015. In fact, Marilyn's career for the last forty years has effectively amounted to popping up on a breakfast TV couch or some 'where are they now'-style TV show, claiming to have signed a new deal and currently working on new music. It's a shame, really. His legacy is likely to forever be something along the lines of being slightly more identifiable than the non-Geldof Boomtown Rats members in the Band Aid video.

It wasn't long before Culture Club's infrastructure began to weaken. The band were getting fed up with the non-stop globetrotting that massive popularity demanded. Wherever they landed, they'd be mobbed by fans, most of whom were donned in George-related garb – an ever-constant reminder to the rest of the band who the star was. Despite all the adulation, songs weren't getting written, exhaustion was coming into view and rumours of a split were abundant. So much so that George felt the need to drop in on *Top of the Pops* to stress they *weren't* splitting up.

Culture Club's 1984 was not without its hurdles. Despite being massively popular in the afterglow of the multi-million selling success of 'Karma Chameleon', the band were too focused on being pop stars – and Boy George had become a cultural phenomenon known for his one-liners on the chat-show circuit. The prospect of sitting down and knocking up some memorable songs was becoming an arse-ache. As Jon Moss told *Smash Hits*, 'we booked two or three weeks to do the songwriting and didn't use one day of it. We had an argument and we left. We tried again three days later and had another argument. We rowed and rowed and George smashed his tape recorder and I threw a chair at him. Then we wrote the album in four days.'

The campaign for *Waking Up With the House on Fire*, the third Culture Club album, kicked off with the release of the single 'The War Song'. The idea of impeding third-world-war doom was everywhere in the pop charts of the early '80s. Post-apocalyptic videos were de rigueur, with everyone from the likes of Kim Wilde, Ultravox and the Human League looking for that extra drama, even if the accompanying songs had nothing to do with bombs or any kind of nuclear activity. The biggest of them all was 'Two Tribes', which saw Frankie Goes to Hollywood's label ZTT going out of its way to push the horrors of war. In adverts for the single, they grimly detailed the nuclear capacity of each superpower, playing on every teen's fear of the threat of annihilation. Culture Club's 'The War Song', by comparison, seemed a little tame. Noble statement that it was, the notion of war being 'stupid' sort of felt insipid and overly simplistic. Culture Club weren't above making grand statements, but the fact that they'd been struggling to compose numbers for *Waking Up With the House on Fire* showed.

After seeing the video for the single, Dead or Alive's catty Pete Burns sent Boy George a wreath, offering condolences for the band's career taking a nosedive. If anything, he had a point. 'The War Song' felt like they'd given up. A number two hit, where a year previously they'd enjoyed the biggest-selling single, felt like a disaster, especially as the single evaporated from the Top 100 after eight whole weeks.

A massive star he may have been, but George was becoming a husk of himself. Quite simply, *Waking Up With the House on Fire* was not a very good album. 'Being a pop star is like being thrown out of a window naked,' George explained of its title. 'Everyone wants to scrutinise you, see you naked. You become property, hot property.

'Only now have we had time to soak up success, seeing it for what it really is . . . Last year, certain things got a bit too much for me, like kids standing on my doorstep day and night. I was a total wreck. I need privacy. Twenty-four hours a day, my life is Culture Club and I need time to myself.'

After a world tour at the end of 1984, each member decided they wanted time out as things had started to disintegrate in the camp. Boy George was bored with being Boy George, the relationship between him and Jon was fractious, and both Mikey and Roy were increasingly fed up with being in the middle of it all. The commitment to new music took a nosedive. Mikey admitted that 'everybody's egos seem to be catching up with them. Of course, we all want our faces in the paper – it's nice to be in the public eye. But I'm beginning to wonder if they set them up or what. I'm not slagging anybody but, yes, all four personalities have changed.'

Jon Moss seemed similarly disillusioned. 'To be honest, I think I'm going to have to do a lot of soul searching over the next year. At the moment, I just go with it, take it as it comes. If you push things too far, you just mess everything up for everyone else.'

Aside from the drama, Boy George's profile eclipsed a fracturing band and saw him achieve a few notable firsts. 'We know we can't change the world but there's no harm in trying. I'm on the Christmas cover of *Cosmopolitan* – the first man to do so. I've also done eight pages of women's beauty in *Harper's Bazaar* – that's history as well. My ambition is to make the cover of *Vogue*. I not only want to break down class barriers, I want to break down sexual barriers.'

The breakdown of George's relationship with Moss, a turbulent one to say the least, had been the background noise throughout Culture Club's initial burst of success. To make matters worse, George had graduated from light marijuana use to full-on heroin addiction in a matter of months. The band's fourth album, 1986's *From Luxury to Heartache*, suffered significantly, thanks to long-winded recording sessions. They began working with industry veteran Arif Mardin, a producer who'd been behind some of the biggest albums of all time. However, even *he* bailed after the process seemed to be taking forever and getting nowhere. George's habits and increasingly unreliability had put paid to the success of both the album and the band. Having had three platinum-selling albums, *From Luxury to Heartache* limped in at number ten in the UK album chart, where it spent a measly six weeks.

The band's worldwide success seemingly formed a protective barrier, but things were moving on and other acts were eclipsing Culture Club for music fans' attention. It didn't matter which country they landed in, George still found himself surrounded by adoring clones. He'd untapped something in youth culture not seen since the advent of Bowie in the early '70s. Despite their music beginning to slip off pop's radar, George still commanded attention.

However, the writing was on the wall for the band when, wanting some time out, George and Marilyn flew to New York, where they engaged on a destructive binge of drugs and partying. 'I packed my bags and went off to New York to have a good time,' George told *Record Mirror* in 1987. 'And, unfortunately, I had too much of a good time. Things started to take their toll.

'I think the more successful you get, the less energy you have. When we first started Culture Club, we played together as a band simply because that's what we were. And then it became a case of when we could rehearse, when we could write songs, when we could fit it into our schedule. And that's when, for me, it got very boring.'

Boy George's story is effectively the most '80s thing ever: scenester at the key clubs; briefly joins a Malcolm McLaren-formed band; forms his own band instead; becomes a massive, global popstar and national treasure at record speed; goes off the rails; gets into hard drugs; and then finds religion and redeems himself by throwing in his lot with acid house and becoming a DJ. That's the perfect '80s trajectory of pop stardom. Unlike his rivals Duran Duran or Spandau Ballet, there were no yacht purchases, nor farms bought with George.

Since then, George has had his fair share of troubles, most notably in 2009 when he was sentenced to fifteen months' imprisonment for handcuffing a male escort to a wall and beating him with a chain. He was initially incarcerated at HM Prison Pentonville in London, but was then transferred to HM Prison Highpoint North in Suffolk. Given early release after four months for good behaviour, he was still required to wear an ankle monitor and submit to a curfew for the remainder of his sentence.

Bar the unpleasantness and the on/off Culture Club reunions, George's ascendancy to becoming a national treasure was because of his relatability and, much like his idol Bowie had done, the doors he opened to millions of fans. He's made himself into a judge on talent shows like *The Voice* and Ireland's *The Big Time* – although the irony here, perhaps, as he'd no doubt admit himself, is that someone as individual and characterful as Boy George would barely make it into the first round of some of these programmes.

George spoke of sexuality and promoted a fearless self-expression at a time when society wasn't ready for it. His influence can be seen in RuPaul's endless *Drag Races*, where several thousand drag queens can now express themselves freely, thanks to a lineage of dressing up that George not only became a massive part of, but also pushed into the mainstream. Respect is due to him for having had the balls to lead the way and show how it's done. He took the knocks. He took the bullshit. And, to paraphrase George in his own words, he took it like a man.

NEWCASTLE PATIENT DIES OF AIDS
Blood plasma from Britain and the United States was used
to treat Mr Terence McStay, aged 33, who suffered from
haemophilia but was not a homosexual.
– The Times, 19 November 1984

SYLVESTER

'I think we could all live together.'

Being Sylvester in 1984 must have been a strange experience. Only a few years earlier, he'd been the figurehead of gay disco, the architect of mirrorball androgyny and the undisputed queen of the scene – the empress of San Francisco[1]. And yet now he found himself at odds with

---

[1] San Francisco in 1984 was not the city it had been. What had originally been regarded as a gay utopia in the '70s, with gay men flocking to live there, had become a shadow of itself due to AIDS. Dr Mervyn Silverman, the city's public health director, had ordered the closure of fourteen bathhouses and sex clubs due to AIDS. The establishments were chosen as they had 'been inspected on a number of occasions and demonstrate a blatant disregard for the health of their patrons and of the community'. This move came after the health department released figures showing an increase in reported AIDS

the world he had created. The year began with his now-legendary One Night Only concert at the Castro Theatre, which celebrated ten years of his career. The charts were full of the music that he'd championed and the biggest pop star on the planet was another man in a dress. Yet it was bittersweet. He was surrounded by copycats, the city that had made him was in decline, and death was stalking his community.

However, the Queen of Clubs label was a bit of a misnomer. 'I work in them [clubs] and don't enjoy the endless noise,' Sylvester told *Gay Times*. He was more likely to be found in church singing in the choir with his backing singers Two Tons O'Fun (aka the Weather Girls[2]). Being gay and going to church wasn't a contradiction for him. 'In my church, people are allowed to be what they are. My faith

---

cases in San Francisco, where officials estimate that 15 per cent of its population of 700,000 was homosexual. The city's AIDS crisis was also being reflected in Armistead Maupin's *Tales of the City* novels, the latest instalment of which addressed the epidemic. 'I realised I had no choice but to let AIDS be part of the narrative,' Maupin told *POZ* magazine. 'Jon Fielding was the first AIDS fatality in fiction anywhere. That was in '83. A couple of novels came out the next year, but this was the first time that anybody talked about the epidemic.'

[2] The Weather Girls – aka Martha Wash and Izora Armstead – had seen their single 'It's Raining Men', originally released in 1982, belatedly become a hit in the UK in March 1984. It reached number two, held off the top spot by Lionel Richie's 'Hello', and its slightly creepy, pottery-themed video where Lionel seemed to stalk a blind student.

teaches me to respect all human beings and I am respected in return for that.'

Growing up in Los Angeles with his mother and siblings, Sylvester was aware of his sexuality from a young age, but a dysfunctional relationship with his mother and stepfather reached its limits when they were unable to accept his sexuality. As a result, he moved in with his more tolerant grandmother at the age of fifteen, whose wardrobe he would regularly raid. He soon fell in with a bunch of like-minded black teenage drag queens and formed the Disquotays. They would flout California's law against public cross-dressing by wandering the streets of south-central Los Angeles in full drag and throwing wild parties. Sylvester later claimed the Disquotays had joined in the 1965 Watts riots, looting shops for 'wigs, hairspray and lipstick . . . just the fun stuff'.

After being wooed to move to San Francisco by a fellow drag queen, Sylvester joined the Cockettes, a hippy-adjacent, drug-hoovering drag troupe. He was soon outshining and outperforming his fellow band members; they could neither match his ladylike conduct nor his vocal range. He was also singled out in reviews, with *Rolling Stone* describing him as a 'beautiful black androgyne'. While the Cockettes gave him the opportunity to showcase his formative jazz, blues and gospel influences, according to Joshua Gamson, the author of *The Fabulous Sylvester*, Sylvester wasn't a perfect fit. 'He usually stood a few feet back. He was *among* the Cockettes but never quite one *of* them.'

The group travelled to New York where, unsurprisingly, they were the toast of the Warhol set, but Sylvester began to distance himself from the other members. The band didn't survive and after the Cockettes dissolved, Sylvester moved back to San Francisco, where, encouraged by *Rolling Stone* editor Jann Wenner,[3] he recorded an album. Although it wasn't released at the time – it was thought to be unsellable – Sylvester was backed by a bunch of heterosexuals called the Hot Band and covered songs by the likes of Neil Young. Sylvester & the Hot Band found themselves opening for David Bowie during his first tour, at Winterland in 1972. Bowie-mania had yet to arrive in the US, and the show was by no means a sell-out. But Bowie was hip to what was happening, 'They don't need me,' Bowie remarked to a reporter. 'They've got Sylvester.'

---

[3] Jann Wenner co-founded *Rolling Stone* in San Francisco in 1967. Initially, the magazine was a countercultural haven and helped to popularise writers such as Hunter S Thompson, Greil Marcus and Tom Wolfe. Wenner also discovered photographer Annie Leibovitz, as well as co-founding the Rock and Roll Hall of Fame in 1983. Two years later, Wenner separated from his wife of twenty-eight years and, since then, he's been in a relationship with fashion designer Matt Nye. Wenner came a cropper in September 2023 when, in the introduction to his book *The Masters: Conversations with Dylan, Lennon, Jagger, Townshend, Garcia, Bono, and Springsteen,* he claimed black and female artists were 'not in his zeitgeist', and that no female artists 'were as articulate enough on this intellectual level'. The Rock and Roll Hall of Fame binned him almost instantly.

Sylvester then hooked up with a new manager who, as well as encouraging him to tone down the drag (in order to secure a record contract), also set up auditions to find his client some backing singers. Enter Martha Wash. She stole the auditions and soon introduced Sylvester to her chum Izora Rhodes. Forging a unique connection, he dubbed them Two Tons O'Fun. Before long, the trio were regularly performing at nightclubs. He attracted the attention of Nancy Pitts, the wife of Motown producer Harvey Fuqua; Fuqua subsequently offered Sylvester a solo recording contract with Fantasy Records in 1977 ahead of his third album. The eponymous *Sylvester* featured 'Over and Over', which was enough of a hit to upgrade him to bigger stages. Sylvester befriended Harvey Milk – the first openly gay man to be elected to public office in California – performing at his birthday, he also made a cameo in the Bette Midler-starrer *The Rose*.

Sylvester was ready to step up, and he did so on his next album, 1978's not-inappropriately titled *Step II*. It featured a song that would catapult him into the stratosphere. Sylvester's guitarist and co-writer, James Wirrick, had come up with a chord sequence for a ballad that intrigued Sylvester, who then decided it would work better as a disco track. He had yet to pivot to disco, but could sense which way the wind was blowing culturally. And the introduction of Sylvester's producer mate, Patrick Cowley, would push things even further. For a record that Wirrick claimed they were 'just trying to get on to the radio', it would go on to do somewhat more than that, becoming a hugely influential blueprint of dance music. That song was 'You Make Me Feel (Mighty Real)'.

Cowley, who was no stranger to the seamier side of gay nightlife, knew what he was doing. The strange and important sound of the synthesiser had already made inroads with Donna Summer's 'I Feel Love', but the disco scene of that time was still very much rooted in funk and soul. Synthesisers were seen as 'other' – aka European and queer – compared to the inherent masculinity and straightness of the guitar. While 'I Feel Love' invented the future, '(You Make Me Feel) Mighty Real' helped to embed its almost otherworldly sequenced throb into pop's landscape. Sylvester made up the words on the spot; he was just discussing his life of clubbing, cruising and sex. This in itself was seen as a radical move – someone singing their existence, rather than deciding that they had to *make* something gay. As Joshua Gamson rhetorically asked in the *Guardian*, 'What is it in that song that is making him feel real, like the most fully me; the most you can possibly be? I don't know exactly what sex act it is, but it's some sexual experience that is transformative.'

You could argue that this might also relate as being one of the first and most high-profile occasions of 'realness', as in 'serving realness', in the wider cultural sphere. However, Sylvester had no need to 'serve' realness as he was literally being himself. What you would see onstage was what you'd get in real life. Here was Sylvester, a gay man singing about how he feels when having sex with men. In 1978, that was quite a moment.

The song proved to be the launchpad for him and was embraced by clubbers of all persuasion. The straights recognised an absolute fucking banger, while the gays saw their existence acknowledged in a global smash. Sylvester had well and truly arrived. After further success in the disco and mainstream charts, by 1984 Sylvester was a name that was being regularly cited by others as an inspiration, even if his records weren't reaching the heights they once did. Part of this could be put down to the death, in 1982, of Cowley, with whom Sylvester had created the bulk of his iconic output. It could also be a symptom of the sound he helped to birth now being everywhere, and of his keenness to move on. 'Sometimes, folks make us feel strange,' he told a New York audience in November 1978, 'but we're not strange. And those folks – they'll just have to *catch up.*' But by 1984, those folks *had* caught up.

When promoting his 1984 album *M-1015* and the single 'Rock the Box' (where he wanted to hear the music bopping across Britain 'from Liverpool to Wales', with his 'unique' grasp of geography not realising this is a distance of a full twenty-three miles by road), he was asked by *Gay Times* what he thought of high energy. 'What is the fuss all about? All my disco records are high energy. That's what dancing is all about. The respect people have for me as a performer is because they simply enjoy the music and not because they are following some craze. I'm not out to shock anyone. The bottom line of talent is that you can stand there and perform, and perform well. I always sing live, and what I look like comes secondary. People are often amazed and say I sound just like my records. Why should they be? It's me!'

Sylvester also offered his opinions on the phenomenon of Boy George. 'When I first was a hit over here, I used to wear sort of dresses because that was the sort of drag I was into at the time. We all wear drag, whether it be dresses or leather or jeans. But people were shocked at the time. When they worked out that I was a man and the gay papers asked me the same stupid questions like "When you are singing are you being homosexual or just sexual?" and I said, "What do you mean? When I'm singing, sex is the furthest thing from my mind." I suppose it was new then and a shock to them.

'Yet, now, the press probably see me as boring and passé . . . I have stood up for my gay rights all my life and never compromised. When I hear the things that Boy George or others say to be outrageous because it's chic now, it bothers me quite a bit because I know what it was like when it wasn't all right to be. I've survived all that.'

By 1986, Sylvester had become an advocate for HIV awareness. He had seen the devastation it wrought on the gay community and had been impacted by the deaths of both Cowley and his partner Rick Cranmer, who died within a year of discovering he had the virus. Sylvester refused to take a test. He just *knew*. And when diagnosed, he refused to take the antiretroviral drug due to the serious side effects it caused. Instead, he decided to dedicate what time he had left to speaking out. In one of his last interviews, during the making of an album he knew he'd never finish, he told the *Los Angeles Times*, that 'it bothers me that AIDS is still thought of as a gay, white male disease. The black community is at the bottom of the line when it comes to getting information, even when we've been so hard hit by this disease. I'd like to think that, by going public myself with this, I can give other people courage to face it.

'I know that, whenever I hear that someone has AIDS, my heart goes out to them. And when anyone I know dies from it, it worries me. I get nervous because I think, "That'll be me someday." But I don't spend a lot of time feeling sorry for myself because of that.'

Sylvester attended the 1987 Gay Freedom Day Parade in San Francisco's infamous Castro area in a wheelchair to huge cheers. And by the end of November 1988, he'd become bed-ridden and was on a diet of drugs to cope with the pain.

'I've been in situations I shouldn't have been in. We all have. But I still think that I'm a good person and I don't regret anything I've done in my life. Down the line, I hope I won't be in a lot more pain. But I don't dwell on that. I'll be fine, because my spirit is fine.'

Shading the comments fellow disco queen Donna Summer had made a few years earlier, he noted that he didn't believe 'that AIDS is the wrath of God. People have a tendency to blame everything on God.' Sylvester died on 16 December 1988 at the age of forty-one. An entertainer until the end, he was buried in a red kimono and full make-up.

In 1984, Sylvester was at a turning point – he was everywhere in the culture, with his talons in the music, the androgyny and the drag that had come along in his wake; he was even being outsold by his backing singers. But he was also at the epicentre of a disease that would play out and define his final years. Sylvester's no-fucks-given approach to life had made him an icon, and his invaluable work speaking out about AIDS only cemented that. While it would be another few years before a far more famous musician would die of the disease and increase awareness, Sylvester's lead would be the one to follow, his impact and legacy forever celebrated by the music he left behind. What an absolute *queen*.

Editorials at the time relied consistently on homophobic biases. An editorial from The Times *in December 1984 fostered prejudiced sentiments, claiming that 'the infection's origins and means of propagation excites repugnance, moral and physical, at promiscuous male homosexuality . . . Many members of the public are tempted to see in AIDS some sort of retribution for a questionable style of life.'*

PRINCE

'I'm not a woman. I'm not a man. I am something that you'll never understand.'

He was the pint-sized purple pop perv who liked to wear women's panties under a flasher mac. He sang about all manner of filth, from masturbation to incest to general bedroom etiquette. He 'wanted to be your lover' and, when he reached the apex of his career in 1984 with *Purple Rain,* that love was reciprocated by millions of new fans. It was the year in which he exploded onto pop's wider stage, where he joined pop's top table, at that point occupied by the biggest star of the era, Michael Jackson.[1]

What differentiated Prince from the other superstars of the era was that while he cut a fine dash as the key brand manager for the colour purple, he was also a grafter, spending almost every waking hour consumed by the creation and playing of music. 'Prolific' barely touches the sides. What some people would consider a power nap, or nodding off in front of the telly between breaks, would be the total of his sleep during a twenty-four-hour period. To look at his achievements across the '80s, and the sheer wealth of ideas and sounds that came out of his head, is to boggle at someone who literally could not stop being amazing.

Prince was a collision of opposites. Rock and soul, punk and funk, black and white, male and female, sex and God.

---

[1] Michael Jackson was at the everyone-has-gone-slightly-mad level of stardom. By April 1984, his sixth solo album *Thriller*, first released at the end of 1982, had spent thirty-seven non-consecutive weeks at number one in the Billboard 200 and was the first album in the chart's history to be the biggest-seller two years running. He'd begun 1984 still fresh from the rapturous reception given to the full-length John Landis-directed video for the album's title track. With the Jacksons, he signed a huge sponsorship deal with Pepsi worth $5 million (approximately $14 million in 2024), the biggest of its kind (although, when filming a Pepsi TV commercial in January 1984, the pyrotechnics went awry and set Jackson's hair on fire, causing second-degree burns to his scalp). Throughout the year, and fuelled by his ongoing retreat into being a hugely successful yet reclusive superstar, Michael would be dogged by questions and rumours about his plastic surgery, his pet chimp Bubbles and his sexuality. And his life would only get weirder from there on in.

That collision came to fruition with the use of purple as his then signature colour. 'All is fair in love and war,' he told *The Face* around the time of the release of his fifth album, *1999*. 'Royal purple, red and blue, the colour of yin and yang when they become one … The war of Armageddon is coming whether we're prepared for it or not, and in [album track] "Free", I talk a little more about the freedom of choice between good and evil. No government gave you that, God did. But governments don't want you to remember that – which is why they put conscientious objectors in jail. But in the war that's coming, there'll be no way to abstain. Whatever you do, you'll have to be behind one flag or another. My flag is freedom, purple, unconditional love.'

Prince Rogers Nelson had a bit of an upbringing. He was born in Minneapolis on 7 June 1958, the son of jazz singer Mattie Della and pianist/songwriter John Lewis Nelson, and was named after his father's stage name from the time he performed as the Prince Rogers Trio – reportedly because he wanted Prince to do everything he wanted to do. Prince actually loathed the name, choosing instead to call himself Skipper, which was widely used during his childhood. He was an epileptic child, suffering from many seizures, and after an apparent encounter with an angel (obviously), he informed his mother that he'd no longer be sick. He wrote his first song, 'Funk Machine', on his dad's piano when he was seven years old.

In 1975, Prince and his neighbour Andre Anderson, aka André Cymone, joined 94 East, a band formed by

Pepe Willie (the husband of Prince's cousin Shauntel) and who were fronted by future 'Trapped' hitmaker Colonel Abrams. Prince wrote 'Just Another Sucker' and played guitar. By 1976, he was focusing on his own music and made a demo tape in a local studio. This piqued the interest of entrepreneur Owen Husney, who signed the nineteen-year-old Prince to a management contract. Husney hawked the demo around several labels and, while Columbia and A&M all took an interest, it was Warner Brothers that won his signature, offering him a three-album deal and creative control. His 1978 debut, *For You*, featured him playing all twenty-seven instruments and, at one point, forty-six vocal overdubs. The album had just a single co-write. Its recording cost nearly three times the advance he was given, and apparently – and understandably – was a knackering process. As well as performing decently on the R&B charts, it gave Prince his Billboard debut, peaking at number 163 on the Billboard 200, while the single 'Soft and Wet' breached the Hot 100.

The wider world was alerted to Prince by the 1980 release of his third album, the slightly rougher and somewhat saucier *Dirty Mind*. It was that transition to a raunchier, rockier sound – complete with more shocking lyrics delivered by a man who'd taken to wearing women's underwear – that forced people to sit up and take notice.

Prince and his outfit made their European debut in June 1981, having just finished supporting Kool & the Gang in the

US. (The mind boggles at what an audience awaiting cheery knees-ups such as 'Celebration' made of fruity old Prince.) He was about to embark on some dates on the latest Rolling Stones tour, when he and his band arrived in London to play their first UK concert at the Lyceum Theatre. 'Prince sings exclusively in a falsetto voice, which he pushes at times to an eerie caterwauling intensity,' noted the *New York Times* review of the London show. 'This style is ideally suited to the theatrical lasciviousness that is central to Prince's act. On stage, Prince displays an unbridled street eroticism. Wearing black bikini briefs, fringed high-heel boots and black thigh-high stockings, he is sexual license incarnate. But Prince is such a charismatic performer that his stylised salaciousness doesn't offend. With his sassy grace and precocious musicality, he is heir to the defiant rock and roll traditions of Elvis Presley, Jimi Hendrix and Mick Jagger.'

Dealing in the currency of shock, Prince's trajectory continued with 1981's *Controversy*, the title track of which twinned a recital of *The Lord's Prayer* with lines such as 'Am I black or white? Am I straight or gay?' that lashed out at his critics. This was followed by 1982's *1999*, an album that foreshadowed the extended Prince universe by featuring the newly-minted Revolution, a band who'd been sidelined until now.

The line-up of the Revolution fully confirmed Wendy Melvoin on guitar and vocals, Brown Mark on bass guitar and vocals, Lisa Coleman on keyboards, piano and vocals, Matt 'Doctor' Fink on keyboards and vocals, and Bobby Z on drums. The multi-racial, multi-sexual and multi-*everything* group – a nod to Sly and the Family Stone's similar set-up – were drilled to perfection by Prince. Not that they weren't too shabby in the first place. But Prince demanded loyalty and he got it. If you're on a date and you ask: 'Who was the best backing band of all time?' and the reply isn't 'the Revolution', settle the bill and leave that instant.

After *1999*, Prince's contract with Warners was up for renewal, and he'd told his manager Robert Cavallo that he would not re-sign unless he was allowed to appear in his own film. The idea of a musician-led film wasn't a prospect anyone in the industry seemed keen on, and while Prince had indeed accumulated a degree of success by this point, every studio that he and Robert Cavallo met with passed on it. So Cavallo decided to produce it himself. He commissioned screenwriter William Blinn, who'd worked on the movie of *Fame*, who created a script called *Dreams* that was far darker than Prince had in mind. After a further song and dance to source a director, Cavallo secured the services of film editor Albert Magnoli, who rejected the *Dreams* script and set about creating something truer to Prince's vision, one that focused on the music – although that vision wasn't helped by the allegation that Warners initially rejected Prince as the film's lead, suggesting that John Travolta would be better.

Once Magnoli was on board, and with the new title *Purple Rain*, Prince arranged for the musicians to attend acting classes. The search for a female lead was on, too. When original choice Vanity, from Prince's female project Vanity 6, left the group ahead of filming, she was replaced by actress Patricia Kotero, one of the twelve models featured on that year's Ridgid Tool Company's wall calendar. Patricia was soon rechristened Apollonia and, despite out-auditioning several hundred other actresses, got the gig primarily because she wouldn't dwarf the 5-foot 2-inch lead.

As MTV's influence grew, the station was called out for not featuring enough black acts by none other than David Bowie. In a 1983 interview with VJ Mark Goodman, Bowie noted that, 'having watched MTV over the past few months, it's a solid enterprise with a lot going for it. I'm just floored by the fact that there's so few black artists featured on it. Why is that?'

And he was right. Michael Jackson may have broken through into daytime MTV with 'Billie Jean' and 'Beat It', but many black acts were reduced to having their videos shown between midnight and 6am – the graveyard slot. Goodman didn't exactly cover himself in glory with his reply, telling Bowie, 'We have to try and do what we think not only New York and Los Angeles will appreciate, but also Poughkeepsie or the Midwest. Pick some town in the Midwest that would be scared to death by Prince, which we're playing, or a string of other black faces. We have to play the type of music the entire country would like.' The idea of parts of the US being scared to death by Prince seemed a little absurd.

While editing the film, Magnoli decided to pull together a montage that would encapsulate all of the trials of Prince's 'character', The Kid. He suggested that the film needed one more song. 'I told Prince it was about his father, his mother, loss, redemption, salvation — all the themes we're dealing with in the film,' Magnoli explained in Alan Light's book *Let's Go Crazy: Prince and the Making of Purple Rain*. Wendy Melvoin's twin sister Susannah also recalled to Light that when the song was unveiled, 'everybody knew this was gonna be history'.

That last-minute track, 'When Doves Cry', was a bassless, sensual clunk of beat and primal moans. It was the first single from the soundtrack and saw Prince smash into the top five in the UK. It was also his first number one in his homeland, ruling the spot for five weeks. The last song recorded for *Purple Rain*, it was the fastest-selling single in Warner Brothers' history and propelled advance orders for *Purple Rain*'s soundtrack to more than a million.

While the film itself was no masterpiece, it did act as a showcase for Prince and his world. If you take away the quality of acting, the thin plot and the questionable portrayal of women, the series of electric musical performances are more than enough. Few movies manage to capture the excitement and magic of a live show, but *Purple Rain* did. It also made the nightclub where the performances took place, First Avenue in Minneapolis, as much of a star as Prince was.

Throughout the second half of 1984, Prince's stock rose to such a level that he could no longer be ignored. *Purple Rain*'s box-office takings were more than $70 million (the equivalent of $209 million in 2024), the accompanying album had shifted more than 25 million copies and, in January 1985, *Purple Rain* clocked up a whopping twenty-four consecutive weeks at the top of the Billboard 200. Along with Jacko, the US now had two reclusive black artists who'd managed to transcend the boundaries between race and genre and had the receipts to prove it[2].

While Prince was adamant that he liked rumpo, he was careful to position himself as an equal-opportunity, almost genderless being. The very words of 'I Would Die 4 U' ('I'm not a woman. I'm not a man. I am something that you will never understand') expressed a level of mystique at a point when he'd given up on interviews to let the music speak for itself. 'The important thing is to be true to yourself, but I also like the danger. That's what's missing from pop music today. There's no excitement or mystery.'

Prince's impact on not just music, but also sexual liberation, resonated with anyone feeling remotely other. To Frank Ocean, Prince was 'a straight black man who played his first televised set in bikini bottoms and knee-high

---

[2] There were only five number-one albums on the Billboard 200 in the whole of 1984: *Thriller* (fifteen weeks), the *Footloose* soundtrack (ten weeks), Huey Lewis & the News' *Sports* (one week), Bruce Springsteen's *Born in the USA* (four weeks) and Purple Rain (the rest).

heeled boots, epic . . . He made me feel more comfortable with how I identify sexually simply by his display of
freedom from and irreverence for obviously archaic ideas
like gender conformity.' The *Slate* writer Christina Cauterucci noted that 'like his gender-bending predecessor David
Bowie, Prince was flamboyant in both his masculinity and
femininity. He wielded his outrageous guitars like exten-
sions of his manhood while vamping under winged eyeliner
and plentiful jewels. He even bragged that his traditionally feminine features lent him a special sexual power.' To
Cauterucci, 'Prince didn't just disregard the boundaries of
gender and sexuality: he kicked straight through them in
platform heels, gyrating his very visible bulge in naysayers'
faces for good measure.'

A keen fan of God, Prince's own religion offered a far
more nuanced take on what he read in the Bible. After
becoming a Jehovah's Witness, he often toned down the
performances of his earlier work, seeming to be making
a statement about repenting on his past life. He was furious when he was misquoted for suggesting he was against
gay marriage and abortion. Speaking to the *New Yorker* in
2008, he appeared to be reinforcing that purple outlook:
'Here's how it is: you've got the Republicans, and basically
they want to live according to *this*.' He pointed to a copy of
the Bible. 'But there's the problem of interpretation, and
you've got some churches, some people, basically doing
things and saying it comes from here, but it doesn't. And
then on the opposite end of the spectrum, you've got blue,

you've got the Democrats, and they're like "You can do whatever you want. Gay marriage, whatever." But neither of them is right.'

The signs were there back in 1982. 'You can look at it two ways. Either other aspects of the wrong way people are using their environment is making people sick, or these diseases are just what they call them – the Wrath of God. All I say is that you shouldn't repress your sexual feelings just because somebody official told you to. In many places in the world today, you're not supposed to fuck, just like you're not supposed to think. Part of thinking for yourself is avoiding people who are going to give you diseases – mental or physical.'

In 2014, he told Arsenio Hall that 'when you're twenty years old, you're looking for the ledge . . . You want to see how far you can push everything . . . and then you make changes. There's a lot of things I don't do now that I did thirty years ago. And then there's some things I still do.'

Whatever Prince was, whatever he believed and whatever he thought, he enabled a generation or two to question and express themselves. Maybe the gentle insistence of not pushing any particular viewpoint or agenda made him far smarter than any other musician of the era. He simply allowed his fans to take what they wanted from him, making straight people hornier and alerting LGBTQ+ people to a whole spectrum of experimentation and inclusivity. He turned everything upside down. And that's what you kinda want from a genius, is it not?

In December 1984, Channel 4 broadcasts Bright Eyes *by video artist Stuart Marshall. The documentary places the AIDS crisis into a historical context, aligning it with the long-term persecution of homosexuals, as well as looking at what activist groups have been trying to do in order to combat prejudice.*

DEAD OR ALIVE

'Watch out, here I come.'

It's easy to look back and reflect that Pete Burns will forever be famous for being Pete Burns, but by 1984, it seemed like he'd been waiting an eternity to take his rightful position as a pop star. He was also slightly terrifying – the bad witch at the dress-up party and almost the antithesis of Boy George, the 'mardy sex threat' compared to George's increasing Mills & Boon inoffensiveness. Yet the real Pete Burns was a bullshit-free, speak-his-mind character who had a slightly wonky upbringing. His mum was German-born and had moved to Vienna to escape the Nazis as her father was Jewish, before meeting an English soldier named Francis Burns, marrying him and moving to

Liverpool. Young Pete was an occasionally shy lad and rarely attended school – and when he did, he'd be asked to leave because he'd done something outré with his hair. He'd stay at home with his mum, and so created a world with her, although by this point, she was an alcoholic who had attempted to commit suicide on numerous occasions. And yet, despite all this, he idolised her.

Pete's first job after leaving school was as a hairdresser. It wasn't a major career move, but it was where he met his future wife, Lynne. Pete was then employed in legendary Liverpool record shop Probe, where he was known to tell customers to fuck off if he didn't like what they were buying. He also sold fashion out the back. He made his stage debut in 1977 as a member of the unlistenable, one-off punk outfit, the Mystery Girls, the fellow members of which included Julian Cope and Pete Wylie. He then formed Nightmares in Wax in 1979 before changing their name to Dead or Alive the following year. Pete was never comfortable with his voice and didn't regard himself as a particularly confident singer. It would be his way with a provocative image and bitchy one-liners that helped propel him into showbiz.

'I almost looked on sex as a journey,' Pete said in his autobiography *Freak Unique*. 'I had something to give and I hadn't found the person to give it to. I lost my virginity to Lynne. That was truly the first fully rounded sexual experience I'd ever had, and that was a very, very frightening prospect . . . It was just a new sensation, a tickly, woozy messy sensation and it happened and it continued to happen. I couldn't believe that this bit down below was doing something that wasn't hurting my bum. It was very vanilla!

'I did sleep with men, but I didn't have sexual relationships with them. I seemed to be drawn largely to impotent men, but I never thought for one minute that it was me causing that impotence . . . I'm sure people have this impression through seeing my performances and the energy I give off that I'm some kind of tacky old queen who gives blow-jobs to taxi drivers for a free ride home. Well, it ain't like that. I conduct myself with a lot of self-respect and dignity.'

Not one to easily pin down sexuality-wise, Pete told *Record Mirror* that 'Gay to me conjures up a moustache, a check shirt and doing twirls to Gloria Gaynor records – and if that's what gay is, then, no. I'm not side-stepping any questions – I go with both. Well, at the moment I go with one of each.'

By 1984, Dead or Alive had been through numerous line-up changes and ascended from independent notoriety onto a major label, with Epic signing them in 1982. 'Epic came to see me at Heaven,' Pete recalled. 'There was nothing I wanted, but they came up with something like a ten-album deal. We wanted a long-term deal, for more than a handful of singles and a launch album. We wanted time to develop and grow, and even then it wasn't easy to find a record company who would let you.

'So, we signed with Epic in the summer of 1982. But then the goalposts moved . . . They wanted Culture Club.

I wanted Bobby Orlando, who'd done Divine's "Native Love". They wanted a ballad. I wanted "Native Love".'

As much as Dead or Alive looked like they were Pete and . . . some others, the hitmaking line-up consisted of bassist Mike Percy, drummer/guitarist Steve Coy and keyboardist Tim Lever. Future Mission frontman Wayne Hussey was the original guitarist, but he'd gone off to be a full-time goth as Dead or Alive pivoted towards wanting to sell some records.

The band had initially worked with Martin Rushent's engineer Tim Palmer and, within twenty-four hours, they'd recorded what they thought was their major label debut, 'Misty Circles'. Epic weren't impressed and demanded it be re-recorded. After hoping to use Sylvester's backing singers Two Tons O'Fun, Epic suggested producer Zeus B Held. Pete's heritage was a help. 'Zeus and I spoke a lot in German and he got it.'

This was just what was needed to get the band to a broader audience, even if at first the broader audience didn't appear to be fulfilling their half of the contract. 'Misty Circles' is all treble-y, metallic clattering and slap bass, with Pete basically yelling over it. Actually, his vocal style could best be described as a throaty, domineering yell – the sort of bellow that you really didn't want to be on the receiving end of. 'Misty Circles' was a US dance success and saw the band make their debut in the UK Top 100 at, well, number 100. It found them on the kids TV show *Razzmatazz*, with Pete's look of Westwood and dreadlocks placing him firmly in the bitchy crosshairs of Boy George, who presumably viewed him as a threat barging into his spotlight.

The follow-up, 'What I Want', continued in the same breathless, high energy vein of 'Misty Circles', even throwing in several nods to New Order's 'Blue Monday'. While it fared better in the chart – look, some people would give a limb to get to number eighty-eight and then eighty-seven a year later on re-release – it looked like the band's chart career was more dead than alive.

By the time of their third single on a major – at which point Epic must have been tapping their watch wondering what on earth they'd been throwing money at – 'I'd Do Anything' was both a rallying cry and a plea for success, serving up the Pete Burns persona in four minutes.

When an act does a cover version, it's usually seen as the last roll of the dice. It carries the faint whiff of desperation, with record executives demanding success and payback. It was now deemed essential, with Dead or Alive's singles having mostly been chart-allergic affairs; indeed, 'I'd Do Anything' managed a what-was-even-the-point peak of number seventy-nine. But the band finally found themselves cracking the Top 40 – and *Top of the Pops* – in March 1984 with their cover of KC & the Sunshine Band's 'That's the Way (I Like it)' from their debut album *Sophisticated Boom Boom*.

'That's the Way . . .' wasn't a full-on cash-grab cover; the band had previously used the chorus from their song

'Black Leather' from when they were called Nightmares in Wax. Almost instantly, that 'overnight' success was finally theirs. Number twenty-two may not have been all that in the greater scheme of things, but at least Pete had a bona fide hit to back up the press and attention bestowed upon him and his band – even if the reissued 'What I Want', peaking at number eighty-seven, brought them straight back to earth. Despite having a great camaraderie with producer Zeus B Held, the sound that Pete was after was still eluding him. But that was about to change.

'Lynne and I had a radio alarm clock next to our bed, and it was always on,' Pete reflected in *Freak Unique*. 'It was on that that I heard two songs that spoke to me. The first came from Hazell Dean. "Wherever I Go (Whatever I Do)" [*sic*] had the polish and the production value I craved. I sat on the bed, motionless, trying to piece together how it was done. Then I heard Divine's new single, "You Think You're a Man". Again, I pretty much froze in the bedroom. It didn't sound as good as "Native Love", but it was still fabulous, still the kind of music I wanted to make.'

To Pete's surprise, he discovered that Bobby Orlando hadn't had a hand in the Divine single. It was actually some blokes based in London. After tracking down Mike Stock, Matt Aitken and Pete Waterman, the two Petes met, and the plan to make a single was hatched. Epic, though, weren't having it. They wouldn't allow the funds to be released for Dead or Alive to work with these essentially up-and-coming producers. In fact, Epic's A&R man, Muff

Winwood, didn't believe that long-time music industry maverick Pete Waterman was a producer. Pete took out a bank loan for £2,500 to record this song that he felt would change everything for his band. That song was called 'You Spin Me Round (Like a Record)'.

'Pete Waterman said we'd got a number one, so we got going.'

Recalling this time, Pete said, 'We were still hungry. We were still fighting. We had no real money, no proper budget. You want a sandwich for lunch? Fuck off – we still can't afford it. But what we did have was a new desire to take it all on again, the studio equipment and the song.' Much has been made of the gladiatorial aspect of the recording process, with some exaggeration about tensions between Dead or Alive and Stock Aitken Waterman (SAW), and reports of any near-violence have long gone into the making of the song's folklore. In fact, the thought of fisticuffs – imagined or otherwise – adds to the *drama* of the thing.

'We made the record "You Spin Me Round" in September 1984,' recalled Matt Aitken. 'By the time CBS got around to releasing the single, we had moved out of the Marquee Studios and into our own facility. We had no idea it was going to be our first number one. I didn't really stop to smell the roses. We were already on to other artists and projects when it hit the top. Working with Pete Burns and Dead or Alive was a little tense at times. But looking back I selectively remember only the good bits.'

'You Spin Me Round' was inspired by Luther Vandross' 'I Wanted Your Love'and Little Nell's 'See You 'Round Like a Record', Pete said. 'It's not the same chord structure, but then that's the way I make music. I hear something and I sing another tune over it.'

Imagine listening back to 'You Spin Me Round' and saying it was awful. IMAGINE. But that was Epic's first reaction. They were still throwing suggestions of other producers at Dead or Alive, as well as threatening not to proceed with a second album if it wasn't a hit. And, well, it looked like Epic were right after all. On its release on 5 November 1984, 'You Spin Me Round (Like a Record)' took its sweet time to get to the top, entering the chart at number seventy-nine. It wasn't until the following February that it would hit the Top 40.

The manipulations made to get the record into the charts would have ended lesser groups. The rise of club records and underground dance tracks into the singles chart had much to do with how the sales figures were collated and where the shops were. If a specialist dance shop was selling 500 copies of a record without being required to submit sales figures to the chart compilers, it was the ten copies sold in a chart-return shop that mattered more. Much like the situation with high energy sales, Martin Wedge recalled how the single was another example of chart irregularities.

'Dead or Alive was probably the biggest example of a north/south divide. It was selling lots and lots, but hardly any sales in the south. It was also a big seller in Scotland. CBS even issued an extra 12-inch mix – I think called the 'Murder Mix'. Again, it was a big 12-inch seller, but the single was a very slow mover. The chart position outside the Top 40 didn't reflect the sales at all. We used to call up Gallup and ask them why it wasn't higher. They used to have a chart coordinator called Chris Naylor-Smith who would come and check sales between the data port and the invoices in the shop against stock levels. CBS were concerned they were going to lose the track, so they deleted it when it was between forty and fifty for two weeks. This built up more demand and, when it was reactivated, the extra momentum pushed it into the Top 40 and then it went from there. CBS then started doing the same with other singles, so "The Power of Love" by Jennifer Rush received the same thing and that charted Top 40, too. These singles had taken a long time to get to the Top 40, often months on end.'

It looked like 'You Spin Me Round' was doing a random grand tour of any position that wasn't in the Top 40. And then, in February 1985, it reached number forty itself. From there, it felt like the gates to stardom were unlocked, leaping to nineteen, then five, then two and then, as February turned into March, number one. Not only had Dead or Alive reached the top, they'd also given SAW their first chart-topper into the bargain.

'You Spin Me Round' was the sound of bombardment, a demonic charge like a battering ram of clattering bigness,

mowing down anything in its path. Lean and bereft of sub-
tlety, it was spiky, demanding and like a box of fireworks.
The colossal rush of the 12-inch 'Murder Mix' was like being
caught in the crossfire of amyl combustion. To dance to it
was to prepare to fight your nemesis, and its gravitational
pull drew in everyone within a mile's radius. It was SAW's
first masterpiece, a calling card that laid down the foundation for the remainder of the decade, and the track that had
Bananarama hammering on the production team's door to
do similar on their version of 'Venus' a couple of years later.

Then the palaver stepped up a gear. And the hostility. 'I'd been invisible up 'til then,' said Pete Burns, 'and
accepted like a mythical creature – a unicorn – that you'd
see from time to time in town. But then I was number
one and people were really angry, especially the people I'd
moved among, the musicians. It was like I'd done a shit in
the Vatican.'

He was finally the pop star that he should have been
all along. And, yet, it was already starting to sour, despite
the global fame that accompanied 'You Spin Me Round'.
Pete wasn't enjoying the constant demands and lifestyle
required to keep things afloat. He was also very keen not
to be chewed up by the demands of being a pop star.
'I don't want to be on the back of a Cornflakes packet,' he
told *Smash Hits*. 'It might happen, but if it does you'll know
I've tried really, really hard to avoid it.'

Ferried around the States in cattle class, and answer-
ing the same questions every half hour, was taking its

toll. Having rush-recorded the album *Youthquake*, which he condemned as 'shit' (although he liked its remixes), the pressure was on for further chart action. But it was starting to dry up, as much to Pete's frustration as anybody else's.

SAW also worked with the band on 1986's *Mad, Bad and Dangerous to Know* album, but the cracks were opening wider, with Pete refusing to let the producers write all the songs. There'd been a plan to record another SAW song, 'Respectable', which eventually went to Mel & Kim, and an invitation to be on Madonna's Who's That Girl tour, which was upended when Pete found himself struggling with his mum's cancer diagnosis. This caused a tailspin and propelled him into seeking every and any cure to prolong her life, spending much of his fortune trying to help.

Pete was aware of the downsides of pop life. 'I think we're in the never-never land of being lumped in with Culture Club,' he had explained to *Melody Maker* in 1984. 'We're in the middle, I suppose, somewhere. Now everybody's gonna jump on anything that's slightly subversive. Everybody wants their token homo band now, I think.

'One thing Frankie has proved that if people think you're slightly subversive, then the airwaves and the powers that be can't stop the public wanting it, if they wanna follow it up. 'Cos if the BBC had their way, it wouldn't have been anywhere, would it?

'Mind you, Frankie were bloody lucky. But I love that record and I'm personal friends with some of the group.

I'd much rather see them at number one than some of the shit that gets there.'

Dead or Alive knew their place, and they also knew what they were capable of. That much was clear. Pete Burns was the star, the focus, the gobby cheerleader. They stood in the wings watching their more celebrated local rivals – everyone from Echo & the Bunnymen, the Teardrop Explodes, Wah! and now Frankie – becoming cover stars and scoring Top Ten hits while they unsuccessfully plied their furrow. More broadly, Burns was often lumped in with Boy George, albeit something that played to his advantage. He also knew how to give good headlines, even if his singles were struggling to get to the same level sales-wise as those of Culture Club or even Marilyn.

Despite the frenemy status with Boy George ('I read people saying that "Karma Chameleon" was a brilliant record, and I think that anybody who says that needs their head reading'), Pete appreciated that the public's acceptance of Boy George had helped him. 'God, it's made it a lot easier for me to walk down the street. I'm delighted – it used to be so heavy. I just think I'm lucky. I could've been badly scarred by now.' He said similar to *Smash Hits*. 'Since the coming of Boy George, there's been not that much aggression to someone of my appearance, actually.'

Pete found an unlikely ally in Morrissey. The pair were friends and were interviewed together in *Smash Hits* in October 1985. Quite what a gobby northerner full of disdain for his fellow pop acts had in common with a gobby northerner full of disdain for his fellow pop acts became apparent: they were two pop outsiders who had each other's back. 'Peter is so detached from the pantomime element of the whole industry and the whole party ethic,' said Morrissey, 'and so are the Smiths . . .' Pete repaid the compliment. 'And I'm a Smiths fan, embarrassingly enough. I'm not supposed to admit that, but it's always exciting when they're on *Top of the Pops*.'

Pete Burns knew the ludicrousness and transient temporary nature of it all, as he revealed to *Melody Maker*. 'Everything regresses quickly enough . . . There's a set amount of things in human nature. I don't think that dressing up as a gender bender or a trannie is going to change anything. There are too many other things to concentrate on. But take Ziggy Stardust. That was a real breakthrough. You used to hear dockers saying "Ah, I'd give Bowie one." That was great. But it'll never happen again.

'When people do perceive me as a tranny or a woman, they're picking up on the identity I created that was part of my character as a performer, which is very different from the person that's underneath. So I am being perceived as a character that I didn't create – they have imprinted that on to me – and if someone creates a role for you, it's very difficult to change that perception.'

Over the ensuing decades, as Dead or Alive became effectively just Pete, he was still very much in demand in countries such as Japan, where he'd earn a small fortune for spending a fortnight there just being Pete Burns. By

2006, he'd divorced Lynne and set up home with his partner Michael Simpson. He also took part in *Celebrity Big Brother*, causing a fuss with a coat he claimed was made from gorilla fur (it wasn't) and befriending fellow contestant and political irritant George Galloway. Despite coming fifth on the show, and a re-released 'You Spin Me Round' reaching the top five again, he entered into something of a reality show afterlife, appearing in confections such as *Celebrity Wife Swap*. He was also jailed for breaking bail conditions imposed on him when he was accused of harassing ex-boyfriends Jason Peters and (his now-ex) Michael Simpson. More bizarrely, Pete was tagged and banned from travelling to London, other than to appear in court, meaning that he had no access to his house in Notting Hill Gate.

He had long been into altering his looks with plastic surgery – 'People redecorate their homes every few years and I see this as no different. Changing my face is like buying a new sofa' – and revealed that he'd spent most of his money on correcting cosmetic surgery on his lips which had gone horribly wrong.

The last few months of his life saw a sharp vicissitude of fortune, with Pete looking a bit of a state, bankrupt and appearing on Channel 5's *Celebrity Botched Up Bodies*, talking frankly about his horrific experiences, which had given him near-fatal blood clots and pulmonary embolisms.

He suffered a cardiac arrest and died, at the age of fifty-seven, on 23 October 2016. His funeral was paid for by

Boy George. The two had long become friends, yet still played up their rivalry. 'I loved Pete Burns,' said George, 'even when he disliked me, because he was genius!'

Pete may effectively be atomised into one tune, but *what* a tune. Even with Dead or Alive's substantial discography, the kismet of 1984's high energy boom and a combination of events where inspiration struck and a pop revolution ensued, not only made him a star, but also set in motion the sound of the rest of the decade. With SAW's help, 'You Spin Me Round' was the one song that distilled Pete's essence and deservedly made him the star he knew he was all along.

According to figures by the Terrence Higgins Trust, by the end of 1984, there were 108 AIDS cases and forty-six deaths in the UK. By the end of 1985, every region in the world had at least one reported case of AIDS, with more than 20,000 cases in total.

WHAM! / GEORGE MICHAEL

'To the heart and mind, ignorance is kind.'

The thing about George Michael – apart from a legacy of classic songs and general amazingness – is that he was never publicly 'out' until a certain incident in 1998 in Beverly Hills. That said, all the signs were there to read if you wanted to. Just two years earlier, he'd opened an album with a near-seven-minute song about his dead lover ('Jesus to a Child'), following that to the top spot with one about going out cruising ('Fastlove'). It seems inconceivable in 1998 that he ever felt like he needed to say (or do) anything at that point. That said, after the toilet-trader incident, he seemed somewhat more at ease with himself, and at pains to address any situation where he felt he may have been opaque about his sexuality.

But first, let's begin: it's a tale as old as time itself. Two schoolfriends form a ska band, but the ska band isn't particularly good. And, let's be honest, the brief window where such a thing as being in a ska band would have made sense has long passed. That's the story of how George Michael (born Georgios Kyriacos Panayiotou on 25 June 1963) and Andrew Ridgeley (born the previous January) came to be in the ranks of the Executive along with Ridgeley's brother Paul, Andrew Leaver and David Austin (then Mortimer). By 1981, ska had lost its allure, so George and Andrew set about embracing pop. They fled the Executive and, thankfully, created Wham!.

Wham! were to be more fun. More pop. More accessible. And, fingers crossed, more famous.

Andrew was to be as vital to Wham! as George was. 'His clothes were always perfect,' George said of his bandmate. 'He was really stylish. All the girls liked him. And that was something I always wanted to be, because I was such a mess to look at. The whole idea of being physically attractive never occurred to me until I met him.' It was Andrew who gave George the confidence he lacked, along with the realisation to fulfil his ambitions.

Wham! began playing in gay clubs, where they would perform short sets, effectively dancing to their own yet-to-be hits. While it's now rude for an aspiring pop turn not to build a gay fanbase, back in the early '80s, it was a novel and somewhat brave move. It can be seen as even braver given that they were still unsigned at the time and that this was an era when record campaigns were unlikely to even think about including gay clubs when promoting their artists. George and Andrew played on their camaraderie and homoeroticism. It was totally the right move. Simon Napier-Bell, who'd famously steered Dusty Springfield, Marc Bolan and Japan among others towards fame, came knocking. It was the perfect match. Napier-Bell claimed they were 'without doubt one of the most vital and interesting groups'.

Napier-Bell recalled how George 'never meant to be in Wham! in the first place . . . He wanted to create a group, but he never saw himself in it. He was the Svengali and the songwriter, and Andrew and some other guy would be the band. So, when he couldn't find the second person, he thought, "I'll join the group and act the part for him." It was like a movie, which is why he was right not to come out at the time, because he wasn't George – who was gay – but a copycat Andrew.'

Once the concept of Wham! was nailed as a duo of Andrew and George, Napier-Bell realised that the partnership would be pop dynamite. 'What I saw immediately was this fantastic image, which has been the basis of the film industry throughout the century. That is, two guys, two straight guys, who care more about each other than they do about the girls. During the film, one of them might fall in love or go to a brothel or whatever, but at the end, they ride off into the sunset together. It's the sort of macho homoerotic image that's never been used in pop. I was certain it would be one which everyone would latch on to.' Napier-Bell had also been told by George that he had one year to make Wham! the biggest group in the world, to which he responded with laughter. As he recalled to the *Telegraph*, 'George was wonderfully, youthfully arrogant, which I liked.' He countered and offered George a compromise. '"Why don't I make you the first group to play in communist China? You'll get non-stop publicity." George said, "Yeah, that's good. We'll do that." So that was it.'

There was nothing particularly gay about Wham! at the time. Queer, yes. The butch man-drag outfits in 'Bad Boys'. The white Speedos of 'Club Tropicana'. The directional choreography of mostly pointing and shouting 'Wham!' They were seen as somewhat more approachable than the likes of Soft Cell or Culture Club, and looked like the lovely-haired boys next door up against the bombast of sick filth that was Frankie Goes to Hollywood.

They courted the cool early on. They were celebrated by the *NME*, and John Peel had played 'Wham! Rap', their debut which extolled the virtues of life on the dole, on his radio show. By the time of the release of their second single, 'Young Guns (Go for It)', the success they felt destined for was having a wobbler. '"Young Guns (Go for It!)" had been released in September 1982,' Andrew recalled, 'but with it only landing at number seventy-three in the charts, the odds of Wham! becoming internationally famous were lengthening by the day . . . However, when the charts came out the following week, "Young Guns" had jumped to number forty-eight and, all of a sudden, the prospects of a Top 40 record and of being included on the all-important radio playlists was within reach.'

It would be the keen eye of a researcher from BBC TV's kids show *Saturday Superstore*, spotting the band playing in a club, that would prove to be the lifeline they badly needed, as Andrew explained. 'The programme was a big deal at the time and always featured bands it knew would appeal to its young audience. Everybody knew that an exciting performance in the studio could work wonders for a new act.' Although it didn't immediately launch them into the all-important Top 40, stalling at number forty-two, another stroke of luck was on its way. '*Top of the Pops* decided they wanted to have us on the show. There's still something of a mystery surrounding the circumstances of our appearance, but apparently another band had dropped out at the very last minute. I don't know who it was and we were never told, but fate stepped in and gifted us our golden opportunity.'

That performance did the trick. The world of Wham! was exposed to a bigger audience, offering up youth, excitement and an almost-military precision level of choreography honed from countless hours of rehearsals in George's parents' living room ('no choreographer was gonna to come up with that shit,' said George). 'Young Guns (Go for It)' bounded up the chart into the top three, turning George and Andrew into pin-ups at last.

'It looks terrible when you look at it now,' George later admitted. 'But at the time, it was considered quite innovative and new, the way we presented ourselves. There's a certain energy through the naffness. It worked in a weird kind of way. Everybody remembered it at the time.'

That initial trilogy of singles was completed by the camp-as-tits 'Bad Boys'. There were hints and moments where Wham! looked gayer and more subversive than the parent-upsetting Culture Club. Even the men-in-pilots-uniform giddy-goating of 'Club Tropicana' played up to it. George and Andrew, along with Shirlie Holliman and Dee C Lee, looked like the gang of mates you wanted to hang out with. Shirlie and Dee weren't there as mere decoration to the centre-stage antics of George and Andrew; they were pivotal to the action. They were the two mates exchanging flirty glances with the boys in 'Club Tropicana', but never quite getting together with them. Nothing, it seemed, was going to get in the way of George and Andrew's friendship. Shirlie and Dee might have saved the unintentionally hilarious video of 'Bad Boys' had they been in it, bringing some light relief to the homoerotica of George and Andrew giving it some mincey routine moves with similarly attired gents in *The Wild One*-esque biker gear at the end.

If the title of their 1983 debut album *Fantastic* hadn't given it away, 1984's follow-up – *Make It Big* – truly spelled it out. With a minor line-up change that saw Helen 'Pepsi' DeMacque replace Dee, who'd left to pursue a solo career, they released half of what would become *Make It Big* as singles, three of which went to number one. There was the pop confection jitterbuggery of 'Wake Me Up Before You Go-Go', the George-as-a-solo-star launching 'Careless Whisper' (complete with pricey video that was re-shot because he wasn't keen on his hair and flew his hairdresser over to Miami to sort it out), and the Motown exuberance of 'Freedom'. The only single not to top the chart was 'Everything She Wants', which had to settle for number two as a double-A-side with non-album track 'Last Christmas'. And the reason why 'Last Christmas' didn't make number one was, as we already know, due to the charity blockbustin' 'Do They Know it's Christmas?' 'Last Christmas' would eventually reach the actual summit of the charts in 2021, thirty-six years after it was first released. It repeated the feat in 2022. And it finally became an actual Christmas number one twelve months later, spending four weeks at the top. According to Official Charts Company data, it now has a combined sales figure, from physical sales and streaming, of 4.88 million. Suffice to say, 'Last Christmas' did fairly well after all.

'I never minded being thought of as a pop star,' George told *GQ* in 2004. 'People have always thought I wanted to be seen as a serious musician, but I didn't. I just wanted people to know that I was absolutely serious about pop music.' After the 1984 he'd had, people got the gist.

The Band Aid single hit the shops on 3 December 1984. It sold more than 1 million copies in its first week, and more than 3 million by the end of the year, at the time becoming the biggest-selling single of all time in the UK. While he might have been smarting that Wham! had been denied the festive top spot, George encouraged his fans to buy the Band Aid single and also donated proceeds from 'Last Christmas' to the Band Aid Trust.

While charity records and concerts were nothing new – Bronski Beat's 'Pits & Perverts' concert in aid of striking miners for one, and Wham! had even appeared at a similar event at the Royal Albert Hall show with the Style Council that September – the huge impact of Band Aid, and its superstar line-up, would set the tone, leading to a series of chart-topping charity singles throughout the rest of the decade, made in response to various events and causes. These included USA for Africa's 'We Are The World', Ferry Aid's 'Let it Be' (following the Zeebrugge ferry disaster), the Crowd's 'You'll Never Walk Alone' (the tragic fire at Valley Parade, home of Bradford City FC), Cliff Richard and the Young Ones doing 'Livin' Doll' for Comic Relief, and Wet Wet Wet's version of 'With a Little Help From My Friends' in aid of Childline. The '80s finished with a Stock Aitken Waterman-helmed Band Aid II delivering a fifth-anniversary re-record of 'Do They Know it's Christmas?'

Band Aid, and the accompanying Live Aid concert the following summer, could also be seen as marking the end of the first half of the decade's 'New Pop' era of frivolity, fun and yacht ownership, and triggering The New Seriousness that dominated the second half. You were never too far away from a bunch of acts bandied together on a concert bill, or in a recording studio, in the name of a good cause or raising social awareness of an issue.

It was ahead of the band's 1984 return that George came out to both Andrew and Wham! co-traveller Shirlie, after revealing that he'd had an encounter with a man when they were filming the 'Club Tropicana' video in Ibiza six months earlier, as Andrew recalled. 'He said to me, "Didn't know how to tell you this, but I'm gay. If not gay, you know, bisexual."'

'Once I realised this was a part of my sexuality I couldn't ignore,' said George, 'I went to come out to Andrew.' However, both Andrew and Shirlie suggested he kept his sexuality a secret. He acknowledged that, while this was a significant moment in his life, telling his close friends might have been a mistake. 'The three of us were so close at the time, but the point being I'd really, really asked the wrong people. At that point in time, I really wanted to come out, but I lost my nerve completely.' So, instead, George popped his sexuality to the back of his mind and threw himself into Wham!'s career.

Andrew suggested that their youth paid a part, what with them being 'twenty years old. Our perspective was a little narrower. When he told me it was like, "Oh, well, yeah. That explains a few things", but it was unremarkable. It was unsensational.'

Was George's sidestepping of his homosexuality a deliberate choice to allow him to push harder and achieve greater accolades? Could it be argued that he didn't want to derail the success they'd achieved in 1984 by revealing his sexuality? Coming out to a few friends is one thing, but having the eyes of the world on you and letting them into your private life is something that very few of us can imagine, let alone know what it feels like. Perhaps we can forgive his motives at the time. Hindsight is a wonderful thing. And what we do know now, is that the biggest pop star of 1984, in Britain at least, was a gay man.

As he told *Desert Island Discs* in 2007, his desire to keep it a secret was driven by not wanting to upset his family. 'So firstly, understand how much I love my family and that AIDS was the predominant feature of being gay in the 1980s and early '90s as far as any parent was concerned. My mother was still alive and every single day would have been a nightmare for her thinking what I might have been subjected to.

'I'd been out to a lot of people since nineteen. I wish to God it had happened then. I don't think I would have the same career – my ego might not have been satisfied in some areas – but I think I would have been a happier man.'

For the next couple of years, George and Andrew oversaw a magnificent run in which they cracked the US, and, yes, became one of the few Western acts to play concerts in China, thus earning their profile as one of the biggest bands in the world. By the time the pair announced their split and performed their final show at Wembley Stadium in June 1986, George had already topped the charts again.

His second solo single was the barely-there melancholic minimalism of 'A Different Corner', by which time Wham! had enjoyed another pair of number ones with 1985's 'I'm Your Man' and 'The Edge of Heaven' in 1986.

If, by the time of his solo debut album, 1987's *Faith*, George's fans were under any misunderstanding that he had discovered sex, he made sure they were aware of it when he released the single 'I Want Your Sex'. Complete with a rumpo-based video, starring his then 'girl-friend' Kathy Jeung, it suggested that George was very well-versed in such matters. Hem hem. However, it was common knowledge among close personal friends that he was actually gay and had been since a teenager. Yet, to the public, 'I Want Your Sex' suggested that he was quite the ladies' man, making racy videos that got banned. When the follow-up single 'Faith' came along, George had taken to wearing tight jeans and a leather jacket, and had invented designer stubble. He'd also started wearing cowboy boots, and donned a guitar (which he admitted he couldn't play), which helped the US audience take him more seriously. He knew what he was doing.

That said, George struggled with the massive success of *Faith*. The album was the first by a solo white artist to hit number one on the Billboard Top Black Albums chart and he felt at odds winning awards traditionally given to black artists in R&B categories. The album sold a whopping 25 million copies worldwide, and the strain of having to be so *present* took its toll.

By the time of his second album, 1990's *Listen Without Prejudice*, there was a concerted effort to pull back and remain in the shadows. Every image came loaded with some sort of meaning. His rejection of being a massive pop star and the oh-so-subtle burning of his *Faith* leather jacket was an 'and this is me' moment. Suddenly he wanted to be taken seriously as an artist and, despite the reluctance to play the pop game at that time, if anything it helped enhance his image and career ten-fold.

George's third solo album *Older* was released in May 1996. It was his first since extricating himself from the record deal he had with Sony[1], where he'd accused them of underpromoting *Listen Without Prejudice*. The new album

---

[1] Following the end of Wham! and the huge success of *Faith*, he'd signed an eight-album solo deal with CBS in 1988. The subsequent album *Listen Without Prejudice* sold relatively poorly, and although he refused to do any promotion and didn't use his image on the sleeve, George believed the low sales were down to Sony being unwilling to promote it because of his decisions. With CBS having been sold to Sony, George was given a whole new set of bosses with whom he'd had no professional dealings, and who didn't really know how to handle him. He also argued that the set-up of the label, and indeed the wider music industry, led to an imbalance of power where the labels had far more control over an artist's work than they did. Although he lost the case and had stated that he would no longer record for the label, in 1995 George saw Sony sell the contract to rival record companies Virgin Records (rest of the world rights) and DreamWorks Records (US and Canada rights). All future releases were co-labelled with Aegean Records, a record company set up by George and cousin Andros Georgiou in 1991.

was infused with loss and paranoia, regret and sadness. 'I wrote *Older* within about, I suppose, eight months,' he told *GQ*. 'I think I wrote the best, most healing piece of music that I've ever written in my life with that album.'

Older's genesis can be pinpointed to New Year 1991 when George's Brazilian boyfriend Anselmo Feleppa flew to London to tell him that he had tested positive for AIDS. They'd only been together three months, and even though Anselmo had known his diagnosis for a few weeks, he didn't want to spoil George's Christmas.

Anselmo eventually died of a brain haemorrhage in 1993, shortly after returning to Brazil for a blood transfusion. George wasn't with him. Anselmo hadn't wanted him to use his 'star status' to get him preferential attention. 'I think he went to Brazil because he feared what my fame would do to him and his family if he got treatment elsewhere. I was devastated by that. The idea that he had the opportunity to go somewhere better but wouldn't take it because of my fame makes me feel very guilty.

'It was untimely, but that way he never lost his dignity, and I suppose I was spared the worst of what some people go through. But I'm still convinced that, had he been in the USA or London, he would have survived, because just six months later everyone was on combination therapy.'

On the day after Anselmo's death, George decided it was time to reveal his sexuality to his family and did so in a letter. His mother's reaction was understandable; she was simply devastated that he hadn't allowed her into his life when he was supporting Anselmo as he was dying. His father's reaction was one of consolation. 'He never displayed any disappointment or homophobia,' said George. 'I'm sure he felt it, and it was hard for him, but he didn't lay any of it onto me, which I have to thank him for. This is sad, but I do feel success can negate a parent's disappointment. I genuinely feel that although his son is gay and not going to give him any grandkids, my dad's consolation is that I have done well in life.'

Anselmo's shadow looms large over the whole of *Older*, especially on the opening track and lead single 'Jesus to a Child' and on the poignant 'You Have Been Loved'. Both songs are beautiful, mournful tributes to the man he adored. In the case of 'You Have Been Loved', it has grown beyond one man's personal grief into something far more universal – so much so that it was adopted by radio stations and played almost hourly following the death of Diana, Princess of Wales in 1997.

The key to *Older* was how it related to George's fans on multiple levels. There were the longtime George fans who were in awe of a pop giant back at the top of his game. And there was the gay audience, an audience that could relate to the album's themes of loss and regret. The ghosts of former lovers and those long gone is part of the tragic narrative that underpins much of the best pop music. George had loved, and lost, and the devastation was relatable.

But also relatable was the fact that, in 'Fastlove', George had gone out for some indiscreet bumming and alfresco intercourse. And, in 'Spinning the Wheel', he was admonishing a lover for abandoning monogamy and playing around having unprotected sex. Again, very relatable to a large part of his audience.

Older may not have shifted the requisite units worldwide as *Faith* had – very few artists are able to repeat the feat of selling 25 million records – but 7.5 million copies was not too shabby at all. He also enjoyed a record six top-three hit singles in the UK across a two-year span. George. Was. Back.

With *Older*, George presented himself as a less distant, more human figure, a flawed perfectionist who knew his strengths and weaknesses. For a private man who gave very few interviews, when he did speak, he was unguarded, open and sometimes hilariously honest. Speaking to *Attitude* magazine, George admitted: 'I think it's important that I can be out there and say that I'm a big tart and still have a big smash album.

'I'm very proud of *Listen Without Prejudice*. But I think the whole experience of losing Anselmo ... the period of grief, which was roughly two years that I didn't write a note of music. And, then, the absolute knowledge that the next album I was going to write would be about grief and recovery. *Older* is my greatest moment, in my opinion. And as I've said before I don't ever want to be that inspired again.'

The standing of *Older* as George's definitive album will surely continue to grow as the years pass. It may not have had the huge success of its predecessors (yeah, just the 7 million copies sold, no biggie), but it's a testament to his talent and soul-baring. It is an album that has resonated with millions of people – not just gay men and women – who can identify with its universal themes of life, love, loss and sexuality. I'd go as far as to say it's his masterpiece. He would go on to make gayer records, such as his reworking of the Ones' 'Flawless – Go to the City', which was his self-confessed first 'queens record' but, to be honest, on *Older* it was already there in all its glory.

Speaking of being a big tart, it was being just that which led to him being arrested after a bit of cottaging in a public toilet in Beverly Hills. On 7 April 1998, he was arrested by undercover policeman Marcelo Rodríguez in a sting operation using so-called 'pretty police'[2], where members of law enforcement spent an unusual amount of time in public toilets aiming to nick anyone attempting a bit of

---

[2] Press attitudes towards homosexuality in 1984 seemed to soften somewhat, especially in the case of Conservative MP Dr Keith Hampson. Hampson was on trial for allegedly fondling the thigh of a male dancer, 'Luscious Leon', at the Gay Theatre Club in Soho in May 1984. It emerged that Leon was in fact an undercover policeman, part of the Metropolitan Police's 'pretty police' who would engage in entrapment. Hampson was then Defence Secretary Michael Heseltine's Parliamentary Private Secretary (PPS). Although the case was eventually dropped, Hampson was forced to resign his PPS position. The *Daily Mail*'s Lynda Lee Potter noted that 'if the destruction of Dr Keith Hampson MP's career results in ending the vendetta against homosexuals which the police have been conducting for years, possibly one iota of good will emerge from this sad and sorry case'.

knob-touch. Naturally, when this hit the news, the press had a field day. Here was someone, who'd they'd known about for many years and were desperate to expose any cracks in his private life, effectively handing out the information they'd been after.

George's response? He didn't so much as publicly come out of the closet; he danced out of the thing and torched it. Quite simply, he reclaimed the narrative and refused to be cast as some tragic, shamed character. His response was the song 'Outside', the video of which sent up his arrest and featured him dancing around in a men's toilet dressed as a cop. It was the perfect fuck you.

As he told *Attitude*, he believed he felt a sense of duty. 'When I was tempted to give up in the middle of making this album, one of the things that made that difficult for me is that I would have felt I'd let down a whole generation of young gay kids, that they'd think, *He's massive, then he comes out and then he's gone.* When I made the "Outside" video, I knew I was helping a whole generation of fifteen-year-olds who are cruising and dying of shame about it. I felt that lightening the stigma around cruising was the most immediately beneficial thing I could do. I know for a fact that, when I was sixteen, seventeen, when I started cruising, that watching the "Outside" video would have taken some of the weight off my shoulders.'

That it did. And, almost immediately, the narrative around gay pop stars started to change. Those who saw him telling his story and showing no shame realised that they no longer needed to conceal their true selves. And even those who felt pressurised to out themselves via the blackmail tactics of unpleasant 'showbiz' editors, saw this example as a reclamation of their path. THEY now had the control – and weren't losing fans either.

In a way, George's outing freed him from the semi-reclusive 'artist' who wanted us to listen without prejudice. This world-famous long-term closeted pop star was now popping up on chat shows and morning TV, able to laugh off his arrest for getting caught hoping to empty the bollocks of an undercover policeman. And he spoke openly about long-term partner Kenny Goss, about how they were in a happy and stable relationship.

A sidebar to this period was the death of his mother in 1997, which sent George into another tailspin of grief. But he took comfort in the fact that he had made his peace with her as regards his sexuality.

After *Older* had done its business – and despite a couple of hits compilations, a live album and a collection of covers – frustratingly George would only release one more original studio album during his lifetime. This was the 2004 chart-topping *Patience*. While reluctant to go on the road again, he did celebrate his twenty-five years in pop with the 25Live tour that took him around the world. However, he was at his happiest at home, sitting on the couch with his beloved dogs, watching the soaps and getting stoned.

George's later sexual adventures seemed to take over his public profile. He'd been arrested on Hampstead Heath while cruising the area, and was also done for possession of drugs, as well as his inability to drive while on them. There's likely no end of men who could come forward and reveal that they'd had sex with George in a bush, but the gentlemen's code of conduct for anonymous sex in such circles meant that no one did, despite efforts from the tabloid press to corner his conquests.

The erratic nature of George's public life spilled over into the private, and he and Kenny parted ways after several happy years together. It's noticeable that George's health then began to deteriorate. In 2011, after suffering chest pains ahead of the first night of his Symphonica tour, he was admitted into hospital and it was revealed that he'd suffered from pneumonia and, at one point, had been in a coma.

After George's death on Christmas Day 2016, among the many outpourings of grief and condolences, it was revealed that he'd been quite the philanthropist. He'd already donated sales from his singles to various AIDS charities and was a patron of Elton John's AIDS Foundation. But there were other stories too – stories of him writing large cheques to various charities, playing concerts for nurses, donating vast sums to good causes and quietly stepping in to pay someone's bills. It was as if the riches he'd accumulated over the years were there to help others in need. It was arguably his philanthropy that helped keep him grounded.

So here it is, the ballad of George Michael. A tale of ambition, success beyond his wildest dreams and a legacy of enduring, iconic songs. A man who may have taken himself a bit too seriously at one point, who had his fair share of troubles and yet who managed to see through the charade and achieve some level of peace. He was the very example of how to be a pop star, and how one can turn their fame into good, unburdening themselves of their demons and becoming a fully rounded decent human being.

He is sorely missed.

OUTRODUCTION

So, 1984: sexuality, pop music, sensationalism, outrage and politics – an accumulation of factors and incidents and artists that would go on to change attitudes, culture and policies, stewed in an occasionally hostile environment not too dissimilar to what is going on today with the rights of the LGBTQ+ community seemingly at risk.

The influence of that year is still being felt, with gay artists – by and large – no longer having to worry if their sexuality will adversely affect their careers. However, with discussions around gender, draconian bills being passed that make Clause 28 look tame, and an atmosphere of fear and contempt in general, our rights are looking ever flimsier and so our voices should be louder than ever.

In the USA, by June 2023, more than 530 anti-LGBTQ+ bills had been drafted and proposed in state legislatures and in Congress. Of those bills, which were submitted between 1 January and 31 May that year, sixty-eight have been enacted into law, with only 122 officially failing so far. In the UK, a proposed ban on conversion therapy has been promised, but it has been in limbo since Theresa May first promised it during her period as prime minister and it was echoed by Boris Johnson after his election in 2019.

Worldwide, the rights of LGBTQ+ people have been wound up with populist parties engaging in culture wars to detract from their failing economies. Draconian anti-homosexuality bills have been passed in countries such as Uganda, while similar moves have come under review in Kenya, Poland and Brazil. In an echo of Clause 28, Hungary passed its own 'don't say gay' law, banning the discussion of LGBTQ+ issues in schools and on children's TV, and Republicans in the US have sought similar, including the removal of any books seen to promote non-family values in school libraries. In 2023, seventy-five new laws were passed that the American Civil Liberties Union (ACLU) considered harmful to LGBTQ+ people. At the time of writing, there are another 484 under scrutiny in the US that the ACLU has flagged. These are mostly targeting trans kids, and include forced outing at schools, denial of healthcare and banning access to facilities.

I could pop my 'I've listened to podcasts about this' hat on and say it's a rise in state-sanctioned anti-LGBTQ+ stigma and a worrying sign of democracies in retreat. Countries once thought safe for sexual and gender minorities are increasingly less so. The rise in populist authoritarianism fuels anti-LGBTQ+ persecution that can drive migration, while also reflecting fewer safe harbours for sexual and gender minorities. Indeed, the dog-whistling ghastliness deployed by the UK Home Office suggested that Britain should not grant asylum to people who simply express fear of discrimination for being *gay* plays well towards a bigoted voter base – and is a statement that detracts from their own ineptness at their job. Bad-faith mouthpieces have gained notoriety and fame for singling out anyone considerably 'other' as bad. Where once the words 'groomer' and 'paedophile' were among the very harshest of language, they are now liberally thrown around on social media by arseholes. It's easy to scoff, ridicule and amplify the deranged theories of certain figures, such as Liz Truss, the temp-staff former prime minister-turned-tinfoil-hatted goon who claimed at the Conservative Political Action Conference at the National Harbor in Maryland in February 2024, that there is a 'whole new problem' with the civil service being 'full of trans activists'. But she is still there with a platform. For every social media condemnation of her derangement, there's a small sector of people who'll claim she has a point.

If you thought that the newspaper columnists of 1984 sounded awful towards LGBTQ+ people, there's a just-as-vitriolic level of ghastliness from today's generation towards trans people. Then factor in the cocktips-for-cash burning Pride flags or driving boycotts of LGBTQ+ friendly companies on social media. These are some extremely powerful voices stirring up hatred and it's promoting a new age of hostility.

There has also been a rise in homophobic attacks across the world, with LGBTQ+ organisations in France, Germany and Spain highlighting this worrying trend. Stonewall has reported that the UK is increasingly unsafe for LGBTQ+ people, while hate crimes on the basis of sexual orientation are up by 112 per cent in the last five years, based on figures released by the Office for National Statistics in October 2023. That is a frightening statistic for a country which is supposed to be quite liberal.

Yet despite all this noise, and away from the world online, there *have* been great leaps in tolerance. The British Social Attitudes (BSA) survey in 2023 reported that the UK *is* a far more liberal society as regards opinions on gay marriage and same-sex relationships are concerned, with 50 per cent of respondents saying they were 'always wrong' in 1983, compared with just 9 per cent in 2022. If you step away from the computer and cease the doom-scrolling, you'll find that there are many more people for whom the culture wars seemingly have no effect.

Yet, culturally, against this backdrop LGBTQ+ people have an increased visibility. *Strictly Come Dancing*, the biggest TV show in the UK, has featured several same-sex couples competing. *Doctor Who* is living up to its multi-universed reputation by featuring gay and trans characters. Soap operas are now *full* of LGBTQ+ characters reflecting and living normal everyday lives. It contrasts somewhat to the dismay that Colin in *EastEnders* caused when he kissed another man in 1989, which led to Piers Morgan's pearl-clutch in the *Sun*, calling it a 'love scene between two yuppie poofs'.

In sport, where once the idea of a gay footballer was seen as taboo, there's now Jake Daniels, Beth Mead, Lauren

Hemp, Megan Rapinoe, Jill Scott and more. Across the sports spectrum, more and more people are feeling comfortable enough to live their true lives. Diver Tom Daley, arguably one of the highest profile and most-decorated of British Olympians, has become a global LGBTQ+ advocate. There have been firsts happening, such as the comings-out of Welsh rugby star Gareth Thomas, the NFL's Carl Nassib, NHL's Luke Prokop and Puerto Rican boxer Orlando Cruz. Where once the fear of admitting sexuality may have come at a cost as regards sponsorship, it's now become increasing irrelevant. You'll find that homophobic chants tend to evaporate once trophies are being lifted.

In politics, where Labour's Chris Smith once seemed like a lone gay voice, there are now numerous LGBTQ+ MPs in the commons, representing all of the parties. There have even been out heads of state and governments, such as Ireland's Leo Varadkar, France's Gabriel Attal and Latvia's Edgars Rinkēvičs.

Movies featuring gay relationships and characters, such as *Call Me By Your Name*, *All of Us Strangers*, *Moonlight* and *Everything Everywhere All at Once*, are no longer niche concerns but are award-hoovering blockbusters. We've also come a long way since the 'scandal' of Rock Hudson, with a range of LGBTQ+ actors such as Andrew Scott, Jodie Foster, Ben Whishaw, Luke Evans, Jonathan Bailey, Sir Ian McKellen, Cynthia Nixon and more.

A host of TV dramas, such as *It's a Sin*, *Heartstopper*, *The Last of Us* and *Sex Education*, have won wide acclaim and huge audiences. *RuPaul's Drag Race* has numerous regional variations around the planet, pumping out new drag queens into the mainstream almost weekly. Musically there have been Scissor Sisters, the xx, Self Esteem, Troye Sivan, Sam Smith, St Vincent, Janelle Monáe, John Grant, Rufus Wainwright, Peaches, Christine & the Queens, ANOHNI and more. Meanwhile, superstar allies such as Lady Gaga, Harry Styles, Beyoncé and Adele continue to speak out against intolerance and embrace their LGBTQ+ audiences.

Yeah, sure, there will always be arseholes with their comments and their sniping. There will always be ghastly morons, with no sense of what the word actually means, who will claim things are now – urgh – 'woke'. Ignore them – you're fabulous. And always remember that bullying ages people *dreadfully*. You've got back-up. There are more people on *your* side than there are on theirs.

Tolerance is an ongoing process, so it helps when we raise a glass and celebrate these moments when progress was made. So, here's to all the artists who've leant against, pushed or, in some cases, demolished the door for the rest of us. The perverts, freaks, drags and groundbreakers who showed another way or illuminated the underground. The icons who spoke up and paid back to the community. Those three or four minutes of exhilaration of being seen and being heard. The moments that said, 'You're not alone' or 'Don't be afraid' or 'It gets better'. Because that's what pop music does.

And pop music is important.

PLAYLIST

Hits and perverts! The official soundtrack of the book with bonus period-appropriate favourites of the author (just in case you might have thought Lloyd Cole and the Commotions' 'Perfect Skin' had some hidden gay context).

'Relax (New York Mix)', Frankie Goes to Hollywood
'What Difference Does It Make?', The Smiths
'Down in the Subway', Soft Cell
'Here Come the Rain Again', Eurythmics
'It's My Life', Talk Talk
'Let the Music Play', Shannon
'Wood Beez (Pray Like Aretha Franklin)', Scritti Politti
'I, Bloodbrother Be', Shock Headed Peters
'How To Destroy Angels (A Slow Fade to Total
    Transparency) (Recorded live at the Air Gallery
    24/8/83)', Coil, Zos Kia and Marc Almond
'Dr Mabuse (The First Life of...)', Propaganda
'Shake it Up', Divine
'Robert De Niro's Waiting', Bananarama
'The Killing Moon', Echo & the Bunnymen
'I Wanted Your Love', Luther Vandross

'Holiday', Madonna

'Girls Just Want to Have Fun', Cyndi Lauper

'It's a Miracle', Culture Club

'Radio Ga Ga', Queen

'Eat Me Alive', Judas Priest

'Thieves Like Us', New Order

'My Ever Changing Moods', The Style Council

'Each and Everyone', Everything But the Girl

'Just Be Good to Me', The S.O.S. Band

'Change of Heart', Change

'You're a Winner', Sharon Redd

'I Am What I Am', Gloria Gaynor

'The Upstroke', Agents Aren't Aeroplanes

'It's Raining Men', The Weather Girls

'So Many Men, So Little Time', Miquel Brown

'Where is My Man', Eartha Kitt

'Another Man', Barbara Mason

'Caught in the Act', Earlene Bentley

'Sad Songs (Say So Much)', Elton John

'I Want to Break Free', Queen

'Lucky Star', Madonna

'Wake Me Up Before You Go-Go', Wham!

'Holding Out for a Hero', Bonnie Tyler

'The Lebanon', The Human League

'West End Girls (Original Bobby Orlando mix)', Pet
     Shop Boys

PLAYLIST

'High Energy', Evelyn Thomas

'Searchin' (I Gotta Find a Man)', Hazell Dean

'You Think You're a Man', Divine

'That's the Way (I Like It)', Dead or Alive

'Smalltown Boy', Bronski Beat

'Love Resurrection', Alison Moyet

'Time After Time', Cyndi Lauper

'When Doves Cry', Prince and The Revolution

'Heaven Knows I'm Miserable Now', The Smiths

'Perfect Skin', Lloyd Cole and the Commotions

'Rock the Box', Sylvester

'One More Chance (Original Bobby Orlando remix)',
    Pet Shop Boys

'Baby Wants to Ride (Original 1984 Demo Radio Edit)',
    Jamie Principle

'Give Me Tonight', Shannon

'Two Tribes'*, Frankie Goes to Hollywood

'War (Hidden)', Frankie Goes to Hollywood

'Eyes Without a Face', Billy Idol

'Self Control', Laura Branigan

'Whatever I Do (Wherever I Go)', Hazell Dean

'Careless Whisper', George Michael

---

* indicates that IDEALLY we'd have the Annihilation mix, but it is currently unavailable on streaming apps.

'William, it Was Really Nothing', The Smiths

'Those First Impressions', The Associates

'Pink Turns to Blue', Husker Du

'She Bop', Cyndi Lauper

'Why?', Bronski Beat

'Love Kills', Freddie Mercury

'The Boy Who Came Back', Marc Almond and the
    Willing Sinners

'Master and Servant', Depeche Mode

'Freedom', Wham!

'Blue Jean', David Bowie

'Purple Rain', Prince and the Revolution

'I Feel for You', Chaka Khan

'Madam Butterfly (Un Bel Di Vedremo)', Malcolm
    McLaren

'Smooth Operator', Sade

'Together in Electric Dreams', Phil Oakey and Giorgio
    Moroder

'The War Song', Culture Club

'You Spin Me Round (Like a Record)', Dead Or Alive

'How Soon is Now?', The Smiths

'Sexcrime (Nineteen Eighty Four)', Eurythmics

'Close Up', The Art of Noise

'It Ain't Necessarily So', Bronski Beat

'Like a Virgin', Madonna

'I Would Die 4 U', Prince and the Revolution

'Last Christmas (Pudding Mix)', Wham!

'The Power of Love', Frankie Goes to Hollywood

PLAYLIST

To listen to the playlist on Spotify, open your app and scan the code below:

To listen to the playlist on Apple Music, scan the code below with your iPhone camera:

BIBLIOGRAPHY

Books

Almond, Marc, *Tainted Life* (Pan, 1999)

Ball, Dave, *Electronic Boy: My Life In and Out of Soft Cell* (Omnibus, 2020)

Boy George, *Take It Like A Man* (Pan, 1995)

Brewster, Bill and Broughton, Frank, *Last Night A DJ Saved My Life: The History Of The Disc Jockey* (Headline, 2006)

Bullock, Daryl W., *Pride, Pop and Politics: Music, Theatre and LGBT Activism 1970 – 2021* (Omnibus, 2021)

Burns, Pete, *Freak Unique* (John Blake Publishing, 2007)

Cashman, Michael, *One of Them* (Bloomsbury, 2021)

Clews, Colin, *Gay in the 80s* (Troubador, 2021)

Easlea, Daryl, *Everybody Dance: Chic and the Politics of Disco* (Helter Skelter, 2004)

Evans, Richard, *Listening to the Music the Machines Make* (Omnibus, 2022)

Flynn, Paul, *Good as You* (Ebury Press, 2017)

Frankie Goes to Hollywood, *And Suddenly There Came a Bang* (Ztaat, 1985)

Gamson, Joshua, *The Fabulous Sylvester* (Macmillan, 2006)

Garfield, Simon, *The End of Innocence: Britain In the Time of AIDS* (Faber and Faber, 1994)

Gruen, John, *Keith Haring: The Authorized Biography* (Thames and Hudson, 1992)

Halford, Rob, *Confess* (Headline, 2020)

Heath, Chris, *Pet Shop Boys Versus America* (William Heinemann, 2020)

Heath, Chris, *Pet Shop Boys, Literally* (William Heinemann, 2020)

Hodgkinson, Will, *In Perfect Harmony* (Nine Eight Books, 2022)

Horn, Trevor, *Adventures In Modern Recording* (Nine Eight Books, 2022)

John, Elton, *Me* (Macmillan, 2019)

Johnson, Holly, *A Bone in My Flute* (Arrow, 1995)

Lewis, Justin, *Don't Stop the Music: A Year of Pop History One Day at a Time* (Elliott & Thompson, 2023)

Light, Alan, *Let's Go Crazy: Prince and the Making of Purple Rain* (Simon & Schuster, 2014)

Moran, Caitlin, *Moranthology* (Ebury, 2013)

Morrissey, *Autobiography* (Penguin, 2013)

Mulligan, Michael, *The Official Christmas No. 1 Singles Book* (Nine Eight Books, 2021)

Paphides, Pete, *Broken Greek* (Quercus, 2020)

Paytress, Mark, *Glam! When Superstars Rocked the World 1970–1974* (Omnibus, 2022)

Pegg, Nicholas, *The Complete David Bowie* (Titan, 2016)

Quirk, Justin, *Nothin' But a Good Time: The Spectacular Rise and Fall of Glam Metal* (Unbound, 2020)

Reynolds, Simon, *Retromania* (Faber & Faber, 2012)

Reynolds, Simon, *Rip It Up and Start Again: Post Punk 1978–1984* (Faber & Faber, 2005)

Reynolds, Simon, *Totally Wired* (Faber & Faber, 2009)

Ridgeley, Andrew, *Wham!, George & Me* (Michael Joseph, 2019)

Rimmer, Dave, *Like Punk Never Happened* (Faber, 2011)

Rimmer, Dave, *Like Punk Never Happened: New Expanded Edition* (Faber & Faber, 2022)

Shapiro, Peter, *Turn the Beat Around: The Secret History of Disco* (Faber & Faber, 2005)

Stanley, Bob, *Bee Gees: Children of the World* (Nine Eight Books, 2023)

Stanley, Bob, *Yeah Yeah Yeah: The Story of Modern Pop* (Faber & Faber, 2013)

Stewart, Rod, *Rod: The Autobiography* (Century, 2012)

Tennant, Neil, *One Hundred Lyrics and a Poem* (Faber & Faber, 2018)

Tennant, Neil, *The Best of Smash Hits* (Emap Books, 1985)

Thorne, Matt, *Prince* (Faber & Faber, 2012)

Waterman, Pete, *I Wish I Was Me: The Autobiography* (Virgin, 2000)

Magazines and newspapers

Attitude

Classic Pop

Gay Times

GQ

Guardian

HIM

Independent

Melody Maker

MOJO

Music Week

Newsweek

NME

Number One

Q

Record Collector

Record Mirror

Rolling Stone

Smash Hits

Sound on Sound

The Face

The Times

Uncut

Vanity Fair

Websites

10 Years of Being Boring – 10yearsofbeingboring.com

80s Hi-NRG & Eurobeat – 80shinrgeurobeat.com

909 Originals – 909originals.com

Advocate – advocate.com

AOL – aol.com

Arcadia – byarcadia.org

Attitude – attitude.co.uk

Bartleby Research – bartleby.com

BBC – bbc.co.uk

BBC Genome Project – genome.ch.bbc.co.uk

Billboard – billboard.com

Bishopsgate Institute – bishopsgate.org.uk

Blabbermouth – blabbermouth.net

Blues & Soul – bluesandsoul.com

British Film Institute – bfi.org.uk

British Library – bl.uk

Buzzfeed – buzzfeed.com

Classic Bands – classicbands.com

Classic Pop – classicpopmag.com

Daily Express – express.co.uk

DC's – denniscooperblog.com

Digital Transgender Archive – digitaltransgenderarchive.net

Eurodance Encyclopedia – eurokdj.com

Far Out – faroutmagazine.co.uk

Fighting Words – fighting-words.co.uk

Forbes Magazine – forbes.com

Gay Birmingham Remembered – gaybirminghamremem-
bered.co.uk

Gay in the 80s – gayinthe80s.com

Gay Times – gaytimes.co.uk

Gender Forum – genderforum.org

GM Forever – gmforever.com

Grammy Awards – grammy.com

GRIN – grin.com

Headteacher Update – headteacher-update.com

History At Northampton – historyatnorthampton.com

History is Made at Night – history-is-made-at-night.blogspot.com

HIV.gov

Huffington Post – huffpost.com

Illness As Art: Archiving Smiths History – illnessasart.com

James Hamilton's Disco Page – jameshamiltonsdiscopage.com

Kerrang – kerrang.com

KFF – kff.org

LA Times – latimes.com

LGBT Archive – lgbthistoryuk.org

LGBT+ Language and Archives – lgbtcumbrialanguageandarchives.wordpress.com

Like Punk Never Happened – likepunkneverhappened.blogspot.com

LouderSound – loudersound.com

Manchester Digital Music Archive – mdmarchive.co.uk

Metro – metro.co.uk

Michael Mouse – michaelmouse1967.wixsite.com

Mojo – mojo4music.com

MTV – MTV.com

My Queer Agenda – myqueerto.com

National Library of Medicine – ncbi.nlm.nih.gov

New York Post – nypost.com

NME – nme.com

NPR – npr.org

Official Charts Company – officialcharts.com

One Vision – rushingheadlong.tumblr.com

BIBLIOGRAPHY

Open Culture – openculture.com

Our Warwickshire – ourwarwickshire.org.uk

Out – out.com

Pet Shop Boys Commentary by Wayne Studer PHD – geowayne.com/psb

Pet Shop Boys Technology – petshopboys.cz

Peter Tatchell Foundation – petertatchellfoundation.org

POZ – poz.com

Prince Vault – princevault.com

Psychology Today – psychologytoday.com

QX Magazine – qxmen.com

Red Bull Music Academy – daily.redbullmusicacademy.com

Research Gate – researchgate.net

Resident Advisor – ra.co

Rolling Stone – rollingstone.com

Royal College of Psychiatrists – rcpsych.ac.uk

San Francisco Aids Foundation – sfaf.org

Scientific American – scientificamerican.com

Sexual Alpha – sexualalpha.com

Simon Napier Bell – simonnapierbell.substack.com

Simon Napier Bell – simonnapierbell.com

Slate – slate.com

Smiths on Guitar – smithsonguitar.com

Song Facts – songfacts.com

Steve Pafford – stevepafford.com

Stock Aitken Waterman – stockaitkenwaterman.co.uk

Street Laughter: A Gay Cavalcade of Comic Stereotypes – ukjarry.blogspot.com

Terrence Higgins Trust – tht.org.uk

Terry Sanderson's Media Watch – gtmediawatch.org

Test Pressing – testpressing.wordpress.com

The Atlantic – theatlantic.com

The Herald – heraldscotland.com

The Quietus – thequietus.com

The Royal Commission on the Ancient and Historical
   Monuments of Wales – rcahmw.gov.uk

The *Spectator* Archive – archive.spectator.co.uk

The World of Italo Disco – italo-interviews.com

Tom of Finland Foundation – tomoffinland.org

Today in Madonna History – todayinmadonnahistory.com

Top of the Pops 80s – totp80s.blogspot.com

Tribune – tribunemag.co.uk

Udiscover – udiscovermusic.com

Ultimate Classic Rock – ultimateclassicrock.com

Ultimate Eurythmics – Archives eurythmics-ultimate.com

University of London – london.ac.uk

Vanity Fair – vanityfair.com

Vice – vice.com

Vogue – vogue.com

Westminster Abbey – westminster-abbey.org

Zeitgayst – thestarryeye.typepad.com

ZTT and All That – zttaat.com

ACKNOWLEDGEMENTS

Thanks to . . .

Pete Selby, whose faith, wisdom and belief steered me through in getting this book to be this book, also, cheers to all the Nine Eight lot.

Mum, Cathryn, Christine, Pauline, Dan and family, Tom, Georgina, Alex and Harry. Also, Dad and Janet.

Siân Davies and Mark Cooper for the love, support and feedback for when I wasn't being Wadey enough.

John Earls for reading my witterings, being a champ and talking me away from the ledge on numerous occasions.

Mark Wood for being so amazing.

Alexis Petridis for wise counsel and guidance.

Neil Corry for the chin-ups and big-ups.

Plus love and thanks to: Andrew Harrison, Andy Morris, Angela Walker, Anna Derbyshire Woolgar, Arthur, Ben Soundhog, Caitlin Moran, Chris Roberts, *Classic Pop*, Dan Maier, Daryl Easlea, Dave Hickey, David Hutcheon, Duckie, Duncan Jordan, Garry Shrimpton, Gavin Hogg, Gemma Williams, Guy Burch, Iain McDermott, Ian Carmichael, Ian Harrison, Ian Snowdon, Ian Usher, James Nicholson, Jamie McKelvie, Jeremy Thomas, John Doran,

John Fitzgerald, John Geddes, John & Flora, Johnny Kalifornia, Jude Rogers, Julian & Mark, Julian Stockton, Justin Quirk, Lauren Kreisler and everyone at The Official Charts Company, Lauren Laverne, Lee Kynaston, Lili Harges, Liz Buckley, Luke Turner, Maria Jefferis, Mark Johnstone, Martin Aston, Martin Wedge, Matthew Horton, Michael Hubbard, Michael Mulligan, Miranda Sawyer, Murray Chalmers, MusicOMH, Nadia Shireen, Neil Kulkarni, Niall McMurray, Nick Linsdell, Paul Flynn, Paul McGee, Paul Noble, Pete Paphides, The Quietus, The Readers Wifes, Rebecca Williams, Record Club, *Record Collector*, Rik Flynn, Robert Leach, Robin Turner, Ryan Minchin, Sali Hughes, Simon Price, Spiritland, The crew at St Paul's, Steve Harnell, Steve Yates, Stuart Maclean, Tony Felgate, Tracey Thorn, Victoria Segal, Wesley Doyle and anyone else I've prattled on about this book to.

Andrew & Dave, Ian & Lisa, Lisa R, Kat & Martyn, Chloe, Gary & Hayley, Teresa, Matt, Emma & Simon. Also, Jaye and Neil Stevens.

And finally, to N. Thank you for everything: the support, the read-throughs in Narvik, the kicks up the arse and letting me wang on. And also, for generally being the greatest. Love you loads xxx